MANAGEMENT OF URBAN PARKS

David Welch

Longman Group UK Limited
6th Floor, Westgate House, The High, Harlow, Essex, CM20 1 YR

First published 1991

British Library Cataloguing in publication Data

Welch, David
    Management of urban parks.
    I. Title
    352 . 7068

ISBN-0–582-07833-4

Typeset by Expo Holdings Sdn Bhd
Produced by Longman Group (FE) Ltd
Printed in Hong Kong

Contents

Chapter 1 Early parks   1
Chapter 2 Functions of parks   12
Chapter 3 Legislation   34
Chapter 4 Competitive tendering   47
Chapter 5 Marketing   77
Chapter 6 Risk management   98
Chapter 7 Catering and recreation management   113
Chapter 8 Children's playgrounds   128
Chapter 9 Native plants and animals in parks   160
Chapter 10 Britain in bloom   214
Chapter 11 Demographic changes   231
Bibliography   235
Index   239

1 Early parks

Parks and open spaces are an old idea. Humanity is essentially gregarious and places in which to assemble were central to every community from the earliest times and in all parts of the world. Modern problems, challenges and opportunities have an echo of earlier experience. Even today's shiny new concept is likely to have had its precursor yesterday. Alphonse Karr said (Les Guepes January 1849) 'The more things change the more they stay the same'.

The public squares of ancient Greece and Rome were gathering grounds acting as places of assembly, meeting, political and philosophical debate, and festival. They find their direct descendants in the piazza, plaza, and place, of today's towns in Mediterranean countries. The market places of medieval and later periods satisfied much the same need. In some places they were little more than a swelling out of the street but in cities like Brussels they were big enough for large public gatherings and assemblies. In Nottingham from early medieval times up to the early part of this century the famous goose fair was held in the market place in the heart of the city where there was room for a large amount of fairground equipment, numerous stalls and the crushed population of the city.

Market places have their counterparts in urban parks and squares. The pedestrian streets of many cities, Cologne, Vienna, York, Perth (Western Australia), Brisbane and hundreds more fulfill the same functions in an extended form. They are places to gather, listen to buskers in the passing, see the work of a pavement artist, pause for a cartoon portrait, watch a game of chess as in Joubert Park in Johannesburg or of draughts in Union Terrace Gardens in Aberdeen, meet friends, and in places like the Rambla in Barcelona to parade, take coffee, buy souvenirs, read a newspaper, see the passing show.

Preserving open space has also been a preoccupation since the first developer hove into view. Isaiah though not a noted town planner recognised the problem. 'Woe unto them that join house to house, that lay field to field till there be no place, that they may be placed alone in the midst of the earth.' (*Isaiah* 5:8). He is the earliest predecessor of the National Playing Fields Association. He was anticipating one of their current preoccupations which has also been taken up by Mrs Thatcher's last Minister of Sport, Mr Robert Atkins.

In presenting new guidelines to Local Authorities in October 1990 he said much the same thing:

> It is particularly important to retain sufficient recreational open space in urban areas to avoid town cramming.

The guidelines aim to halt the sale of valuable urban recreational space for commercial development and say that local authority planners have probably miscalculated how much recreational land will be needed in the next ten years by failing to look at the increased birth-rate in the last two or three. 'Many local authorities have sold off land because they projected a drop in demand — in fact there will be a mini boom in the number of school children around in the next decade' said the Department of the Environment to which the minister is attached. Oh for an Isaiah!

One modern fetish is sponsorship. Governments all round the world urge local authorities to look for it when they are unwilling to spend money themselves. It is a very old device indeed. Many Victorian parks were given by benefactors, sponsors by another name, and even they were following in an ancient tradition. Anthony explains of Julius Caesar 'Moreover, he hath left you all his walks,..... His private arbours, and new planted orchards,..... On this side Tiber; he hath left them you,..... And to your heirs forever: common pleasures...... To walk abroad and recreate yourselves'. *Julius Caesar* 111.2.248 to 253. He did indeed bequeath his grounds to the people of Rome. It was an early recognition of the utility of urban open space. He was not alone and the centre of imperial Rome was eventually endowed with many other similar gifts. It was the outlying areas which were so deficient and produced the mob. The sponsorship might have been better directed.

Ramesis III who reigned in Egypt up to 1166 BC founded public pleasure grounds and gave, it is said, more than five hundred gardens or the space for them to various temples. Such gardens were and still are a feature throughout the world. Even the ancient buildings which form the Roman Church of the Holy Sepulchre in Bethlehem are grouped around a garden and many great cathedrals York, Chester, Durham, Westminster Abbey, have cloisters with green spaces at their heart. They permit contemplation in peaceful places free from the hurly burly of life. This is one of the functions of the modern park.

A contrary pressure also exists to turn open space over to active pursuits. Practising archery in medieval times for military reasons meant reserving open land for the purpose within or close to towns. In one Scottish burgh it was felt necessary to ban golf because it interfered with archery practice. Charles I opened Hyde Park in London to the public early in 1635. The 800 hectare Phoenix Park in Dublin was opened in 1747 it is one of the biggest urban parks anywhere. The commons and common land offered similar outlets for exercise and activity. In 1990 the North East of England region of the Sports Council commissioned a study intended to stimulate the greater use of parks for sport and active recreation.

In 1600 Grays Inn in London was built. It was the start of a new kind of urban open space. It began a fashion. The earliest of the Paris squares, now called Place des Vosges was built four years later. It was not long before the idea spread and by the beginning of the 19th century there were more than twenty squares in central London alone. The idea was echoed and developed in cities like Bath, the New Town of Edinburgh the spa towns, and seaside resorts like Brighton and elsewhere.

At first they were places in which to leave carriages, and in which the horses could be exercised from time to time whilst they were waiting, but they soon started to fulfill the same function they perform today: that of small, often private parks, fenced and reserved for the residents and used for walking; the enjoyment of plants and verdure; sitting in the open air in pleasant surroundings; and as a background of greenery when viewed from the surrounding houses. They were the precursors of the Victorian public park with the same range of activities. Housing schemes are still being designed on the same principle.

Early in the 18th century the pleasure garden developed. Ranelagh Gardens is a famous example, the vestige of it still remains beside the Royal Hospital at Chelsea where the Chelsea Flower Show attracts hundreds of thousands of ` people every year. The gardens opened in 1742 and survived for sixty years. They were used for music and dancing and the young Mozart played at Ranelagh on his visit to London with his father in 1764. Firework displays took place there and the walks were illuminated at night.

Vauxhall Gardens were opened in 1661 and continued until the middle of the 19th century. They were not large, only about 12 acres, but they were packed with attractions to compensate — just like a modern park might be. Illuminations, a cascade, entertainments, music, pavilions, a supper room. They were superseded or rather eclipsed by Cremorne Gardens on a site at Chelsea alongside the Thames where an esplanade was built so that boats could land their passengers. The entertainment included music, dancing, balloon ascents, a maze, a circus, a variety of special

events, and other attractions. The gardens were built over when
they closed in 1877.

All the pleasure gardens were the victim of changing tastes, no
doubt of increasing land values, and of competition from the
expanding system of municipal parks which were free and which
opened all the year round every day, unlike the pleasure gardens
which were open only in the summer and charged for admission.
The attractions that they tried however are the same in substance
as those which enterprising parks managers still use today.

Other pressures were at work. The Industrial Revolution started
early in Britain and the rapid uncontrolled expansion of the main
urban centres began. The experience is being repeated in developing countries today. A flood of people is being drawn to the
cities and the better life they seem to offer. High birth rates add to
the problems of overcrowding, bad sanitation, and inadequate
public facilities.

In Victorian Britain these were associated with low life expectancy, high infant mortality, epidemics of cholera, typhoid, and
typhus. The pressure to provide parks as one of the solutions for
these problems stemmed from the idea that bad air of itself caused
ill health and that parks and open spaces would act in William
Pitt's words 'as lungs for the city', they were to be green venti-
lators. Air pollution in some parts of the world from the smog of
Californian cities to the pall of wood smoke across those in Africa
is still regarded as a risk to health.

There was also a belief that the countryside was the natural and
most beneficial milieu for man. The urban park was seen as simu-
lated countryside. There were economic reasons for providing
parks. Recreation and exercise in the open air would improve
physical fitness it was said. This would increase productivity, and
prolong the economically active life of city dwellers. There were
moral motives as well. The Parliamentary Committee on Public
Walks in 1833 was convinced that 'some open places reserved for
the amusement of the humbler classes would assist to wean them
from low and debasing pleasures'. These ideas still echo in todays
debates about leisure provision. Only the language has changed.

The enclosure of common land had proceeded rapidly in 18th
century Britain. It had been good for farming, bad for people. It
had materially reduced the amount of land to which they could
obtain access. Today it would be called privatisation. By 1834 the
feeling was gaining acceptance that it had gone far enough and
that people were being deprived of too much recreational space.
A bill to facilitate the enclosure of commons was defeated that
year but despite that, common land continued to go and the small
residue that still exists today shows how little was won from the

fierce disputes of the time. Today's countryside commissions and their access agreements seek to restore one of the advantages of common land. The larger urban park and the community forests which are now proposed, do so too.

Efforts in 1835 to pass legislation allowing parks to be made failed to get support in spite of advocacy by the Select Committee on Public Walks. The election of 1837 changed the composition of Parliament. The impetus was lost. Some parks were laid out in places as far apart as Bristol, Leicester and Preston but the investment in land, the cost of design and layout, and the expense of maintaining them in perpetuity were daunting even then.

The sheer awfulness of life in the industrial towns and the epidemics that arose there caused Parliament to set up another Select Committee in 1840 this time on the health of towns. It evolved a long shopping list of improvements low down on which were open spaces, though still only for public walks, and playgrounds near schools.

These pressures produced an aside is the *Towns Improvements Act 1847* allowing the rates to be used to provide parks and a line or two in the *1848 Public Health Act* repeated the provision. There were even government grants available — though small. Once the laws were in place civic pride saw to the rest. It expressed itself in philanthropy and public spending. Just as British local authorities felt that they must have a leisure centre in the 1970s and 80s — these increased from one or two at the beginning of the period to several hundred by the end — so the urban park was the fashionable leisure provision a century before and its numbers increased even faster though in real terms they were no cheaper to provide.

Duthie Park in Aberdeen was laid out during the period. It contains a statue to Hygeia the goddess of health. Hers was the altar on which philanthropists laid their gifts of open space. Parks were highly prestigious mechanisms for improving the health of the population. Everybody wanted them. They immortalised the name of the donor. The human desire for a lien on the future is worth keeping in mind by those who look for sponsorship even today. They were impressively popular — more and more were built — they became an accepted cost on the rates: the parks department was born.

Not all the Victorian parks were in the right place of course, many were at the edge of the then *urban centres*. Some were provided to buffer one district from another, usually inferior, as a sort of *cordon sanitaire*; some were former private estates that had been engulfed by the spreading town; some provided a stimulus to selling rather up-market houses nearby which was the effect of Birkenhead Park, the Arboretum in Nottingham, Victoria Park in Aberdeen, Regents Park in London and others. Some were put on ground that could not be developed for anything else: a circumstance familiar to today's manager who often has to thank the cleansing superintendent for so tipping domestic and other refuse that parkland is the only possible after-use of sometimes large areas.

Park design was influenced by the work of the two most popular landscape gardeners of the time. John Claudius Loudon wrote extensively and was influential in adapting and developing the ideas of Humphry Repton a dominant landscaper and garden designer for nearly thirty years at the end of the 18th century and the start of the 19th. Loudon designed the Birmingham Botanic Gardens in 1831 and the Derby Arboretum which was opened in September in 1840. He also produced possibly the first management plan for a public park in respect of the Arboretum.

Sir Joseph Paxton designed Princes Park Liverpool; Birkenhead Park; Kelvingrove Park in Glasgow where he also had a large hand in the designs for Queens Park; Peoples Park in Halifax; and parks in other towns. His most famous work the Crystal Palace built in Hyde Park for the Great Exhibition of 1851 was later moved to Sydenham where he designed a park with formal gardens, winding paths, large scale tree planting, and perhaps the first example of what was to become, and still remains, a feature of parks department gardening: the extensive use of flowering plants as a public attraction. In fact floral entertainment.

His work set a pattern that was to be followed for much of the following hundred years modified by the efforts of William Robinson who railed against the use of bedding plants later in his life, and of Gertrude Jeçkyll whose fragile gardens and careful use of plants and their colours became a vogue and have recently undergone a revival.

Victorian park designs reflected the wish to see elements of the idealised countryside brought into the city. The concept that they were walks rather than play areas produced numerous paths and the now famous 'keep off the grass' signs though these were not used in every town and some specifically rejected them as early as 1872. Most have now been confined to the reserve stock of museums. The design had to be hard wearing. The flood of plants entering Europe from plant hunters, explorers, and missionaries from all round the world was found a place. Parks were embellished with statues, lakes, fountains, guns captured by belligerent Empire makers, bandstands, rockeries, aviaries, flowers. They were triumphantly successful, thronged with people who had few other distractions. Little wonder that they spread.

Another idea was looming. In his book *Tomorrow a Peaceful Path to Social Reform* published in 1898 and reissued as *Garden Cities of Tomorrow* in 1902 Ebenezer Howard propounded a new form of urban development based on community land ownership. He saw that simply expending the existing conurbations by yet more additions at their periphery caused all the problems of urban life to be exaggerated and made worse — congestion increased; people had to travel further to work; the countryside became ever more remote; facilities that made city life worthwhile like a wide range of shops, theatres, concert halls, museums and other institutions became harder to reach for those that lived on the outskirts. Those that did get there found them full of pushing crowds.

He took the view that after a certain ideal size a city should stop growing and another should be built. It should be connected with the first so that together they could support more sophisticated facilities but remain physically distinct and separated by countryside that would be protected from further development. He chose the number of 32,000 for his ideal population of whom most would live in the city itself, and 2,000 in the country around it. He judged this population would be enough to sustain all the social and cultural needs of the population and provide sufficient sources of employment, without the disadvantages which came from greater size. They would have public parks and open spaces for amenity and recreation and to preserve the sweetness of the air. Every house would have its own private garden.

He was not only a theorist. He put his ideas into practice. With others he established the Garden Cities Association in 1898 and the town of Letchworth was planned in 1903 on the principles he had laid down. Welwyn Garden City followed in 1920. Both are in Hertfordshire. He lived long enough to see that his ideas were a success and that the two towns were working in the way he had predicted and were financially sound. He was knighted in 1927. He died in 1928. He was profoundly influential. He had evolved a theory and made it work. It was the seed from which grew today's green belts, and new towns.

He furnished the idea of a community planned at the outset with parks and a full range of facilities. He demonstrated the use of street trees and showed how green space could reach right to the heart of a town and be interlaced with its other components. His thoughts led to the Green Belts round British cities. They are intended to protect against sprawl and coalescence. By 1990 more than one and a half million hectares of green belt had been designated in England alone nearly an eighth of its surface area. There were two hundred thousand hectares in Scotland.

Parks managers should make a pilgrimage to Letchworth to see one of the greatest modern influences on the work they do. The model villages of Port Sunlight with its open front gardens, Bourneville, and Hampstead Garden Suburb share the same organised picturesque leafiness with interlocking diverse open spaces made integral to the urban fabric. They have a weakness. The abundant evenly spread open space makes it hard to get the sense of the town as an *urbis*, little appears as the product of happy accident, there is less of the thrill experienced in wandering the crowded urban centre of towns like York or Durham with their sense of organic development and surprise and exploration.

The idea of a city in a garden can be seen in its ultimate form in Canberra. It was purpose built as a capital city. The American architect Walter Burley Griffin was appointed to design and lay it out. He planted the trees before he finished the roads. He got the sack, but Canberra is magnificent because of its space and trees. As the city grew his vision was better understood. The great lake he designed for the front of the parliament building is now named after him.

Active recreation was the next trend. The government sought to encourage physical fitness not to confer comeliness and eternal life, but to fight a war. A national fitness campaign was instituted in 1937 and in the same year the *Physical Training and Recreation Act* thudded onto local authority desks encouraging them to build playing fields for field games. The bleak if grassy landscapes that resulted were all too often the green deserts that later conservationists were to denounce. Some still exist unmodified by the large scale tree planting that alone can resolve their problems of scale.

The emphasis on active recreation produced thousands of additional playing fields, pitches for soccer, hockey, rugby, cricket, occassionally for lacrosse and shinty, even more of the tennis courts and bowling greens that had made a much earlier appearance. Golf courses grew in number especially in Scotland where some district councils provide as many as eight. In autumn 1990 the Minister for Sport said that British Government policy was to encourage greater participation in sport and to promote excellence.

Elsewhere than in Britain the same processes were at work. In America Andrew Jackson Downing wrote about parks and garden design propounding a similar view to Repton and Loudon in England. He campaigned for public parks including a major park in the centre of New York. He laid out the most filmed garden in the world — that of the White House, also the grounds of the Smithsonian Institute and the Capitol in Washington.

Central Park New York is one of the most famous parks in the world. It was the subject of long campaigning. A competition for its design was announced in 1857. Frederick Law Olmstead who was already employed as the superintendent of the park joined with the architect Calvert Vaux who had been Downing's partner. Together they submitted the winning design which was influenced by the ideas of Downing and by Paxton's work at Birkenhead Park.

They went on to design Prospect Park in Brooklyn, Golden Gate park in San Francisco, Riverside Chicago, and many others. Olmstead laid out the famous Arnold Arborethum and Franklin Park in Boston and developed the idea of a system of parks connected with parkways so that instead of separate units they could be seen as parts of a whole. Their influence is still felt; their designs still generate comment; and their ideas, especially about the separation of traffic and pedestrians, are still used.

It is natural in a new country to collect and exhibit the local flora and to import and exhibit familiar plants from home. Botanic gardens are thus a relative common place in countries like Australia. Botanic gardens at their best have many of the attributes of a public park, the Royal Botanic Gardens at Kew are a leading example. They are influential in introducing new plants, showing how they can be used, and training people to grow them.

The Melbourne Botanic Gardens are another case in point. They were first proposed in 1842 a mere ten years after the colony was established. Today they still fulfill the role of a Botanic Garden but are also among the busiest public open spaces in the city. They combine a landscape idyll with a major plant collection and vigorous public use. They are a lesson to anyone wishing to combine education about plants with pure public enjoyment and they show that gardens in the best manner can attract large crowds for the classic reasons: relaxation; strolling at leisure in the open air; picnicking; sitting; playing on the grass; feeding the black swans and the ducks on the lake.

I once spoke to a summer school of the Indiana State University. It was held in Edinburgh and it attracted people from all walks of life and from all over the United States of America. I mentioned that the year, 1988, was the centenary of the birth of one of the greatest of all park developers. He was Robert Moses who was dominant in New York for forty four years. A lady came and spoke to me afterwards. She had been one of his secretaries up to the time he was ousted from office in 1968. We talked about him.

His first important post was as the President of the Long Island State Park Commission which he took over in 1924. In four years he built up the parks and beaches there from virtually nothing to nearly four thousand hectares; he built tree lined roads which he called parkways to get people out to the new developments. He believed that the parks should be filled with happy relaxed people and he provided the resources they needed: playing fields, restaurants, snack bars, marinas, boats for hire, thousands of picnic tables, bathhouses, places for children to play, golf, pitch and putt, roller skating rinks, bandstands, dance floors, huge car parks for tens of thousands of cars. By the time he had finished even these were not enough. There never was a grander vision of what parks ought to be.

He became the head of the New York State Park Commission which extended his role further. Long Island became only one of his concerns. He preserved the battle fields at Saratoga and Fort Stanton; obtained the Whiteface Mountains; and preserved the woods there. He bought large parts of the Adirondacks and the Catskills and preserved them from felling. He made campsites, footpaths, bridle trails, picnic places, nature trails, gave access.

In 1934 he became the Park Commissioner for the City of New York. The department had become almost derelict under the mismanagement of the Tammany Hall regime. When Robert Moses started work in New York there were 119 playgrounds he built six for every one he took over. During the depression he had an army of tens of thousands of men refurbishing the city parks, adding skating rinks, tennis courts, golf courses, baseball diamonds, footpaths. He built beaches out of mud flats importing the sand on barges.

He removed nearly a hundred miles of fences opening up areas that had long been caged; refurbished nearly three hundred statues; formed a parks department band more than sixty strong; put new equipment in the playgrounds and added benches so that parents would be encouraged to accompany their children; put down surfaces that would not tear and scratch the child who fell on it. He cleaned the granite walls in Central Park; restored the buildings; replanted the Shakespeare Garden; rebuilt the zoo. He also refurbished the zoo in Prospect Park and made a new one on Staten Island.

He searched for unused pieces of city land throughout the slums, took them over, made them into parks. He planted trees, made lawns and used flowers on a scale not seen before, but it is not so much the statistics of his work that are important as the philosophy and the invention that underlay them: he saw the places he built as bringing pleasure and delight.

He found money for all these projects wherever he could by hunting for sponsors and donors — he looked in the obscure corners of the city and the state accounts — and took full advantage of grants from the federal and state governments. It was one of his greatest skills.

He was the hero of New York: life in the city was profoundly better for the work that he had done in the parks and because of the green spaces he made.

Oscar Wilde took the view that history is gossip. Perhaps he is right. Still, a moment's gossip is needed to say what happened to Robert Moses. His was a long career. He held many public positions. He built bridges and parkways and housing, accruing more and more power. He also made enemies. In the end they brought him down but not until he had changed the face of his own city and affected many others by his example and ideas.

2 Functions of parks

Parks are still important though they are no longer the high fashion they were in the three decades at the end of the 19th century. Their place has been taken by the sports hall and leisure centre. There is a drawback. Parks and open space systems have not always or everywhere had the investment they need to modernise and refurbish, still less to develop. The make-work schemes of the 1970s and early 80s — periods of high unemployment in many western countries — allowed some redress but they were not sustained for long enough.

Shabby parks with their structures languishing for want of investment attract fewer people. Falling attendances produce lower status. Diminished status results in lower priority. Management is buried deep in other administrative structures. Lowly functionaries lack the clout to demand the cash the systems need. Cash starvation reduces standards and more customers are lost. This is not true everywhere of course. There are shining examples of the conservation and development of parks and others of rescue and recovery but it is true enough in some places.

Parks should be full of people enjoying themselves. They have other roles as well but that is the basic one. They are essentially places of public resort.

They are a big investment in land alone and often occupy sites of considerable value. Add to that the cost of layout, landscaping, internal roads, buildings, playgrounds, shelters, pavilions, and access roads, and the investment can be seen as the biggest most local authorities have in their portfolios after housing. There is an obligation to it as well. The investment cannot be justified by the income it produces or the value it adds to surrounding property, though it does both. The only possible return on the scale required is in public use, entertainment, enjoyment and happiness. Achieving this should be the central objective of management. The truly successful manager requires not only the technical skills of the profession but also the fervour and zeal of the missionary, and the panache, éclat, style, flair, élan, and pizzazz of the showman.....

Well managed parks can provide services that nothing else can. That is why they have antecedents going back to the start of mankind. They uniquely allow use by very large numbers of people and can sustain it over long periods, the capacity even of a medium sized twenty hectare park is perhaps a hundred times greater than that of a large leisure centre.

The running costs of a park for each hour of use is a fraction of that of even a riotously successful sports hall. The sums are easy to do. Parks permit every member of a family and every generation to enjoy themselves together. Larger parks allow areas of high intensity use to be interlaced with a wild and natural landscape, preserved or introduced, so that they widen and enhance the urban experience.

The General Household Survey in 1986 showed that in Britain 46.3 per cent of adults over sixteen years old participated in a sporting activity, including walking, in the four weeks prior to the survey taking place. That means that more than half of all adults did not. They are however quite likely to have visited a park as indeed would most of sports men and women themselves.

There have been a number of surveys that show that visits to parks are high. The General Household Survey (OPCS 1979) estimated that as many as 1.7 visits for every adult in the population of Britain are made to urban parks each year and that does not include visits by children who are among the principal groups of user. In part this stems from the much wider age and social range of people that can use open spaces.

Management should ensure that all can feel at home including those who feel inhibited elsewhere: adolescents chased out of a shopping centre; old people wanting a place to get warm as well as somewhere to sit, talk, watch the world go by, get a half price tea or make their own; teenage youths seeking a place to play a vigorous uninhibited game of football; the unemployed; ethnic minorities; disadvantaged groups like single parent families. To these the park may be their only accessible leisure resource. They should be able to feel at ease there along with all the others.

Parks are flexible they allow easy adaptation to accommodate changing tastes and varying individual needs. They cannot be packed with people continuously so at times they provide for solitude and courtship for walking and contemplation for the lonely introverted exercise of the jogger; and at others for great community occasions bonfires, firework displays, orchestral and other concerts, great sporting occasions, displays, exhibitions, demonstrations, galas, fairs, flower shows, highland games, son et lumières, steam engine rallies, jousting tournaments, ballooning, parachuting, whippet racing, horse shows, pop concerts, festivals, open air aerobics and exercises in the oriental manner, visits by celebrities, coaching schemes by the heroes of their sports, family parties, picnics. All of them in the open air surrounded by plants and a glimpse at least of the natural world, stylised perhaps, limited and regulated certainly, but enough to give the taste for more and to act as an antidote to traffic infested urban life and an escape from the motor car which civilised or not is an alien.

Corbusier in addressing the third International Congress of Modern Architecture which was held in Paris in 1930 said 'the street becomes appalling, noisy, dusty, dangerous:..... How can anyone achieve the serenity indispensable to life, how can anyone relax or give a cry of joy, or laugh, or breathe, or feel drunk with sunlight? How can anyone live!..... The man in a city is a lump of coal in a brazier: he is being burned up simply for the energy he produces'. The park is the antithesis of all that — it allows escape.

The considerations which affect all leisure provision affect parks too. There is more leisure time. Interesting opportunities are needed to allow it to be used advantageously. *Genesis* records six days work in which the earth was made. The seventh was used for rest. It was a pattern followed for centuries. Even the seventh day was often taken up with work. Richard Henry Dana in his book *Two Years Before the Mast* (1840) said 'Six days shalt thou labour and do all thou art able,..... And on the Seventh — holystone the decks and scrape the cable'.

Saturday half-day-off only became widespread in 1880 in Britain. Not until 1914 was there a 52 hour average working week. The 42 hour week only became common after the Second World War. The five day week was an introduction of the 1960's. The 35 hour week is only now starting to appear in industry and when it does is quite likely to produce an equivalent increase in overtime. The average working week has only dropped by an average of 0.6 of an hour in the last twenty years. The leisure explosion we were all warned to expect has not come as predicted through an ever shortening working week. Instead it has expended in other ways which make different demands.

In 1970 only a few people got more than three weeks' holiday a year and there were fewer public holidays. Now more than a quarter of manual workers and more than half of all office workers have more than five weeks. The amount is still increasing. The trend will probably continue with comparatively slight falls in the actual hours worked in a week and a bigger increase in holidays.

Unemployment creates leisure time but we are not trained to cope with it. Most people between leaving school and retiring expect to spend about 65,000 hours at work. We are educated for the purpose. The new National Curriculum in Britain stresses the skills of the work place.

Even the tradition of physical education though enshrined in the curriculum up to the age of fourteen is under threat from several sources, there is a shortage of trained PE teachers; all teachers are less willing than they were to spend time out of school hours supervising games and other leisure activities; and the system of assessments during the school life of pupils will put pressure even on the time that is available. A survey by the Secondary School Heads Association in 1990 showed school based sports activity in sharp decline. They said it had fallen by a fifth in three years.

Teaching people who are abruptly thrown on their own resources may fall to the manager, organising classes for sail boarders, gardeners, trampolinists, botanists, hill walkers, naturalists, bibliophiles. 'He hath no leisure who useth it not' said George Herbert in *Jacula Prudentum* more than three centuries ago. 'To live a life half dead, a living death' said John Milton in *Samson Agonistes*.

As for retirement it represents a very considerable increase in leisure. It is not only occurring earlier in life it is lasting longer as life expectancy increases. Earlier and earlier retirement is one of the easiest ways of coping with the effects of the new technology and of administering the necessary spread of wealth that it produces.

As a result of these factors, long holidays, unemployment, longer retirement, leisure is available in lengthy periods. The manager has to learn some of the skills of tour operators and holiday promoters who have learnt to plan for whole days and weeks on end.

They would consider that a system of parks is more important than individual ones; that managers in neighbouring authorities should cooperate to provide a package of visits and coordinate their entertainment programmes; that there should be closer contact with hotels and guest houses and coach operators; that the parks should offer a wider diversity of sports, games and occupations, and encourage the development and pursuit of hobbies; and that the opportunities should be marketed.

Longer leisure opens the way for more volunteers; managing facilities, supervising, making improvements, planting, building, and doing that range of jobs that used to form parks department winter work programmes before competitive tendering was introduced. The Government statistical service estimates that there is quarter of a million voluntary organisations in England and Wales alone. The manager should start some more, as friends of the park.

Australians have an instinctive genius for poetry, it is expressed in the names they give to the Eucalyptus thus the Stringy Bark Gum, Cabbage Gum, Swamp Gum, Small Leaved Gum and others. They have invented a new word in the same tradition; volunteerism. Nothing could be more expressive. In some local authorities they have networks of people able to work as volunteers on park and amenity projects. In the City of Nunawadding in

Victoria there is a system that park managers all over the world would do well to study. The parks department there has a thousand voluntary leaders on its books each of them undertakes to find ten other voluntary workers and to encourage them to come forward when suitable projects arise. They have the capacity to call on the aid of ten thousand people. It is an important way of recovering the ground lost through the financial stringency and retrenchment which has been the recent lot of departments worldwide. More important it is a means of generating community spirit, civic pride, community protection of community assets.

Parks today must compete for customers. Although there is more leisure time there are also more distractions. Television is now the major consumer of free time. In 1969 we spent sixteen hours a week watching it. By 1979 it had risen to twenty hours a week. By 1989 twenty five hours. By 1987 ninety British households in every hundred had a colour television set. Fifty five per cent of all British households had a video cassette recorder by 1990. Satellite and cable television, a multitude of channels, high definition pictures, stereophonic sound, bigger screens, better videos, are increasing its competitiveness. As well as competing with parks for trade it can help them by providing publicity.

It is generating interest in particular sports and pastimes. In a single year British television coverage of sport increased from 2,850 hours in 1987 to 3,240 hours in 1988 this is partly because sports coverage has an hourly cost which is a fraction of that of drama: a factor which is causing it to increase everywhere in the world. It brings different sports to the attention of the public, for example the British Channel Four programmes of American football have generated a demand for pitches on which to play the game and has stimulated the formation of British teams.

Television programmes increase the affection for wild life and the environment, and they create celebrities the better to plant trees by. Managers should keep an eye on programming, observe and respond to its trends, cooperate with the local management, use them for joint promotions, seek coverage for what is being done.

Shopping, or rather window shopping, is the preferred leisure occupation of most people in western societies after television. There is no reason why the park cannot participate, offering space for shops, garden centres, craft fairs, florists, weekend markets, fashion shows.

In retrospect perhaps the most important leisure change this century will be seen as the improvement of the home as a place in which to spend time. The fall in household numbers throughout the period has produced more space for each individual. There is now a greater chance of following personal hobbies and interests; less need to go out to find privacy; more opportunity to invite friends to the house instead of to a rendezvous elsewhere; it is possible to view television in one room whilst another programme is watched in the next. By 1990 more than 50 per cent of British households had two or more television sets. How to compete? Appeal to the gregarious instinct of humankind. Make the park a meeting place, busy enough always for the visitor to be sure of seeing other people. Every park manager will be aware of a community of regulars. The things they want are the same that every one will respond to: warm, or in some countries, cool places to sit; attractive things to see; pleasant surroundings that are clean and well kept; a restaurant for refreshment; a diversity of entertainment; flowers; trees; birds; and most of all, other people. Popularity once gained feeds on itself.

Horticulture as recreation

A twenty hectare park in an urban area represents an investment at current values many times that of even a major sports hall. In spite of this it is highly unlikely to have a manager and in these days may not even have a regular staff based in it. Still less will it have the garden demonstrations, guided walks, open days, plant identification competitions, classes for rose growers and pot plant enthusiasts, naturalists, tree lovers and garden historians that are the horticultural equivalents of the coaching schemes that a sports centre would undoubtedly provide.

Managers do not always exploit the major international hobby of horticulture though the park can be its apotheosis. Six million people in Britain are alleged by various surveys to say that gardening is their principal recreation. Surveys have shown that a large majority of United Kingdom households have access to a garden. Moreover it is a developing hobby. The British market in plants and garden equipment is now a billion pounds a year. It has increased tenfold in twenty years. There are eighteen million gardens here. More people now go to the gardens of the National Trust than to their great houses and other properties.

The *Sport Council Digest of Sports Statistics* and various other surveys including those by the Office of Population Census and Statistics assess the numbers of people in Britain who follow various sports. Football is the most popular. Estimates suggest that over ten million adults and about two million children play in an organised game of football at some time during the season in

England and Wales. Scotland contains ten per cent of the British population and although football is played better there it can be assumed that the figures are roughly proportionate to the distribution of people. Golf attracted 1.1853 million adults in 1986, tennis 614,600. Add them all together and the number is still less than those who go gardening. The same is true throughout the developed world even in places as sports conscious as Holland, Australia, New Zealand, and the United States.

Parks department clients can, and variously do, provide advisory services, garden visits, soil testing, plant identification, advice about pests and diseases, promote garden competitions, provide speakers, slides, videos, cooperate with the library to increase the range of garden books available. This stimulus to private gardening encourages visits to the parks; improves the standards of private gardens; and through them enhances the appearance of the town or village.

Urban amenities commission

There is no organisation with the title used to head this paragraph and none that has a national role that reflects it. Shame! It is a missing element in the British system of quangos which support recreation and its associated services. In 1989/90 the Sport Council received £52million in grants from the government. The Arts Council received £155million. The Countryside Commission for England and Wales got £22million. They have used the money to publicise their own concerns and to generate interest and enthusiasm for them. Quite right. Through grants they have been able to encourage local authorities to spend in the directions they have chosen for them.

There has been no equivalent organisation for urban amenity that could focus on towns, and the parks, open spaces, natural landscapes, trees, squares, and pedestrian streets that make life so much better in them. The result has been to distort priorities. Local government spending has naturally followed the grants and been directed away from urban amenity as a consequence. Managers should exert steady pressure to redress the balance and campaign for a properly funded new national body to help.

Hierarchies of open space

There has been a good deal of theorising about the relationship that different types and sizes of spaces have to one another. They are sometimes billed as a hierarchy of open spaces and seek to impose rational planning principles over the chance and opportunism that have brought most actual open spaces into being. My advice is do not abandon opportunism.

The first British essays on the subject stem from the garden cities movement led by Ebenezer Howard and find physical expression in places like Letchworth, Welwyn Garden City and in British New Towns. Port Sunlight founded in 1888 on the Wirral peninsula south of Liverpool and Bourneville founded in 1879 near Birmingham embodied the same idea — though the first was built of soap and the second of chocolate. In the United States its advocate was Frederick Law Olmstead.

Sir Patrick Abercrombie produced the Greater London Plan in 1944. It advocated a system of open spaces and listed what they were. It grew outwards from the play space and city square to the countryside outside and around the town. Since it defines the territory his system of parks is included here: children's playgrounds; town squares or amenity spaces; school playing fields and playgrounds; landscaped town parks; large playing fields for adults and older children; recreation and sports centres (these in the superseded definition of outdoor sports and games areas); connecting and radiating parkways; wedges of open land; small green belts and strips of open space for defining the boundaries of communities; commons and heath land; river embankments; green belt; areas of high scenic beauty and farmland.

To this list must now be added shopping malls; pedestrianised streets; linear parks, that range of secret spaces often out of sight behind buildings; the front gardens which were a characteristic of housing developments between the wars and in the immediate post war era; the natural landscape that has survived or been introduced; and the green spaces scattered throughout post war housing schemes as planning authorities applied the minimum standards which by then most had adopted.

In 1968 the Greater London Council conducted a survey of the parks in London. The council's parks department at the time was one of the biggest in the world but it was later split up and eventually disappeared along with the council itself. The planners evolved from the study a hierarchy of spaces. They suggested the kind of distance people would travel to get to them. Naturally the bigger spaces are expected to be less numerous than the smaller ones, and, to have a wider range of facilities, buildings, and equipment.

Their suggested hierarchy was as follows:

1. Local parks two to ten hectares in extent with a catchment area of a quarter of a mile.

2. Larger but still local parks of about twenty hectares with a catchment of three quarters to one mile.
3. Large parks of about sixty hectares with a catchment area of between one and five miles.
4. Parks over one hundred and twenty hectares with a catchment extending for more than five miles.

Nothing is in fact so neat but it does address the important question for those trying to locate open space of how far its effect might be felt. It was also incorporated in the *Great London Development Plan* and affected other plans all over the country.

After lasting for twenty years the scheme was revised by the London Planning Advisory Committee in 1988 and the amended form is given here including fuller definitions of the space. The hierarchies are really planning ideas relating to the physical attributes of the spaces and naturally they generalise. They do however imply a rather inert management and see open spaces as performing a traditional range of functions.

In practice a park, even quite a small one, can draw people from a wide area if its facilities are attractive enough and if it is marketed well or if its location is central. St James Park in central London for example is only about thirty three hectares yet it is never empty and is often thronged and behaves as a metropolitan park might do. (It contains the best fed ducks in the world).

1. Linear open spaces intended for visitors arriving on foot spread through the urban area wherever feasible. They are defined as including canal towpaths, footpaths, disused railways and other routes which provide opportunities for informal recreation including nature conservation and which are often characterised by features or attractive areas which are not fully accessible to the public but which contribute to the enjoyment of the space.

2. Small local parks and open spaces. These are expected to provide for visits by pedestrians especially by old people and children and are seen as having a particular value in high density areas. They are defined as being two hectares in size and at a distance from the home of 0.4 km, they include gardens, sitting out areas, children's playgrounds or other specialist areas including those intended primarily for nature conservation.

3. Local parks are also expected to be used by visitors who arrive on foot. They are defined as areas of two hectares and at a distance of 0.4 km and are expected to include provision for court games; children's play; sitting out areas; nature conservation; landscaped environment; and playing fields if the parks are large enough.

4. District parks are thought of as being twenty hectares in extent and at a distance of 1.2 km. They are said to be for weekend and occasional visits by foot, cycle, car and short bus trips. They are defined as landscape settings with a variety of natural features providing for a wide range of activities including outdoor sports facilities and playing fields; children's play for different age groups; and informal recreation. They should provide for some car parking.

5. Metropolitan parks of sixty hectares with a catchment of 3.2 km or more are meant for weekend and occasional visits by car or public transport. They are defined as either natural heathland, commons, woodlands or formal parks providing for both passive and active recreation. They may contain playing fields, but to comply with the definition would also have at least forty hectares for other pursuits. They should have adequate car parking.

6. Regional parks and open spaces cover four hundred hectares in extent and thought of as having a catchment of between 3.2 and 8 km. They are large areas and corridors of natural heathland, downland, commons, woodlands, and parkland and may also include areas not publicly accessible but which contribute to the overall environmental amenity. They primarily provide for informal recreation with some 'non-intensive active recreation uses' and with car parking at key locations.

The Countryside Commission for Scotland also produced a hierarchy of spaces in their report published in 1974 and called *A Parks System for Scotland* except that their vision extended from the city centre out into the furthest countryside.

The problem with all the studies is that they give insufficient weight to factors other than size. They could just as well be, and might be more useful as, a hierarchy of use. For example the small Piccadilly Gardens in the centre of Manchester is intensively used all day and evening. At lunch time on fine days it is so flooded with people that it cannot physically accommodate more. Its success is in part a product of location but also of appropriateness and suitability of design for its main purpose which is to provide a pleasant sitting area and a bright focus of flowers in the heart of the business district. If the same number of users were to visit a country park a hundred times bigger it would be hailed as a triumph by the manager.

Numbers alone are not proof of success. It is necessary to look at the way visitors enjoy themselves: to see if they are willing to linger; whether they are cheerful and relaxed and feel at home; whether they are engrossed in what they see; whether they are sufficiently at ease to talk to other visitors. Attendance does not by itself imply satisfaction with a park any more than a crowded train is evidence of public satisfaction with British Rail. Even a heavily used and ostensibly popular park may well require improvement and change to produce greater pleasure in its users.

If the number of hours of enjoyable use is the test of success for an open space then the factors that induce the public to go there, and having got there which stimulate their interest, are much more important than size except insofar as this is a factor in itself. Location; accessibility; relationship with the developed area around; management attitude; the quality and range of facilities; wealth of wild life; layout; extra items that give special or eccentric interest; entertainment that the visitor can expect to find; provision for special groups like the disabled or the young can be weighted along with the visual effect of the open space and formed into a numerical model to test its usefulness and to measure it against others.

In the past planning has been hampered because of lack of information about open spaces. Not now. Tender documents contain comprehensive lists of the spaces and their measurements. When recreational management has also been documented there will be complete schedules of games and other facilities. These should be accompanied by statements of management intention and council policy. Test the public response — find out what they want or expect: and a long step has been taken towards systematic assessments of the values of both relative and absolute of individual parks and open spaces and of the systems of which they are part.

Small open spaces

A distinction can be drawn between parks and other large spaces and the smaller pieces of ground that are scattered throughout the community and which are valued mostly for their appearance. These small incidental areas are just as important collectively as the bigger ones. Threats to develop or erode them are less likely to produce the angry tumult of exasperated protest that greets a similar threat to a park so they deserve even more of the manager's protective care. They can if handled with daring — contribute a strong character to a place; generate local pride and sense of community; attract tourists. At their best they give unity and consistency to the built environment, introduce aspects of nature to otherwise barren uninviting places, bring dappled shade and colour; give a human scale; define spaces; affect private gardens as neighbours copy what has been done and emulate the standards that have been achieved. They can bring decoration and adornment, ameliorate the ills of urban traffic; mitigate the ugliness of an unloved development; declare the change of seasons. The aim of the manager should be to achieve a city that seems to have been built in a park.

Bold amenity planting and extensive interesting open spaces are one of the inducements to industry to come to town. Incoming businesses are not likely to settle in down at heel neglected places still less to bring their staff to live there.

We only have to consult our own hearts and to ask where we would wish to live given freedom of choice and what attracts us and then to inject these characteristics into the communities we serve. Beauty should be part of everyday life not separate from it. Consulting the public about the layout of spaces; getting them involved in planting adds to diversity, makes the areas self policing and brings a thousand minds to bear.

Design considerations

Parks are functional places and the layout must reflect this. Their role should be established before the design even starts. If an architect is invited to plan a building he first asks for a design brief forcing the client to think in detail about exactly what is required, what kind of use is to occur. The parks client should systematically plan a brief as well.

It is necessary to decide what the park is expected to do, who it is hoped to attract, what special facilities if any it has to provide; what the balance is to be between active use and passive enjoyment, and between wildlife areas and high intensity ones; where different maintenance regimes have to prevail; where the customers are to come from, how they will get there, how long it is hoped they will stay; how the park is to relate to its immediate surroundings: whether these are to be hidden and the park made into a quiet oasis or are to be visible and made a feature.

The design should express the result of public consultation and customer surveys and of an understanding of the district and its nature; the age groups it now contains and projected changes as time goes by. Even the most successful parks rely for their regular daily visits upon people who live close at hand.

A park can attract people from a wide area but to do that it has to be rich in interest. The manager has to consider what will make it distinctive and worth visiting. Surveys in several towns have indicated that to act as magnets parks must usually be twenty hectares or more in size. There are exceptions. The popular Royal National Rose Society garden at St Albans is an example. It is busy throughout summer when the plants are in flower because it has specialised and made itself a Mecca for rose growers or for anyone wanting to enjoy floral spectacle. It has done so despite being only twelve acres, though it is now being expanded to increase its range. A small park can do the same by specialising in a similar way. The topiary gardens at Levens Hall in Cumbria show the power of the unique. Centuries of clipping have produced an eccentric, cheerful diversity of shapes which are in piquant contrast to the sombre box and yew from which they are made. The National Trust Garden at Hidcote near Chipping Campden in Gloucestershire is only ten acres but it attracts people from far and near because its intricacy and the richness and diversity of its planting allows the visitor to spend a long time exploring it.

Parks have the same potential, but most of them have to provide for many uses and a certain minimum size is needed to accommodate and to separate those that conflict with one another, and still find space for an exiting or interesting and distinctive development to act as a magnet capable of drawing people from a wider area. Parks have to adapt with time and to different demands. Just as flexible design has been a motivation in architecture so it should be in a park.

The design of a park is a matter for the special skills and judgement of the landscape artist but the universal principles of proportion and scale apply to it as they do to all other three dimensional works of art. Although plants are a vehicle for the creation of usable spaces they have to be employed with respect for contrasts of form, texture, colour, mass, the provision of focal points and landmarks just as they would in a garden where they are intended as the predominant element.

Landscape designers frequently employ too limited a repertoire of plants and the current disdain for horticultural varieties that is evident round the world excludes valuable and useful material. Those who reject brightly coloured plants are at odds with the taste of the park customer who occasionally likes to gasp in surprise at a piece of horticultural drama or even effrontery. Such plants need using with care and placing with skill but they have a role in the functioning of a park in the same way that natural vegetation does.

In the countryside only native plants or those which are so familiar as elements of the landscape that they seem as if they are native should find a place. Garden plants there look garish and ill at ease. The exceptions are in the vicinity of buildings or within an enclosure; where the garden is a distinct element defined by trees or land form; or where it is on such a scale that it matches that of the countryside beyond for example at Cliveden near Taplow in Buckinghamshire.

Planting should not be bland or mundane. In parts of the park, sometimes in all of it, growing, exhibiting and displaying plants chosen for their individual beauty, educational interest, effect in the mass, or for delight, it itself the function. The reason people are attracted there is to see and admire the plants and to sit or walk amongst them. Planting should also confer shelter, divide the park into hospitable useful spaces, give a sense of enclosure and containment, screen an unwanted view, mitigate an unlovely one, draw attention to a fine one, provide shelter from wind and stem the turbulence produced by tall slabs of building. People spurn the naked park.

Paths should follow logical routes through the space. That does not mean that they should be straight, far from it. Left alone to form by themselves paths will curve as they follow land forms and may even jink as they negotiate an obstruction or a tree. In the designed landscape they are important as one of the components of the design and the picture it creates. They must also be practical. They should be wide enough for people to pass in comfort without feeling threatened by those who approach. Paths should also be in scale just like the other components of the space. If they fail other paths will be formed or the edges will degenerate as people are forced off them.

One of the ideas present in the design of Central Park New York is that of separating traffic from pedestrians. It is an important lesson for all urban planners not only those concerned with parks. In the largest parks there is always pressure to allow access for motor vehicles. Except in the very biggest areas where there may be a case for giving access to interior car parks, or for letting in specialist vehicles for the disabled, cars should be kept out. The reason: they interfere with the pleasure and relaxation of everybody else especially parents who should not have to worry whether their child is at risk from passing motor vehicles. The lobby to get them into parks suggests that drivers are responsible enough to behave reasonably. Do not believe it.

If cars are admitted the park must thereafter be managed on the assumption that the drivers will behave like those everywhere and forget the erratic vulnerable frailty of pedestrians and children. Managers must take precautions accordingly and these include introducing undesirable landscape elements like barriers, fences, sleeping policemen, warning notices, road signs and markings. Better by far that the car should be left at the gate in appropriately located well landscaped car parks, screened from view. If necessary provision can be made for an internal transport system, horses and carriages, trains, trams. Observe with what invention the problem is dealt with at garden festivals.

The linking of open spaces is desirable. In this way several smaller spaces can behave in the way a big one does and act as a greater attraction. Together they can offer the chance of long walks through the city free from conflict with motor vehicles and away from noise and fumes. One of the best examples of this is in the Texas city of San Antonio where the extensive system of waterways interlaces with the city fabric but at a different level and separate from the streets. The river banks have been turned into a major attraction. They are lined by paths, overhung by trees, and are flanked by cafes and shops. Citizens and visitors flock there.

The British New Towns have all found it easy to plan landscape corridors between larger open spaces and to associate these with walks and cycle ways. They give the sense of a town growing out of the country around it and continuing thereafter to exist within it. Though they have also sometimes fallen into the trap of sundering communities so that the sense of town is lost in all the verdure.

Like other open space the small incidental ones and those that act as corridors should be planned to give delight and pleasure, and a sense of surprise and exploration, give scale, contrast and shelter to the buildings and other elements in the town. Its purpose should be expressed in its design. Such a treatment also improves the chance of wild creatures finding room in the urban space since it will behave for them as a single great habitat.

In older towns a network of open spaces and corridors between them is harder to achieve. Managers must make do with the spaces they can find, river and stream sides, old railway tracks, incidental open space and wedges of greenery, shelter belts, tree lined and planted streets, reclaimed derelict ground, school playing fields. The long term object of building up a network of related spaces and binding them into a unity by trees and planting has to be constantly in mind so that the opportunity to further it can be taken with bustling energy whenever the chance arises. In the meantime the greatest advantage has to be taken of what exists or can be adapted. Fitzhugh Ludlow whose brief life ended in 1870 wrote, 'While we wait for the napkin the soup gets cold,..... While the bonnet is trimming the face gets old,..... When we've matched our buttons the pattern is sold,.... And everything comes too late, too late'. Waiting inertly or reacting sluggishly is no way to serve the public.

Not many parks have been designed as a vehicle for the display of art even though some have powerful sculptural content. The

Parc Guell in Barcelona is an example of how an architect artist in this case Gaudi, created a park so extraordinary that it is one of the major tourist attractions of Europe and toast of every taxi driver in the city. Anyone considering a new park might perhaps look at this possibility. The combination of space, considerations of texture, colour, and form are essentially artistic matters and the engineering and horticultural vehicles of realising the concept can be furnished by others. All good design is the product of adjusting a concept to practicality.

Computer assisted design

Computer software is advancing all the time. The park designer can make use of it just as architects do. It speeds up the process of design, mechanises the once laborious job of drawing details. It can even be used to select trees and shrubs. The designer is left with the essentials of the art, judging scale and proportion, creating useful workable spaces, injecting flair. There are several applications.

A number of programmes are now available to help select the most suitable plants for the conditions of a particular location or to secure a desired effect. There are occasional eccentricities. Nurserymen tell stories of being asked for rare plants in numbers that represent the entire world production this century or for plants that are so obscure they had never heard of them. It is an aid, not a substitute for common sense. There is software for depicting contours; showing cross sections; mapping topography; drawing perspectives, projections, and of course plans. Computers are used for calculating volumes and quantities; recording the data from tree surveys; producing the standard elements of specifications. The draftsman with a 3H pencil, a set of french curves, and a slide rule whilst not yet an obsolete figure is certainly of antiquarian interest.

Programmes are now available for placing a sequence of orders; controlling a flow of goods; issuing instructions for maintenance work; recording expenditure, matching it with estimates; showing the proportion spent and the amount left and measuring these against expected results for the time of year. The use of graphics is also very advanced converting statistics into graphs, pie charts, and block charts and using other illustrations. The manager is not absolved from the responsibility of management and the job can even be made harder because of an information flood. Some of the old skills should be kept honed: judgement, experience, scepticism.

Maintenance

Economy of maintenance should be a central concern. The cost may have to be supported over many generations. Victorian parks have already been kept for a century or more. The investment in design and layout is negligible compared with the accumulated cost of upkeep. It deserves careful thought. The way the park is to be maintained should be considered at the outset and included in the brief, it is not just a question of cost. A design will not survive if it cannot be maintained easily, it will change as adjustments are made over a period: as ground is worn away by the tramp of feet across an unexpected short cut; or as the gardener whittles away at an awkward angle that cannot be reached by the machine that is used; as fragile plants unsuited to the robust life in a park fail and have to be replaced or in wild areas as nature takes its own course and the elements of the vegetation compete, strive for dominance, and suppress their less successful neighbours.

Maintaining areas that have been laid out with native and wild plants so as to form a near natural landscape is cheaper than high horticulture and the areas that are formed in this way enrich the urban landscape and the public experience of it. They are part of a necessary balance and are one of the options that should be considered along with other elements of park design just as Olmstead included them in Central Park New York in the last century and many others have done so before and since. There are also parts of most urban parks for which traditional more intense maintenance programmes are required by reason of the amount and nature of use to which they are put and because of public choice and response. Within these areas the design can affect the cost of maintaining them.

The type of mowing machines and their dimensions should be stated in the brief. The designer can then space trees and borders so that mowers can pass without the need for a smaller machine following behind, picking up the left over areas. A contractor's problem? Certainly, but the cost is relayed straight back to the client. Formal bedding which is very expensive to keep may have to be omitted unless it is to be done on a scale that turns it into floral entertainment, or replaced with flowering shrubs like roses or heathers which give the same class of show without the same annual expense. Plants in borders should be close enough so that they smother weeds quickly without the need for cultivation or chemical weed killers.

Short cuts should be anticipated and made into paths or paved, if they form spontaneously they should be acknowledged and the design adapted to accommodate them and a surface made appro-

priate to the location to allow convenient public use. The lines of a
design should be free from needless obstructions or sudden angles
that cause maintenance equipment to gyrate. Games and sports
facilities should be grouped so that they can be managed by a
single attendant. The natural contours of the site should be retained if possible because altering them may produce a generation of
drainage difficulties. Slopes should be gentle enough to be
maintained by machine because pedestrian guided equipment is
expensive to use.

Fences should be only used where they are essential for practical reasons, around a tennis court or golf driving range or to stop
an impetuous child running onto the road, otherwise the brief
should presume against them not just because they are costly to
provide but because they are expensive to keep afterwards. If they
must be introduced use tough long lasting materials. If chain-link
fencing is chosen use plastic covered wire. Support it on low
maintenance plastic coloured pylon posts. They last longer and
merge into the background. They are many times stronger than
angle iron or its variants. Incidentally choose black for chain-link
so that it sinks out of sight. Green sounds better but in fact plastic-
green shouts in loud self assertion and is incompatible with every
natural colour in the landscape.

The best most durable materials should be used. It is wasteful to
skimp. If paths are paved with slabs these should be thick and
well founded — enough to withstand even the weight of a lorry. If
not they will crack when the first one comes by and be sure that it
will whatever the expectation. If tarmac is to be used then choose
hot rolled asphalt instead. It is far dearer but lasts much longer —
nature designed it for skateboards and roller-skates. If pergolas or
posts are introduced they should not be made of cheaper
softwood because it will need frequent maintenance. Prefer
durable oak in spite of its price. Graffiti prone buildings should be
easy to clean or paint, and be planned for the vandal.

Horticulture is a means of making parks attractive and useful:
not an end in itself. Flowers should be planned as part of the
structure not scattered afterwards as floral litter and those that are
introduced should be chosen and arranged for the function they
perform in attracting the public. Mixed borders which are easier
to keep and which can be designed for all the year interest should
be preferred to herbaceous borders or flower beds.

Shurbs that need annual pruning should be avoided whatever
their charm unless they are interesting for a compelling reason as
roses may be. Even then consider using the so called landscaping
roses which are like their floriferous garden cousins but which do
not need annual pruning and which are on their own roots and

thus free from suckers. Plants that cannot stand the weed killers likely to be used should be excluded even though it robs the park of sweetheart plants like lilac.

Small trees are cheaper than big ones and establish quicker but if they are likely to be scythed down in their youth by stem snapping vandals then bigger dearer ones are better value. As an alternative, and where the design permits multistemmed trees can be chosen, or clumps of several or many trees can be planted very close so that they grow into a natural looking thicket which will prove harder to damage and is more likely to be self healing — just as the gardener puts several plants together in a single pot to give a quick result.

Water areas should be shallow so that they are easier to clean and are less of a risk to those who might blunder into them. The edges should slope gently. Ponds that are small enough should have some kind of circulation system to keep them fresh and lakes are best if they have a stream to feed and cleanse them. Overhanging trees are lovely, but too many of them cause cleaning problems in smaller ornamental ponds because of the amount of leaves that descend in the autumn.

Grass seed mixtures must be chosen for their durability and dwarf low maintenance varieties should be used. There have been many improvements in grasses and the presumption should be in favour of modern hybrids even if their names are foreign and unfamiliar and their price seems high.

Wild flower mixtures are fine but where a sward is to be subjected to heavy wear they are less likely to survive. They will only produce an interesting mixture of herbs on poor soil, without fertiliser. Some recommend the removal of top soil if the layers below are sandy and sowing onto that. Wild flowers need the opposite treatment to garden plants.

Grass areas should be simple in outline so that they are easy to cut. Trees planted in lawns should be at such a distance as to permit the easy passage of the equipment likely to be used. Manhole covers should be aligned with the ground surface even if this means they have to be placed on an angle. The tops of the covers should not be buried otherwise access is difficult and the ground has to be disturbed and restored periodically. There may also be the cost of a time consuming search to find where they are. If fine turf is to be irrigated for example on a golf green, pop up sprinkler systems should be considered at the outset. The chance of finding money for them later is slight.

Where turf may be subjected to intensive wear or incompatible uses for instance a cricket wicket in an open park, then artificial substitutes should be considered. They should also be used where the demand for games like football and hockey far exceeds the capacity of the park to sustain it. If a park is very small as might be the case in a city centre square and the use expected to be heavy, hard surfaces should be considered over its entirety to confer durability and to increase the useful surface to the maximum extent. Planting in such a situation is a secondary element introduced along with seats or statuary as a means of increasing diversity and interest or for shelter or screening.

Pricing

The way prices are fixed in local authority leisure is about to be changed out of recognition by compulsory tendering. The cost of subsidies will be clearer than they have ever been and more subject to deliberate scrutiny. A frequent way of fixing prices was to see what other authorities were charging and to conform. It is a bad method because the results have no relationship to the cost of providing and running the facility. A private business would go bankrupt. Prices should be fixed in relationship to costs and the desire for profit, and then modified by a judgement of the effect on demand. Special groups like the old or the very young can be encouraged by deliberate subsidies or passports to leisure schemes. The costs are then clear.

There are circumstances when a sharp reduction in prices may produce more revenue because of a surge in demand. Managers should be given freedom to experiment with a range of prices, varying them in response to demand, offering inducements for off peak use, arranging special offers, giving discounts for block bookings, subsidising season tickets.

Sponsorship

Sponsorship is not only a matter of money. Companies can offer help in kind, the use of premises, printing and distributing, advertising space, expertise. Most companies fix a budget for advertising. Recent surveys show that it is usually between one and two per cent of turnover. Of this only two per cent is spent on sponsorship. Sponsorship of sport in Britain increased to £50million in 1981 to £200million a mere five years later. The *Arts Council Annual Report* in *1988* said that sponsorship of the Arts was only £500,000 in 1980 but £30million last year. There is money. The problem for the manager is to get some of it for parks projects.

In seeking sponsorship of any kind the important question to answer is what is to be offered in return. The Institute of Marketing says that 'sponsorship aids the corporate image, creates goodwill, increases public awareness of a company through repeated media coverage'. Publicity, advertising, access, are the things the manager has to offer. The English Tourist Board an 1980 said that '... modern sponsorship is a mutually beneficial arrangement between sponsor and sponsored to achieve defined objectives'. Adam Smith in the *Wealth of Nations* said it better two centuries before 'The propensity to truck, barter and exchange one thing for another is common to all men and is to be found in no other race of animals'. Shakespeare explained the technique in *Twelfth Night* Act 2 Scene 5 'Here comes the trout that must be caught with the tickling'. If the manager is skillful and persistent, it is likely that some sponsorship will be forthcoming. The possibility of direct collections from the public might also be considered and the fund raising techniques of other voluntary groups should also be examined and exploited with the aid if necessary of Friends of the Park.

Sponsored planting has been used get bulbs and trees planted. It is easier to measure and more useful than the sponsored walk. The manager will have to make a direct approach to youth groups sports clubs and others with the idea. It has to be made easy by providing support, staff to give instruction, transport and equipment. The group will also respond to publicity just like any other sponsor and the support of the local press and television should be obtained. Sponsorship is also a good way of getting a facility that a committee is unlikely to approve if it had to pay out of public funds: a talking cactus; a frog to blow bubbles; musical play equipment; sculptures; fountains.

It is possible to get money for park developments by many means. At the entrance to Stirling gardens in Perth, Western Australia there is a wishing well. It is an idea as old as water. It is meant to take money. It does. In Fitzroy Gardens in Melbourne there is an area of sponsored paving. It is made of bricks. Each is inscribed with the name of the donor, their nominee, a poem, cartoons, names of companies or best of all with a wisecrack. It raised money, laid a pavement, and created a feature full of interest. Each sponsor got a tiny monument, a toe-hold on immortality. The park gets money to use on something else. Similar things have been done elsewhere.

Some parks are funded by promoting group picnics. The park provides catering, clowns, games for children and adults, the physical equipment, and the catering. In the city of Leeds traffic islands are sponsored by companies in return for a small sign saying who they are. In the Roman baths at Bath up to the third century AD, it was possible to make a sponsored curse. It was a very good idea indeed, much recommended to outgoing Prime Ministers. York holds a busking festival each year from June to July with support from British Rail who give free tickets for the performers; the Yorkshire Evening Press also gives support. There are many forms of sponsorship. The possibility of raising money by ingenious ideas not only offers the chance of fun, it transcends the restrictions on spending that local authorities experience in every country in the world.

3 Legislation

'When I use a word' said Humpty Dumpty 'it means just what I want it to mean neither more nor less'. 'The question is' said Alice in reply 'whether you can make words mean so many different things'. 'The question is' said Humpty Dumpty 'who is to be master — that's all'. Lewis Carrol in *Through the Looking Glass* was making a point that has often vexed lawyers. In finding what a law means, judges start by looking at the exact way a statute is worded. Sometimes it is not clear, then they interpret it and make a little or a large law themselves. It is thus not always enough to look at the legislation that affects parks and open spaces, it may also be necessary to know how the courts have understood it. Sometimes parliamentary orders can be made which ministers present to Parliament and which amplify the act concerned. These have the effect of law too. Managers should go to a specialist when they want a legal point cleared up.

Even so, take a case to a lawyer and the question 'What do you think about it?' is quite likely to be asked back. 'Where shall we start looking?' comes next. A thoughtful personal response is enough for the first question because the work done every day is shaped, limited and regulated by a variety of laws and statutes and the current literature on the profession will contain references to new ones that are proposed or which have been recently enacted. Probably the best answer at present to the second question in Britain at any rate, is to recommend a reference to *The Law of Public Leisure Services* by Michael Scott published in 1985 in London by Sweet and Maxwell.

Every country is different but developments in one have sometimes started trends in others, so British legislation on parks and recreation will seem familiar to those concerned with them elsewhere. Scottish law is different from English but most statutes follow similar lines and some legislation applies to the whole of the United Kingdom. This is made clear in the opening sentences of the statute concerned.

Local authorities in Britain cannot do anything unless Parliament has said they can. If they do their action will be *ultra vires,* that is, outside the law. They can be challenged if they try to step outside their limits by their own officers, by citizens, by people directly affected, or by their auditors. The courts can stop them taking the action and the penalties can be high. Local authorities are sometimes called the creatures of statute. As a result there is a large body of legislation which affects every aspect of local government including general laws like the *Health and Safety at Work Act* and specific ones like the *1906 Open Spaces Act.* Advice will be given by the council's legal officers and anyone proposing a novel action should consult them beforehand.

In some countries local authorities have what is ostensibly a greater freedom in that they are allowed to do everything except what has been forbidden to them: what is called a general competence. There is a disadvantage. Subsequent local government legislation becomes negative and prohibitory rather than positive and having within it a flow of ideas. Nor is it true that the laws will be fewer. Central government will find a multitude of things that it does not want local government to do.

John Stuart Mill in his essay *On Liberty* chapter three, says 'The liberty of the individual must be thus far limited; he must not make himself a nuisance to other people'. Local authorities like everyone else are affected by Common Law relating to such matters as nuisance and negligence. It also deals extensively with contracts.

British legislation about local government takes two forms. It may permit local authorities to take an action if they want to, or compel them to do something whether they like it or not. *The Countryside Act 1968* gives them the power to provide Country Parks and leaves them with the choice as to whether they want to do so. Most of the legislation about the provision of Urban Parks is like this as well. The clauses concerning the control of dogs in the *Environmental Protection Act 1990* imposes a duty, which leaves them with no choice at all. The legislation may be limited to one kind of authority for example District Councils in which case it does not give authority to the others.

The law related directly to the provision of parks and open spaces in Britain is scattered through a number of statutes. They successively chart the development of the service and the way it has broadened over the years though there are some which give wide authority: for example clauses in the *1972 Local Government Act* which brought about the reorganisation of local government in England and Wales and consolidated and extended some of the powers contained in earlier legislation about parks and recreation. The Scottish legislation followed a year later.

The idea of public parks is an old one dating back to antiquity but the modern British system began in Victorian times with private acts of Parliament promoted by individual local authorities seeking permission to make parks. One of the early examples was the *Third Birkenhead Improvement Act* a private act of Parliament promoted by the Improvement Commissioners for Birkenhead. It made provision for the purchase of land, at least 28 hectares of which were to be set aside for the free recreation of its inhabitants. In the event were used for the purpose and Sir Joseph Paxton started work in 1844 on what was to become Birkenhead Park. This in turn influenced Frederick Law Olmstead and his design for Central Park New York as well as many of the public parks developed subsequently in Britain.

Later on general legislation was introduced beginning with the *1848 Public Health Act*. The clauses which it contained about parks were echoed and superseded by Section 164 of the *Public Health Act 1875*. This important statute was the begetter of many of todays urban parks. It allowed the purchase or lease of land by urban authorities and permitted them to layout, plant, improve and maintain lands for the purpose of public walks and pleasure grounds. The powers it gave were clarified and extended by further legislation over a long period right up to the *1972 Local Government Act*.

The *1906 Open Spaces Act* was also far reaching in its effect. It took the parks service a major step forward. It defined open space as 'Any land whether enclosed or not, on which there are not buildings or of which not more than one twentieth part is covered with buildings and the remainder of which is laid out as garden or is used for the purposes of recreation or lies waste and unoccupied'. It allowed the land to be taken into council ownership and to be maintained for the good of the community thereafter. The urban park could step outside its railings.

The *Public Health Amendment Act 1890* had already let local authorities make charges, arrange closures, regulate boating pools and even support pleasure grounds outside their own boundaries. Another amendment act in 1907 allowed them to provide seats, games, apparatus, pavilions and refreshment rooms. There was a rather damp squib on the topic of playing fields in the *1925 Public Health Act* but the *1937 Physical Training and Recreation Act* gave authority to layout and equip playing fields, children's playgrounds, athletics stadiums, community centres and to lease them to clubs and voluntary organisations.

The *1948 Local Government Act* section 132 allowed a generous sum to be raised for use on entertainments and perpetuated and expanded the band concerts that had been endemic in parks since they were established. They had been developed during the war into a wide range of entertainment as a result of the Holidays at Home schemes. The descendants of the schemes continue to attract the public into the more vigorous parks systems today. The

1972 Local Government Act gave the powers a new lease of life in section 145.

The *Education Act 1944* laid a duty upon education authorities to secure the provision for their areas of adequate facilities for leisure time occupation and in respect of schools and colleges under their control for adequate facilities for recreational social and physical training. This not only spread the phenomenon of the school playing field it sometimes led to an unspoken competition between local authorities and their departments and eventually to the faltering progress of the movement to secure dual use of school facilities sharing them in effect between the pupil and the member of the public. Even this has been given a new twist by the *Education Act 1988* which vested considerable powers in schools councils not all of whom wish to provide a subsidised recreation service for the public and who may see in the playing fields pavilions and other games and recreational facilities a useful source of income. Some by contrast are proving as protective and resentful of public use as the most recalcitrant authorities used to.

The *1972 Local Government Act* and its Scottish equivalent a year later are still the first reference points for anyone researching the legislative authority for a particular local government activity. They consolidated much of what had gone before. They contain clauses which give wide powers to local authorities to provide leisure facilities. But the most profound consequence was the shock they administered to the of structure of authorities. The distinct independent parks and recreation department had been a feature for much of the century. In most of the large local authorities it all but disappeared. It was subsumed into others usually concerned with a wide range of other leisure activities and resources, among these were arts centres, swimming pools, theatres, libraries, museums, art galleries community centres, civic catering, and as the decade progressed the burgeoning leisure centres. The thread that was seen as linking them all together was the use of leisure time. Some departments had been growing organically and had initiated or taken over some of these other roles anyway. The progressive changes would have continued even without the stimulus of the legislation.

Nothing is static, everything is subject to change. Local authority structures are simply mechanisms for performing a series of services and they need adapting as the times progress. Tennyson in his poem *In Memoriam* says 'The hills are shadows and they flow..... from form to form and nothing stands..... they melt like mists the Solid Lands..... Like clouds they form themselves and go'. It is a fundamental truth about the structure of local government in all countries. In Britain the 1972–73 legislation not only turned apparently solid structures into clouds it swept them from the skies with the force of a hurricane.

Compared with the 1972 Act the changes which followed during the next fifteen years were trifling though important for what they touched on. The *1976 Local Government (Miscellaneous Provisions)* allows local authorities to provide such recreational facilities as they think fit either within their boundaries or outside them and to make grants and loans to voluntary organisations. The *Zoo Licensing Act 1981* is intended to raise the standards of zoos. There was legislation to improve the safety of sports grounds and this affected the stadiums which many departments provide. The *Local Government Planning and Land Act 1980* among many other things, allows land held under the *1875 Public Health Act for Public Parks* or the *1906 Open Spaces Act* to be released and used for other purposes or even disposed of if it is no longer required for its original purpose. The *Local Government (Miscellaneous Provisions) Act 1982* codified the law on entertainment licences for singing, dancing and music including pop and rock festivals.

Garden Festivals were introduced and in the long term will be seen to have affected the design and contents of new parks as they are made. They stretch the concepts of using plants as components in a general entertainment and extend the already well established idea that parks can accommodate sculpture in many exiting or even controversial forms. Also they can be a home for the other arts and provide venues for eccentric as well as conventional entertainment. Other new laws tinkered with local government powers in a variety of ways.

Legislation intended for general effect like the *Health and Safety at Work Act*, the *Unfair Contract Terms Act 1977* which prevented the evasion of liability for negligence by notices and clauses printed onto tickets, the *Litter Act 1983* and a variety of other measures produced by a series of busy parliaments, all had an influence on parks and open space management.

They are part of a process of continuous adaptation, but one Act contained the seeds of major, even disruptive change. It was the *Local Government Act 1988*. It introduced compulsory tendering and this has had the effect of sundering the parks function dividing it in two. One the client — the other the contractor. The effects are discussed elsewhere.

The changes are not conclusive. Further structural change is on its way. Local Government financing will be reviewed yet again. Even the new certainties will disappear.

By-laws

Park by-laws used to be displayed at the entrances to many parks in a forbidding list of prohibitions and multiple negatives. These notices have largely though not entirely disappeared. It is questionable whether any by-laws are needed at all. The common and statute laws cover every malfeasance and deviation common to mankind with others in addition. Even the most imaginative local authority would find it difficult to cook up more. They should not try.

Petty rules are seldom effective they are difficult to enforce, put righteous people off and suggest interesting ideas to the ill intended. In Scotland the *Civic Government (Scotland) Act* superseded the by-laws that then existed though the local authority can publish management rules which have much the same effect.

Local Government Commissioners

The Ombudsman is now a familiar term in Britain as it is already or is becoming elsewhere. It is applied to the commissioners set up under the *1974 Local Government Act*. They investigate complaints about the way local authorities do their business when this leads to an allegation of injustice. They have no authority to question the merits of a decision or the policy behind it if there was no maladministration and their investigations cannot start until the complaint has been addressed to the authority either directly or by a representative or a councillor, and a reasonable time has elapsed in which the complaint might have been dealt with, or a response made to it. Even after their investigation has started they give the local authority the chance to comment and put a point of view. They may try to settle differences by negotiation.

Most deeply felt grievances are about housing and planning, some concern highways, and personal services like social work and these regularly feature in the Ombudsmens reports. Parks and open spaces do not frequently produce complaints to the Ombudsman but they can. For example if the authority refuses to deal with trees that it owns and which cause annoyance to the complainant, or if a noisy playground is near to houses.

The Ombudsman can report on investigations and will find the local authority guilty of maladministration if an injustice results from unfairness, malice, sloth, bias, incompetence, neglect, high handed committees or officials, if procedural rules have been flouted or if any of the seven deadly sins not named above have been committed.

The commissioner can recommend action to remedy the injustice or suggest compensation. The local authority has to say what it has decided to do, if anything, in response. If this is not satisfactory a second report is prepared. It is rather like being beaten by a sponge. The only strength of the reports comes from the publicity they get. No local authority likes to be accused of maladministration. It embarrasses councillors and officials alike and they usually though not always take steps to put things right. Sometimes they may disagree with the conclusions and ombudsmen are fallible like everybody else, in that case there is no power of compulsion.

Audit Commission

The Audit Commission is the child of the 1982 Local Government Finance Act and was established in England and Wales a year later, there is a separate commission for Scotland. Its task is to appoint auditors for every individual local authority and to promote efficiency through the process of the audit. The commission is a quango, that is to say it is composed of appointees of government ministers, to carry out a public function independently. It is headed by an official called the Controller of Audit and it has a paid staff.

The Commission took over the work of the former District Audit Service which still does about 70 per cent of all local government audits, the rest is the work of private auditors who are also appointed by the commission. The traditional function of audits is to make sure that the local authority stays within the bounds of the law and that its business is conducted honestly. The act gave them another function that of promoting value for money.

The commission cannot determine the policy of a local authority, that is the province of the council itself, but it can influence the way the policy is conducted by showing ways in which it might be done better. Sometimes the commission is outspoken and embarrassed local authorities may have felt the weight of George Canning's plaint now nearly two centuries old, 'Save me, oh save me from the candid friend'.

Value for money studies

Value for money studies are starting to appear in a number of countries. In Britain the Audit Commission undertakes a number of general studies each year pointing to what they think is the best practice, making the case for change, saying what changes they would prefer to see, comparing performance and output, identifying the unit costs, saying whether the job might be done better or for less money or both. They give case studies and examples of good and bad practice. They consult widely. They are sometimes outspoken and critical not only of local but also of central government. Every manager should study their reports. They may have a valuable direct application, they make lucid, well reasoned recommendations and they allow an interesting comparison to be made between local, and the best national, practice.

Some departments are occasionally insular. Oliver Cromwell said in dismissing the rump parliament 'You have accounted yourselves happy on being environed with a great ditch from all the world beside'. The Audit Commission and its reports have breached any isolation that local authorities may have felt, obliged comparative judgements to be made, and in the local auditors they have an assiduous corps of active local agents. Even Louis XV had nothing like them.

Local value for money studies are now also well established in Britain. They can be undertaken by the council's own staff or they may be proposed by local auditors to the Audit Commission who can approve them. They study an aspect of the service with a view to seeing if the money spent on it is giving the best result and to suggest ways in which it might be improved. Value for money is not necessarily the same as cheapness or low cost but it does embrace the ideas of economy and efficiency and effectiveness. The studies may also make comparisons with the nature and price of similar services elsewhere.

Value for money is, as it always has been, everybody's concern but in the main it will be a function of the client who decides on the nature of the work to be done. Contractors have related interests: reducing costs, buying wisely, increasing production and obtaining the best results from the materials and plant they use.

One should remember two contradictory sixteenth century utterances when faced with critical studies. Oliver Cromwell's famous words in a letter to the General Assembly of the Church of Scotland on 3rd August 1650 should be always kept in mind. He said 'I beseech you, in the bowels of Christ, think it possible that you may be mistaken'. Existing practices and performance may be ineffective, or too costly, or be out of date or complacent and in need of change. The opposite proposition can be found in the motto of the Earl Marischal of Scotland of the century before 'What they say, let them say'.

Reports from whatever source and however distinguished should not produce a suspension of judgement. Sometimes the local authority may be of right and the others may be wrong.

Countryside

Other legislation that affects the park system in its broadest sense is contained in the *National Parks and Access to the Countryside Act* in *1949*. It established the National Parks, allows the designation of Areas of Outstanding Natural Beauty, and introduced the idea of access agreements to allow the public onto privately owned but open land for recreation. *Countryside Acts* were passed in *1967* for Scotland and *1968* for England and Wales. They made a number of important introductions and their effect was considerable at the time. Among other things they set up the Countryside Commissions and gave powers to establish country parks, though may local authorities already had areas which were country parks in all but name, Newstead Abbey Estate and Wollaton Park both owned by the Nottingham City Council are examples. The *Wildlife and Countryside Act 1981* and legislation like the Commons Acts and those relating to footpaths can also impinge on the work of the parks manager.

The *Environment Protection Act 1990* will result in the amalgamation in 1992 of the Countryside Commissions and the Nature Conservancy Council. The new bodies like the commissions they replace are to be composed of members appointed by the Government. In Scotland the proposed new body is to be called Scottish Natural Heritage, in Wales the Welsh Countryside Council. Their concerns will be conserving nature and landscape, access to and understanding of the countryside, designating national parks and areas of outstanding natural beauty, promoting the development of country parks, establishing long distance footpaths and bridleways like the Pennine Way and Offa's Dyke Path and sustaining rural communities. The present role of the Countryside Commission starts at the edge of the town. The Nature Conservancy Council has urban as well as rural interests.

The new bodies will make much noise in the world. Be sure that there will be further change. They will cast an eye in the direction of the Forestry Commission whose lands and forests, and the grants they administer have formidable effects on the countryside, the urban fringe and the natural heritage. The Sports Council for Scotland reacted quickly to the new arrangements by pressing for an extension of its own powers so that it can promote access for sports in the countryside. The counterparts of all these groups in other parts of the world will be keeping an eye on the changes and the ways they develop.

Sports Council

The Sports Council in Britain was established in its present form by a Royal Charter in 1972. It replaced an advisory body set up in 1965. It has nine regions each with its own staff and offices and there are sports councils for Scotland, Wales and Northern Ireland though they all work closely together. The council is independent but it gets most of its money from the Government and ministers appoint its members.

It has a considerable influence on the way parks operate through its desire to widen sporting opportunities and the advice and grants that it gives. It aims to promote not only sporting excellence at the highest competitive level but also widespread participation in sport. Its structure has just been altered. It is the subject of yet further study. The Government may look for further change, other ways, perhaps other institutions to further its aims. These are to encourage the greater participation in sport; to promote excellence; to secure better use of existing resources; to increase participation by groups that are at present under represented; to promote the best practice in ensuring that sports facilities respect environmental concerns; and to find further ways of curbing the abuses such as spectator violence and doping which have afflicted sport in recent years.

The Institute of Leisure and Amenity Management

The Institute of Leisure and Amenity Management (ILAM) was established in Britain in 1983 as the result of an amalgamation of four organisations concerned with an associated range of activities, parks, amenity horticulture, recreation both outdoors and indoors, entertainments, and sports management. Among them was the Institute of Parks and Recreation Administration which up to that time was the specialist in parks and open spaces though its range of interest was wider than this. The new institute embraces its concerns. Its formation reflected the changes that had occurred as a result of the 1972–73 reorganisation of local authorities in Britain and the new compendious departments it had produced.

Overseas there are equivalent organisations in Africa, Australia, New Zealand, throughout Western Europe, in the United States, and in other countries. There is an International Federation of Parks and Recreation Administration the members of which are drawn from many countries. They all have the similar aims of providing a professional base for the service, offering training and in some cases systems of examinations, promoting seminars, meetings and conferences, publishing journals, and representing the views of members in national and international forums.

Tourist Boards

The *Development of Tourism Act 1969* is the legislative basis of tourist administration in Britain. Tourism affects parks and open spaces and they affect tourism. Open any tourist guide national or local and you will see that at least some of its contents will concern the amenity that parks and open space systems provide.

There are Tourist Boards for England, Scotland, Wales and Northern Ireland. The British Tourist Authority has the task of attracting tourists to visit Britain from overseas. There are also regional and local tourist boards. They can give grants to develop tourist attractions; they encourage visitors; persuade tourists to come from abroad; and encourage holiday makers to use the resources of their own country. The economic power of tourism is such that nearly all countries in the world seek to take some of the market. The European Commission already recognises its importance and gives grants in assisted areas to encourage tourist developments. Beat a path to Brussels.

The Arts Council

The Arts Council of Great Britain was established by Royal Charter in 1967. Its objects are to develop and improve the knowledge and practice of the arts, to increase accessibility of the arts to the public throughout Great Britain, and to advise and cooperate with government departments, local authorities and other bodies on any matters concerned with the arts. The council operates through a regional structure which is being strengthened even further. There are councils for Scotland and Wales.

The Arts Council may on first sight seem to have little to do with parks and open spaces and it has not yet acknowledged landscape and garden design as an art form. It is true that a large part of its money, which originates from the Government, goes towards sustaining the national drama, ballet, and opera companies and the great orchestras but they do also have cash to promote sculpture and sculpture exhibitions some of which can take place in parks; There is no reason why artists in residence which they also support cannot also take up their home there. It is a matter of taking an initiative and exploring what can be done with the grants that are available.

Drama and music can also be performed in the open air and the seasons in Kenwood Park in London have long attracted large audiences and visitors. Overseas the climate makes open air performances of artistic events easier and more reliable. The Retiro Park in Madrid stages performances of the country's greatest flamenco artists; in Port Elizabeth the Shakespeare play that is part of the syllabus for the matriculation examination for the year is performed in St George's Park; the open air theatre in Woodthorpe Grange Park in Nottingham used to attract thousands of people each summer to performances of plays, and there are plenty of other examples round the world. These are all areas where support from an Arts Council might be sought to develop lively interesting even novel programmes.

Ministerial responsibility

There is occassionally pressure for a Minister to be appointed for the whole range of leisure services in Britain. These are at present distributed between the Minister for the Arts, the Minister of Sport, the Secretary of State for the Environment, the Secretary of State for Education, the Scottish, Welsh and Northern Ireland Secretaries. The gain that is expected from a single functionary is a more powerful voice. It is not at all clear that one voice is such a good idea. If it is a weak one it will be ineffective over the full range of leisure services and they will all decline together. I prefer a chorus as at present. There is also the admirable colonial adage of divide and rule. There is advantage in the status quo.

Local structure

The local arrangement for controlling the parks function varies from place to place. It is mainly in the hands of district councils in Britain and their equivalents in other countries. Within each local authority there may be any number of permutations but the function is now rarely left on its own. Not only has it been taken into other departmental structures it is usually under the control of a committee concerned with a wide variety of services. It is now rare in Britain to find anything called a parks committee.

There is every reason for parks' staff to aspire to the leading posts in the local authorities they serve. At present in Britain and to an increasing extent elsewhere they are finding themselves slipping into roles that are secondary to the main thrust of the department concerned, community services, leisure services, technical services, direct service organisations. The loss of status may not seem important in itself but it can affect access to committees, access to the media, influence in the whole of the budgetary process as opposed to making the initial bid, even the ability to try the novel, or eccentric, or the outrageous. It may not be feasible to think of a change in Britain until local government is reorganised again — an alert ear should be kept tuned to that debate.

Staff should take any opportunity that comes along to apply for the chief posts in departments that contain their function 'A man must take his opportunity as oft a he finds it' said Francis Bacon in his book *On the Advancement of Learning,* nor should they hesitate to apply for the Chief Executive and other senior local government positions when they become available. 'Dost thou not know, my son, with how little wisdom the world is governed?' said Count Axel Oxenstierna in a letter to his son in 1648. True. Parks' staff should not be held back by assumptions about the qualities or experience of others. Their own role in customer care, finding out what people want, responding to the needs of a community, working with voluntary groups, administering large budgets, managing a complex and demanding service is good equipment for the top job. They should get the posts if they can and the intrinsic merit of municipal self assertion should never be underestimated. 'Do something. Do good if you can, but if you can't, do something,' was my mother's favourite adage. I am glad to pass it on. '... fly upon the wings of the wind' says *Psalm 18.*10.

4 Competitive tendering

A modern Rip van Winkle waking up today would find it hard to recognise local government in Britain even had he snoozed for a mere two or three years. Long established departments have disappeared. Ancient time encrusted practices have gotten the boot.

The changes are not over yet. Each of the political parties who will contend for office at the next election have said they want further change and contemplate proposals that would amend the local government structure itself. Central Government has been fidgeting with the form, function and finances of Local Government for most of the last hundred years so the chances of further change are very high.

At present local government responsibilities are divided between Counties and Districts in England and Wales, and Regions and Districts in Scotland. The only all purpose authorities are to be found in the large English conurbations which are divided up between Metropolitan Borough Councils and on the Islands in Scotland where the Shetland, Orkney and the Western Isles councils also administer everything that local government is empowered to do. Every authority is affected by the laws compelling a range of services to be put to tender.

Compulsory competitive tendering (CCT) has been responsible for one of the most profound upheavals in the internal structure of local authorities for many years. The phenomenon is not confined to Britain. Competition for work that was traditionally done by local authorities using their own personnel is being introduced in other countries and has been long established in the USA.

Mention compulsory competitive tendering to any ordinary citizen and the words will almost certainly elicit a look of blank incomprehension. It is a municipal phenomenon, a private misery or a private opportunity depending on the point of view. It is essentially domestic, internal, and organisational. It has changed attitudes, work practices, atmosphere, the conditions of service, the staff structure, it may even have destroyed careers but what has happened should not at any point be evident to the customer. For local authorities the change has been massive and fundamental but its customers should not even know that any change has occurred at all.

Inviting competitive tenders for the work of maintaining grounds, cleaning streets and buildings, rubbish collection, catering, recreation management, and vehicle maintenance was made compulsory in Britain as a result of the *Local Government Act 1988.*

The legislation also leaves the way open for other services to be subject to tender and indeed the minister then responsible envisaged that local authorities would simply perform what was called an enabling role; specifying the work that was to be done through tender documents; seeing that the work was carried out accordingly; and paying the winning contractor to do it. Where the total work amounts to less than £100,000 it is exempt but this sum has already been eroded by inflation and only permits the smallest authorities to claim exemption from the requirement and even some of these opt to go to tender voluntarily.

Governments are not immortal, Edna St Vincent Millay says in *A Few Figs from the Thistle* 'Come and see my shining palace, built upon the sand' but whatever its future, the legislation has already caused irreversible changes as departments have been broken up and their parts rearranged in order to separate the functions of the client from those of the contractor.

Some change was prompted by the view that the local authority workers would win tenders more easily if they were combined together to form large units able to compete for the full range of work exposed to tender. It is assumed that some staff which all contractors use — such as quantity surveyors, accountants and cost controllers, and some facilities like sophisticated computer systems can most easily be shared if they are part of a single organisation. The overheads can be reduced in this way and then spread over a greater volume of work. Outside contractors have not joined together in a similar way.

The departments that resulted were called Direct Service Organisations or DSO's. Like all jargon the term will eventually seem very old fashioned and will fall out of use but it is well established at present and seems likely to form part of the municipal vocabulary during the immediate future.

A few local authorities decided not to compete at all in some fields of work and instead rely entirely on contractors. Tendering is compulsory — competing for the work is not.

All this has produced a bonanza for management consultants though most of the changes could have been introduced on the advice of Chief Executives and management teams. However, draconian change is sometimes easier to bring about when it is proposed by an outsider, and not everyone at the highest levels of local authority management was able to institute changes on the scale necessitated by the legislation. Luckily for local authority staff their competitors were no better prepared.

Effect on park management

The management of parks and open spaces is affected by the requirement to tender for grounds maintenance, catering, recreation management and insofar as it is not done by one of the other groups, building cleaning. Local authorities cannot do any of this work by means of their own direct labour unless it has first been exposed to competitive tender and private contractors have had the chance to compete for it.

The process was introduced in stages for grounds maintenance because of a view that the contracting industry was not in a position to compete for all the work if it were put out at once. This proved to be true. A fair proportion of the first tranche of work was awarded to direct labour organisations without a competitor even looming on the horizon. However, the value of the work being proffered is so large that contractors in Britain have established themselves or expanded, new ones have appeared, their numbers are still being augmented, and others have been attracted from abroad. As the years progress the competition will become more earnest and aggressive.

Occasionally Local Authorities have sought to improve the chances of their own staff winning the tender by using a number of devices. Some put all the work out in one very large contract so big as to inhibit even the largest firms and to completely prevent small local ones from competing or new ones setting up. Others have refused to make their depots available to an outside contractor. Some have produced tender documents of such elaborate complexity that they are not only a barrier to a contractor but also to their own understanding should they happen to win themselves.

In some cases work was included which was never normally done and which would not be done if the Council's own staff won. Outside contractors had to take it at face value and include the full cost in the prices they submitted. On occasion ill assorted work was put in a single tender making it hard for a specialist outsider to compete. Some local authorities have set large redundancy payments against the cost of a cheap outside tender thus making their own the lowest.

All or any of these practices may be seen as uncompetitive by the Government Ministers concerned. These are the Secretary of State for the Environment and the Welsh and Scottish Secretaries.

The problem was addressed in the *Department of the Environment Circular 19/88*. There were equivalent documents from the Scottish and Welsh Offices. These did not illustrate many uncompetitive practices. Local Authorities were more inventive.

The Secretaries of State have tough powers. They can invoke Section 13 of the Act and demand that a local authority explains and justifies what it has done. They can order a local authority to go to tender all over again under Section 14, and they can tell the local authority not to compete itself. Complaints can and have been made by aggrieved contractors and others. Local auditors will also make comments and recommendations under their powers to promote value for money and to ensure compliance with the law.

The client

The legislation does not stipulate the kind of internal arrangements that local authorities have to make, but many have already divorced the client function from contractor. It is likely that more and more will do so. This has meant separating old colleagues and placing them into different departments.

The parks and open spaces client is usually attached to Leisure and Recreation or Community Services Committees depending on the internal structure of the council and its committee system. They often do the client work for others as well or at least get asked for advice. Housing, Education, Highways, Social Work and other departments all have grounds to maintain. The parks and open spaces client has the majority of this work and staff with the necessary expertise. Sometimes these other groups have chosen to perform their own client role or they may be located in different authorities. They are also being subjected to change.

Schools are able to opt out of the Local Authority education system and even within it headmasters have been given their own budgets to manage. School councils have more power than they did. As financial pressures increase on these almost independent institutions expect the grounds maintenance costs and standards to be looked at more critically than ever. There are some 25,000 state schools in Britain so DSOs collectively have to market themselves to a formidable number of potential customers.

Local Authority housing is also in the throes of change. Individual properties are sold. Entire housing estates can opt out of local government control and when they go they take their grounds maintenance with them. The client may need to take its services to market too.

Evaluating tenders is more plainly fair when done by an independent client. The Audit Commission has also expressed the view that the roles should be separate. The clearest way of accomplishing this is to place them in separate departments answerable to separate committees. Like Caesar's wife local authorities must be above suspicion.

There is obvious potential for a conflict of interest if both the client and contractor work is the responsibility of a single director and are within a single department. No matter to what extent it may have been restructured internally there is a risk that the client side will favour the internal contractor at the expense of the outsider. It will certainly seem to do so no matter what the reality. The so called Chinese Walls that theoretically allow separation within the same structure have not always been a success in the financial institutions of the City of London following their own massive changes and are not likely to be effective in a local authority either.

There are potential gains in the division. The arrangement allows a sharper distinction to be made between the role of council committees in determining the principles and policy of a service and the officials role in deciding how this should be put into effect. Radical new ideas may flow faster from an independent client free from concern about the attitude and the interests of the work force which were sometimes overriding considerations in the past. More efficient work under the spur of competition can mean savings. These can express themselves in a better service or lower tax and rate bills.

There are also losses. The management of parks and amenity horticulture is now sometimes buried deep in the bowels of a department that has other more pressing interests and imperatives. It is at risk of being given low priority or receiving no informed attention at all so that a major resource, the system of urban parks and open spaces, is allowed to atrophy and wither or at best remain unchanging and progressively less relevant. Even the energy that is still available for this work and which ought to be expressed in adaptation and innovation is in some cases being dissipated in disputes with the contractor and concern over the minutiae of tender documents.

Local auditors report on what they find in the individual local authorities to which they are attached. There seems no doubt that the split between client and contractor will attract their attention. Where the same department is in charge of both sides of the work even though the contracting arm has a separate trading account, it is likely that the auditors will recommend a split and that eventually this will occur.

The most obvious role of client departments is in preparing the tender documents then placing and managing the contract. The first step in this process is to decide what is wanted from each park or area, and what will be required in the future. These are sometimes called the objectives of management and they should be made clear because they affect the details which eventually appear in tender documents. These targets may change as time goes by and should be subject to review. Only when this has been done should the next step be taken — setting standards, writing or re-writing specifications and quantifying the work required.

The client is responsible for inviting potential competitors to submit their names, assessing their suitability and their capacity to do the work, placing the contact, setting up a system of communication with the contractor so that instructions are passed efficiently, completed work is inspected, certified and passed for payment, defects remedied or deductions made from the sum to be paid. The progress of the contract has to be monitored throughout its life. Variations must be approved, and expenditure controlled and kept within the agreed budget. The client should be concerned with getting value for money, and with the standards that are achieved.

The client also has a duty to think about the situation that would ensue if a contractor were to fail or be dismissed. Contingency arrangement should be planned. Contractors have been dismissed from contracts for poor performance but it is not a step to be undertaken lightly. Such a decision should be made only after the fullest discussion with the council's legal advisors and after efforts to resolve the problem. Complete records should be kept. A contractor is not likely to go without testing the matter in the courts afterwards seeking not only compensation for the loss of the contract but also for the injury to the reputation of the firm.

Clients must prepare estimates which include their own costs not only those of the contract, negotiate funding from the local authority coffers, seeks grants and sponsors and try to increase income from charges. Clients are responsible for budgetary control, and ensuring compliance with the council's financial regulations. They are crucially concerned with contract administration not only with its technicalities.

The client may retain some operative staff in addition to controlling the work of others. Park attendants, security staff and countryside rangers need not be included in the competition nor are zoos or model farms or entertainments subject to compulsory competition though of course they can be included in tender documents if the authority wishes.

Changes to specifications

One of the risks of writing down the details of what is done and enshrining them in tender documents which may be in force for up to five years is that the service may become fossilised: fixed like a fly in amber. For the first time grounds maintenance work has been quantified and specified in detail and two groups brought into being each with an interest in maintaining something like the *status quo*. The client has the role of ensuring that contractors do not get away with anything and that they comply with the specifications, not omitting to do work nor varying it on their own authority. The contractor's interest is not to do more than he has been told without an order and extra payments.

The first step of some contractors in other industries is to go through the documents with a fine tooth comb to find the potential for seeking and charging for variation orders. Therein may lie the profit. It can be expected that this practice will eventually extend even to the amiable world of horticultural maintenance and into the much more ambiguous areas of recreational management. The wise client will resist but every time a tender is due to be renewed it should first be reassessed and corrected where deficiencies or omissions have been revealed.

There have to be periodic changes in specifications. The client department should be aware of changing demands from the public and should respond to them. It should be concerned with development of the service, and one of its most important roles is in seeing that this adapts as time goes by. The client should be lively and innovative and entrepreneural. It is this side of the divide which will be the eventual motor for change.

Specifications now exist for practically all the local authority grounds maintenance work in Britain, but writing them should not be seen as conclusive. It is merely a stage. They need adapting to changing circumstances, and adjusting in the light of experience when contracts are renewed. They should incorporate good ideas and effective practices from elsewhere. The time to introduce change is when successive tranches of work are offered or when contracts are renewed, not in the middle of contract periods. Change then will prove expensive.

I have been surprised at the sometimes wide variations that have existed in the specifications that I have been shown. The approach that has been taken in writing them and the degree of detail that they contain is sometimes markedly different even in adjacent authorities. The strength of local government is that it does permit individual solutions to local problems as well as a degree of experimentation, but expect auditors to compare the cost of work from place to place. They will nag if the price of what on the face of it is the same job seems to vary much from one authority to another. The figures for the first time will be easy to get. They will exert a strong pressure towards standardisation.

Writing and revising specifications allows traditional methods of work to be reconsidered and assessed. It gives the chance to change them. Standards of maintenance can be also varied. Where these were low the effect of the early phases of tendering was to improve them in many places. The reverse was also sometimes true where standards were previously high. The problem of the client is to ensure that these changes are considered and deliberate and are not the inadvertent result of inadequate specifications of inattentive supervision. There is no theoretical reason for competition to lead to deterioration.

Standards can vary between different areas even of the same park. They always have. Specifications causing needlessly elaborate maintenance or inappropriately high standards, add to the cost of a service without commensurate gain to the user. Accuracy of playing surface is essential to some games. Golf and bowling greens are examples. High standards of planting and upkeep may be part of the attraction of a park. For these the specification should be capable of producing high quality work and enforcement should be exact and demanding. Different standards are possible elsewhere. If these have been exceeded the specifications should be changed when the tenders are renewed.

Ground maintenance

The Local Government Act defines grounds maintenance as cutting and tending grass including returfing and reseeding but not initial re-turfing or re-seeding, planting and tending trees, shrubs, hedges, flowers, and other plants and controlling weeds (but excluding landscaping any area though this work is affected by the *Local Government Planning and Land Act 1980* Section 20(2). In practice CCT affects virtually all the horticultural maintenance done in parks and open spaces and since it is rarely worth making a distinction between this and small scale landscape projects such as minor improvements or alterations it in effect includes these as well.

Tenders for grounds maintenance had to be placed in minimum amounts of twenty per cent over a maximum period of five years so that by the end of the period all the work will have been subject to competition. The first contracts had to be in place by the beginning of 1990.

Many authorities chose to put out the work area by area. A few put it out on the basis of activities for example mowing grass verges. Many exceeded the minimum. Sometimes the judgement about these matters was coloured by what was thought to be best for the existing workers.

The problem in competition for grounds maintenance is that standards of upkeep are very variable and expressing them in words is not easy to accomplish. Moreover horticulture permits shortcuts to be taken which may not be identifiable at the time or which an astute contractor can hide but which show up later in inferior growth or dying plants. By then the true cause may be impossible to identify with the degree of certainty necessary to penalise a contractor. Specifications need to minimise these risks just as good supervision helps to do so. There also has to be a spirit of cooperation between client and contractor and the best results are achieved where a vigilant partnership exists based on precisely worded contracts.

A number of sample grounds maintenance specifications and tender documents have been published including one that resulted from collaboration between the Institute of Leisure and Amenity Management and Longman. They all required adaptation to the particular conditions of each individual locality and varied with the factors that affect all horticultural work, climate, soil, the nature of the planting, the topography, size and shape of sites, and the standards required. The existence of these documents which many used as a guide and *aide memoire* if not as a model allowed local authorities to introduce a very considerable change in a short time.

A tender once accepted is a legal contract which places enforceable obligations on those who are party to it whether they are clients or contractors. This is the case whether an outsider is engaged or whether the work is won by the local authority's own staff. It therefore has to be worded with care and should be subject to consideration by the council's lawyers as well as horticultural staff and quantity surveyors. It is much more than a technical statement of the work that has to be done and if things go wrong the documents will be pored over by the lawyers of both sides.

The documents consist of several parts.

The first might be a preliminary statement of the general aims and objects of the contract and an outline of the work that has to be done. It might for example say that the work is intended to provide an attractive setting in which members of the public can find pleasure and recreation in the open air and that to allow this to be achieved high standards of maintenance are required. It may stipulate that the areas must be managed and maintained for the convenience and use of visitors and with regard to their safety. If playgrounds are included it may indicate that the aim is to provide an interesting and stimulating environment in which children can play safely. It may say that the contractor must use competent personnel having the skill needed to do the work to the desired standard. It may call on him to observe the appropriate British Standards.

These conditions are of course pious and are not in themselves capable of enforcement because they are vague and generalised but they provide the setting in which the rest of the contract can be read and in most cases the work is a matter of cooperation between partners rather than confrontation between opponents. Certainly it should be approached on that basis and the process is assisted if the potential contractor understands what the client is seeking to achieve.

The preliminaries can also be used to give details of access to the sites and any limitations that may exist or they may pass the responsibility over by demanding that the contractor goes and looks for himself, saying that claims from difficulties he could have discovered in this way will not be allowed. They may also tell the contractor that he must provide an out of hours service for work that has to be done at the weekends.

The conditions of contract are a substantial element of all tender documents. The Royal Institution of Chartered Surveyors and others publish standard examples and most local authorities use these or similar ones in the work they put out to competition. They are concerned with the business management of the tender and are used to describe matters such as the procedures for resolving disputes; the insurances the contractor must take out including third party insurance; the use of subcontractors; the way new instructions are to be given or variations from the specification or the bill of quantities are to be treated; they describe how the work is to be certified on completion; the methods of payment; and all the other details which allow the rest of the document to be managed and enforced.

Specifications

The second large element of a contract is the specification which develops the policy and aims of the service in a series of statements about the way in which the work is to be carried out.

Specifications for grounds maintenance must either describe all the work that has to be done and do so in sufficient detail to enable the desired standards to be reached and sustained or they must stipulate the standards themselves. In this case it is left to the contractor to work out the means of achieving them. For example it might state the minimum length of grass on a lawn below which it should not be cut and the maximum above which it must not be allowed to grow. It may say that it should be free of weeds and worm casts and be healthy and that the space should be available for public use to the maximum possible extent, leaving the contractor to decide how to arrange all this. It makes life harder for the contractor and might in theory be thought to favour the existing workforce who already have the experience needed to judge with reasonable accuracy what might be involved. In practice it has sometimes led to low tenders resulting from a misunderstanding of the true work involved and later on to bitter disputes as to what is meant for instance by healthy or weed free. The system can only exist successfully where there is a thorough programme of quality control based on *BS 5750 1987* applied both to the client and the contractor, a mutual understanding of the actual quality that is required and a shared desire to produce high class work.

Most authorities have chosen to make detailed stipulations and the Longman guide to tender and contract documents, *Competitive Tendering: Management of Sports and Leisure Facilities* follows this route. In my experience, as an outsider sometimes brought in to arbitrate in disagreements between client and contractor it is the one least apt to produce misunderstanding and aggravation. This kind of specification seeks to explain in words a complete operation, in sufficient detail to tell the contractor exactly what is expected, and with the clarity necessary to permit ready understanding.

Obscurity assists no one and convolutions of language may easily result in misunderstanding or error. It should contain clauses which protect the clients interest as well as describing the task. For example there should be clauses ensuring that nearby paths are not left covered with grass clippings, that litter is removed before mowing and not shredded by the passage of the mowing machine or that damage resulting from vandalism is put right as soon as it is seen. Each section and clause in the specification must be numbered for ease of reference.

A typical clause might be as follows and is used merely to show the degree of detail which can be appropriately included in specifications. It relates to grass cutting which is the biggest and most costly single part of most contracts for grounds maintenance:

All general grass areas will be cut to a uniform height of 12mm using cylinder machines. The work will be completed in a single continuous operation at each location. The machines must be properly set and sharpened so as to make a clean cut and leave an even surface free from ridging.

The contractor must follow a previously agreed system of mowing to ensure that all areas are cut in a regular sequence and to permit ease of supervision. The contractor must notify the client at the commencement of each cycle of mowing.

Prior to mowing the contractor must clear the area of molehills and of large stones, paper, tins, and all other debris and litter, and remove these materials off the site to a previously approved tip.

If the surface is excessively wet mowing must not take place or if it is in progress must stop until conditions allow it to occur without damage and permit the grass to be scattered uniformly without lumping. Where work is delayed for this reason or due to inclement weather the contractor must provide the staff and equipment necessary to ensure that the cycle of work is completed timeously.

The contractor will be responsible for removing all grass clippings which have been scattered or carried during the mowing operation onto adjacent paved areas and will take them off the site to a previously agreed tip.

Mowing will take place over the full area and right to the boundaries of the grass.

If the work is unsatisfactory the contractor will be required to mow the affected area again without payment.

The mowing machines shall be of a type notified to the client in advance. Operators must be trained in the use of the machines concerned and must be conversant with the safety requirements of using them.

The number of occasions of mowing and their frequency will be determined by the client and will vary depending on the season and growing conditions, and cannot be predicted in advance. For the purpose of tendering and as an indication only a number has been included in the Bills of Quantities. The contractor will only be paid for the number of occasions that mowing is in fact required and this may be less or more than the number shown. Payment will be made for each occasion at the rate quoted.

Specifications should be clear and precise but they ought not to impose officious conditions which do not affect the finished job. For example it is not necessary to stipulate with what equipment work is to be done except when this materially affects the quality of the product. On this basis it is reasonable to require a cylinder rather than a rotary mower to be used since this may affect the quality of the surface and it is also reasonable to say that a golf green must be cut with a ten or twelve bladed mower since this is an important factor in obtaining a smooth even surface suitable for the highest quality of play but not that the mower should be of a particular make.

The contractor ought to be allowed reasonable freedom to innovate and explore different and more efficient ways of doing the work. It is reasonable for the client to ask for a list of the equipment that is to be used but only so as to be satisfied that the contractor is adequate for the task.

Bills of quantities

The other major part of the tender documents are the Bills of Quantities which give details of the areas and numbers involved in each of the operations.

Prior to the need to put work out to tender many authorities had scant information about the areas they maintained except where measured bonus schemes had been installed. Even in these cases most areas had to be measured and assessed again. The process is essential and should be done with painstaking care. If the sizes of areas are wrongly stated or if work is omitted completely variation orders will be needed. Be sure the cost will be high. Contractors take advantage of such situations and the client is usually left without an alternative but to accept whatever is asked. DSOs will exhibit the same tendency.

The bills contain a brief description of the work, the measurement of the area over which it has to be done, the frequency, the unit of measurement for example square metres. The contractor must state the rate he wishes to offer for each unit and the total cost. Mathematical checks are necessary when documents are received. It is a job for the client using a quantity surveyor. Errors nearly always creep in. Together they can be enough to affect the outcome of the tender.

The tenderer will also be asked to submit his price for day work. This is used for jobs that crop up which have not been included or specifically quantified in the tender documents. The prices relate to the hourly rates for skilled or unskilled work or for any other grades of staff that it is anticipated may be required or for the use of a stated item of equipment. Watch out. Day work is the most effective vehicle ever devised for over spending.

Bills of Quantities may also be accompanied by plans. These should be checked before issue to be sure of their accuracy. An outside contractor may have difficulty in identifying all the numerous scattered locations in an open space system, the plans should permit this to be done as well as showing the shape, boundaries and features of the site. Photographs are also useful. So are videos. They can illustrate the standard that is expected better than anything else. Later on they may be useful quides in cases where an arbitrator has to be introduced to help in resolving disagreements.

Quantities change as the area to be maintained expands or diminishes during the period of a contract. Where this is a simple variation of the work that has already been specified the process is easy. The contractor's existing rates are simply applied to the new areas or quantities. Where wholly new tasks are involved a quotation should be obtained and scrutinised with care and if necessary compared with prices obtained by authorities elsewhere. It may not be feasible to obtain other competitive prices but they should be sought if the quotation seems unreasonable and the new work can be conveniently separated.

Member involvement

Most local authorities and their client departments have wanted their DSOs to win. It is a matter of pride and loyalty. A few have even let this wish express itself in framing the tenders so as to help. As time goes by however the separate DSO will start to be seen like any other hungry contractor. It will be just as likely to fall out with the client and may be able to pursue a disagreement with more vigour than is possible to an outsider. The DSO has direct access to the client department's own employers. Memories linger.

The councillor will also find that a largely independent DSO separated from the main stream of the system and having a management with considerable freedom of action and with strong commercial tendencies is not the vehicle for pet schemes that the old arrangements used to be. There is no longer scope for diversions like campaigns to improve messrooms, to insist that protective clothing is all in Lincoln green, or that priority in employment is given to particular groups of applicants.

Council members are still involved of course but in a different way. When the DSO has been completely separated from the rest of the system they will form the board which controls it. They have to set objects for the organisation, decide what it has to achieve and make sure it does. They will approve its budgets, set its targets and decide on matters of principle for example whether the DSO is to accept or to seek work from other local authorities and public bodies. In this respect the Audit Commission have cast doubt on the so called cross border trading if it is done for profit. There may be reasons of public principle for work being done for others for example an interest in seeing that hospital grounds are kept to the best standards, so whether the Audit Commission opinion is sustained or not when it is challenged, some possibility for wider trading seems to exist.

The board must set financial targets decide whether or not there is to be a profit sharing scheme and find out what went wrong if a tender is lost and ensure that corrections are made. They have no role in management and should not try to make one. Things will go wrong if they do. Committees cannot act quickly enough for one thing and are very likely to be subject to outside pressures that have nothing to do with the commercial realities which the manager has to face.

They should be quite separate from the client committees and should not try to duplicate what they do. They have no role in setting standards, dealing with complaints, deciding levels of supervision, setting service budgets, planning the development of the service. They should look on themselves as the directors of a business. How can councillors do this? Easy! I have always been surprised how council committees differ in their atmosphere and in the decisions they take even though they are derived from the same group of people and may have a large common member-ship. Members soon fall into the various roles they are invited to play and respond to the nature of the business as well as its details.

DSO management

The contractor has a different set of imperatives to the client and looks at the same set of problems from a different and in some cases the opposite point of view. That is why in the long term the functions of client and DSO are better separated. They have different motivations and principles. In some circumstances they may even become adversaries.

The primary concerns of the contractor are winning tenders; working to the standards demanded in the specification without exceeding them; confining and paring costs and overheads so that the work can be done within the prices quoted; getting the maximum productivity from the resources employed in the business including its personnel, plant, equipment and premises; getting prompt payments for the work that has been done or for any extra unspecified tasks that have to be performed and making a profit.

In the case of the DSO the profit must be at least to the minimum amount stated in the legislation which requires a return of five per cent to be made on the capital employed in the business. In time more than this minimum return will be looked for. Many local authorities of all political persuasions will want to see larger profits from their DSOs and will judge their success on the basis of them. After all they provide money that can be used on favoured projects. In time the DSOs themselves will view profits as the main test of their own success. We are already in the age of the profit sharing scheme and be sure that auditors will make comparisons on the basis of profitability.

To do these things effectively the DSO manager has to behave like other successful commercial managers and develop the same attitudes. In time DSOs will be barely distinguishable from other commercial contractors in their work practices and will require the same degree of alert supervision by the client. Cosy relationships even when they survived the first shock of the culture change are not likely to persist.

It perhaps goes without saying that the DSO manager should have full authority to employ the staff that are needed when they are wanted and should have the authority to dismiss them if discipline or the economics of the operation require it. Local authorities have long established and cherished disciplinary procedures and have in some cases been loath to dispense with them. In the long term even these authorities will develop sharper commercial imperatives. A lost contract marvellously concentrates the mind.

In the same way the manager may need the power to obtain plant, equipment or goods quickly and should be free to do so subject to normal commercial considerations like obtaining the best price and being able to demonstrate later on to the auditors that this has been done.

Changes in practice

DSOs also have to keep a sharp eye on the opposition. They must constantly review their methods of work, see that the equipment and materials that they use are the best and most efficient for the purpose and that they remain competitive. This has meant casting a querulous eye over such long cherished possessions as central nurseries. Many of these have closed, reorganised, or changed into trading entities selling plants to other local authorities and surpluses to the public and using staff and facilities to offer training and instruction in gardening to members of the public. They have thus generated income and reduced the overheads attributable to competitive activities.

The DSOs have not only had to change their attitude. Many have changed working conditions including such matters as the method of pay for overtime in some cases eliminating the so called enhanced rates for work at weekends or reducing the double time that used to be paid for Sunday work.

Many have arranged to work longer hours in Summer and compensate the regular staff by shorter ones in Winter when work out of doors is less productive and when there is less of it. A typical arrangement is 45 hours a week from the beginning of May until the end of October and 33 hours a week for the rest of the year. The basic weekly payment however remains the same throughout the year. There are many variations. Some are very much more elaborate but it can be expected that these will be simplified as time goes on. They should not preclude more radical solutions for instance longer hours in Summer and no work at all in the depth of Winter in Britain say in December and January.

Holidays are now sometimes expressed as an entitlement in hours not days as used to be the case. This encourages staff to take their time off in less productive winter when the same number of hours can be spread over more days. Some prohibit staff holidays during the busiest seasons. In that they are reverting to an old parks department practice in which holidays were never taken in the summer bedding season which was the main peak of work. Some have varied the working day and at the extreme some work shifts in the height of the mowing season so that expensive plant can be kept fully employed and the capital used by the business kept to the minimum.

The problem of absenteeism has had to be tackled with vigour. It is an expensive waste. The idea that somehow there was a sickness entitlement rather like the holiday one drifted into local authorities when the national conditions were changed and no longer demanded a medical certificate for the first three days of sickness in a given period. The idea that 'I'll have to hurry to get my sick leave in before the end of the month' soon followed. A tougher view from managers and sterner discipline have reduced absenteeism and attendance allowances have already made an appearance and can be expected to spread.

Staff are now more flexible in what they do. The idea that different grades of staff can only do certain work was the product of national grading schemes which sought to reward skill but introduced job demarcation as well. In the best examples these barriers have gone altogether.

Casual staff are still taken on for the summer and indeed this was always the cheapest way of dealing with sharp fluctuations in the workload but some authorities have introduced loyalty bonuses the equivalent of two weeks pay to encourage casual staff to stay to the end of the season. This minimises the disruption caused when personnel leave unexpectedly in the midst of a busy season and avoids the expense of retraining new staff. Casual staff are paid for the hours they work since they cannot be compensated by shorter winter hours of working.

Bonus schemes — the product of a fashion of the 1960s have been radically changed. In some places they have been abandoned altogether. No one weeps. Expect more to go. The cost of managing the old ones was often disproportionately high. Where they still exist the cost of administering them should be measured as a proportion of the amount of bonus paid. Expect a surprise. The difficulty of obtaining accurate original documents is profound. The time taken to write them often by people unused to clerical work is sometimes considerable, the trouble taken to verify their truthfulness though variable takes valuable time, and even after that bonus clerks are employed to work out the sums. These costs should be set against the value of any putative gain.

Under the threat of losing members if contracts are lost public sector unions have given up these and many other cherished work practices. Even the once inviolable tea break has come under scrutiny and is now almost certain to be taken at the actual place of work and not in a sometimes remote mess room or bothy. Cashless pay has been extensively introduced. Curiosities like supervisory staffs working different hours to the people they control have also disappeared.

The result of all these circumstances was that in the first round local authorities won more than three quarters of all the grounds maintenance tenders that were offered.

The changes were essential and others like them are still taking place. They should. Contractors have a number of financial advantages over local authority DSOs. They are unlikely to contribute to superannuation; they offer shorter holidays, minimum sick pay; make more use of casual labour; are more ready to lay off staff when work is short; less likely to train their staff beyond minimum instruction; likely to pay only flat rates for overtime; in many cases their basic pay is less and they can negotiate locally so that their labour costs relate specifically to the conditions of the market in which they are trying to recruit. They are better able to control and limit their own central overhead charges and they can freely spread these over both public and private sector work. DSOs need to be constantly on the alert in order to increase production and effectiveness.

A vigorous competitive DSO is likely to keep contractors on their toes. If they do not think they will get much opposition contractors will increase their prices and profits accordingly. Where a tender is lost in its entirety it is difficult for the authority to muster the people, expertise or resources to compete for later ones since these will have been dispersed. Not all need be lost. There is one local authority where the grounds maintenance DSO won back a street sweeping tender that had previously been lost by the authority's specialist staff who had then been made redundant.

The DSO has an advantage in being completely familiar with the work that is involved. This can turn into a drawback if the tender documents are not read with care and fully understood. Work that has been omitted for whatever reason should not be costed even though it has always taken place and will still have to be done. It is the client's problem not the contractors and outsiders will certainly not assume it in their prices.

Selecting contractors to tender

Local authorities must advertise for interested contractors to come forward and the Government has stipulated that this must be done by advertisements placed locally and also in the appropriate trade journals. Section 7 of the *Local Government Act 1988* (Part 1) even goes so far as to stipulate what information the advertisements must contain. Every authority must consider at least three competing tenders. If more contractors put their names forward they can choose from among them. If there are fewer then each of them must be given the opportunity to submit an offer.

DSOs from elsewhere can be considered but they must be extra to the three not part of the number to prevent any risk of collusion.

The possibility of contracts being fulfilled by other local authorities may be cut at by a view of the Audit Commission who said in October 1990 that so called cross boundary tendering is contrary to the *Local Government Goods and Services Act 1970*. They believe that this does not allow local authorities to trade outside their own areas with the view of profit or to maintain employment for their own staff. The risk is borne by residents and businesses who are compelled to pay taxes to meet losses from ineffective local government trading. If losses are made whilst providing services for other communities they are in effect giving an involuntary subsidy. If this opinion proves to be correct it will not only inhibit or stop contracts for maintenance being sought by other authorities it will also stop plants from central nurseries from being traded between authorities as has become the practice.

Contractors must have the capacity of doing the work in the time available and attaining the standards that are required. Not all can. This has given rise to the problem of assessing whether all those that offer to tender are fit to do so. It can be assumed that all in-house contractors are in this position but in the long term they have the same problems as other contractors. They have to ensure a supply of skilled personnel; keep a stock of efficient machinery be capable of accurate costing and cost control; have staff trained to read and understand tender documents and capable of negotiating with clients both informally in discussion and in writing. They must be financially sound and capable of withstanding the effects of a fluctuating cash flow which will vary seasonally through the year and from year to year as future constraints on local government spending take their toll.

The authority is sometimes faced with a tricky job in compiling a short list from the firms who respond to an advertisement. Contractors who have no track record in the work may put their name forward though they may be established in other fields or they may have been newly formed and have no financial history or they may be thought too small to do the work efficiently and on time. They might even have earned a bad reputation either with the particular local authority or elsewhere. As more contractors establish themselves this is likely to be less of a problem, the market will become more competitive and the reputation of the competing firms will become better known and easier to assess.

When unknown firms come forward it is reasonable to find out where they have done work and to go and see it or ask for references or better still to do both. Their financial status should be checked their accounts examined, their health and safety record scrutinised and their quality control mechanisms assessed. A contract has elements of a partnership and quality should not simply be left to the superintendence of the client. In all this the client's object is to try to ensure that none of the work will suffer whichever short listed firm gets the contract.

In grounds maintenance there are also technical points that should be raised. Contractors should have enough staff with a certificate of competence, approved by the Department of Agriculture under the *Food and Environmental Protection Act 1985*, for the application of horticultural chemicals. The act also makes stipulations about the safe transport and storage of chemicals. Even the storekeeper should hold a certificate. If chain saws are to be used trained staff certified as competent in their use should be available. In the case of high class sports turf contractors may be asked to prove that they have, or can recruit, experienced staff capable of the work.

Once the short list has been compiled the tenders can be invited from the selected firms. If fewer than three outside contractors expressed an interest they must all be allowed to offer for the work. This may mean that potentially unsatisfactory contractors are still present at this stage of the process.

Local authorities are not obliged to give work to a firm even though it may have submitted the lowest tender but they must be able to explain why they chose not to and demonstrate that they acted in good faith. If it has been possible to vet all the firms before they were asked to tender then the lowest offer should normally be accepted unless new information has come to light, circumstances have changed, or the offer is so low that there is justification for saying the work cannot possibly be done to the standard required for the price that has been offered. There is nothing improper about a firm pricing itself low in order to win with a view to future advantage stemming from a presence in the area.

The client has to make sure that if a firm is rejected at any stage the authority is not at risk from a successful appeal to the Secretary of State on the basis of unfair competition. Proper records should be kept of the whole process. If trouble is anticipated it is desirable to get outside advice so that the authority is able to demonstrate its good faith.

The contractor

The client has to consider the contractors in preparing the programme. The first advertisement ought to be clear and informative. It has to say enough to allow firms to decide whether it is worth troubling to get more information and submitting their names for consideration. Even simply doing this triggers a demand for information about the status of the company, a request for copies of recent accounts, names of referees, a list of work that has been done recently, health and safety statements and other details.

The great travail starts when a firm is accepted onto the short list. For them the receipt of the tender documents is the start of the period of intense activity. They have to assess the work, search the documents for discrepancies, compare them with the submissions of other authorities and with the jobs they have priced elsewhere, weigh up the opposition, find and check the sites concerned, identify special or peculiar difficulties like a wet climate or intractable soil, assess the standards that have been achieved and record them by photograph or video as an *aide memoire* or to keep against the day when disagreements arise in future, meet the client's representative, talk over the tender and resolve any points that are obscure and decide whether there is a chance of winning.

Then they must go into the sometimes considerable work of looking onto the logistics of moving into the area; the availability of labour and its likely cost; the possibility of recruiting staff displaced from the present workforce; availability of depots. After all that they must price and check the documents.

They have to make a judgement as to whether the client is likely to be reasonable, difficult, or even downright hostile. It is hard to word documents so that they have no element of confusion or need no interpretation. There are many examples of ambiguity even in the most carefully and precisely worded specifications. They derive from the nature of horticultural work and its variability.

The ILAM/Longman publication in specifying shrub planting for example says of replacement planting that the contractor 'will be required to replace all dying, dead or unsatisfactory plants...' The word unsatisfactory leaves a wide discretion and could be costly to the contractor if the client is awkward or pedantic. In a similar way a hostile client could penalise a contractor for failing to mow an entire park in accordance with the specification if his mower caused even a small section to be ribbed when it was cut, or deny payment for the whole job if a small patch of weeds was left in a shrub border which the specification said should be kept weed free.

Many tenders stipulate that weedkillers and chemical sprays cannot be applied in inclement weather mainly meaning when rain is falling or is expected; or when the wind is strong enough to cause the spray to drift onto neighbouring areas. Staff could be held up at great expense whilst a debate occurs between the client and contractor as to what inclement means in the context.

Deductions or hold ups in payments whilst small points are put right can interfere with cash flow and put pressure on a company's finances. In the end a judgement has to be made as to whether small errors will be used to impose large penalties. The conclusion that is reached will affect the price that is offered.

Tenders should be judged without delay so that contractors are told the result promptly. If they have won they have to embark on a major task of gearing up for the work: appointing extra staff arranging work schedules; organising depots; possibly getting extra equipment; and familiarising their staff with the new areas. If they have lost they will want to find other outlets for their capacity.

The value of accepted tenders is public information and is usually published in the minutes of the client committee. Contractors study the results. A firm or DSO bidding high in the absence of competition one year will probably find next time it has caught the eye of more formidable opponents.

There have been cases of contractors failing either financially or organisationally and clients should be ready to meet that contingency. They may have to deal with difficult circumstances without much time to prepare. In the growing season they may have to move quickly to avoid a disaster. The contractor should be made to provide a performance bond so that in the event of a failure the authority is able to obtain compensation for the expense that is involved.

Quality control

All work has to be supervised even that done by direct labour. The presumptions of what might go wrong are different — that is all. In the past the supervisor had to be most concerned on that work started on time and continued thereafter with reasonable application. No more. These are now problems for the contractor.

The client's inspection has to concentrate on the quality of what is done and its quantification so that payments can be made accurately. This should be done in concert with the contractor who also has these concerns. Liaison should be at all levels. The management from both sides have an interest in avoiding damaging and costly disagreements.

The amount of supervision has to be sufficient to ensure proper work and correct payments but not more than this. A lot of money is wasted by excessive numbers of supervisors without a commensurate gain. The cost of supervision is another of the figures that can easily be extracted by auditors and comparisons made between authorities. Expect a lot of comment to be made and many explanations to be demanded.

The amount of supervision may be reduced if contractors participate in a system of quality control because it obliges them to take a large responsibility for the quality of what they do. It is more expensive for them and must be stipulated in the tender documents. Their prices will be affected.

Quality control is important to both parties to a contract and system of quality assurance as described in *BS 5750 Quality Systems 1987* or the international system *ISO 9000* should be considered. The contractor should be asked to participate in the scheme. The client should do so too because both have a part to play.

Once fully in place the system makes supervision easier because the contractor has to be accredited by an independent group as having reached its standards of quality control. This is valuable to a contractor who wishes to compete for other work. It can be withdrawn if things go wrong. It is a useful spur to high endeavour.

The British Standard propounds a system: it does not define the quality or the standard that is wanted. That is a function of the specification. If this is deficient no amount of control will produce quality.

Unfortunately the idea has suffered an accretion of jargon and cliché. The following was a quote taken from a *Press and Journal* report in October 1990 about the work of a quality forum, itself a good idea and intended to let a number of participating firms, local authorities and other organisations, share experience; help one another by example; share knowledge; and give mutual encouragement (rather like a slimmers club).

> Total Quality Management is really an attitude of mind. It is getting everyone playing in the same team. Everyone is a winner; there are no losers. There is nobody at fault; the only area that merits consideration is problem solving. It is job satisfaction. It is ownership of the job, it is commitment, everyone pulling in the same direction and knowing what they are trying to do at the end of the day is really only to produce a better quality product or better service in the internal and external area of a companies activity.

Gosh!

Quality control has long been a concern of industry and local government officials should learn from their experience. Those most closely concerned should be encouraged to join the specialist group the Institute of Quality Assurance and to participate in local campaigns. Hope that whilst they are doing so, they learn to shear cliches, and translate the language which shrouds this good idea, into English.

The contract manager has a backup team. The public is a vigilant superintendent. Complaints are a supplementary way of keeping a check on the performance of contractors. There are always some complaints even in the best managed system but an abnormal flow means that something is going wrong, perhaps fundamentally. Complaints should be dealt with promptly but they should also be recorded and used as one of the tests to see whether the contract is going as it should.

Value analysis

There is a rising star. It is value analysis. Managers can expect to hear a lot more about it. It has been taken up by the EC to help in preparation for the single market though it was evolved as long ago as 1947 in the United States and is used in industry in the USA, Japan, and Britain where there is an Institute of Value Management. It systematically analyses each part of a function or service and then seeks to improve it and make it better, more efficient and economical.

The method is formalised into five stages. Firstly all the information is gathered about the service, the costs, the staff engaged in it, the materials that are used, and so on. Nothing is omitted. The second stage is to assemble a team of people including specialists in the process as well as those who are directly concerned and together they look for ways to improve what is done and find better methods. This is at the heart of the system. It draws on the invention, imagination and insights of many minds. Thirdly there is a process of evaluation, sorting out the ideas that the debates have produced. Fourthly approval is sought from those who have to authorise change and those who are to be subjected to it are consulted. Lastly the ideas are put into practice.

If it sounds familiar it should. It describes what all managers ought to have been doing. The process is given momentum and discipline in some organisations by appointing specialist staff to initiate and lead the analyses.

Performance reviews

How was it? Is the commonest enquiry known to mankind. It invites a subjective performance review. The Almighty might have enquired whether the earth could have been made in five days instead of six and whether it would have been better if it had been. That would have been a fundamental performance review.

Realistic targets should be set in advance, then tested to see if they were reached or could be bettered, or to find what went wrong. Comparisons should be made with others. All work should be measured against an ideal.

Councillors and officials both have an interest in performance reviews. The phrase has received new and recent prominence but the concept is an old one. Students and managers alike should attend a housing committee meeting and see the probing intensity with which the statistics of house repairs and vacancies are discussed. This is a performance review of long standing. The same vitality of debate and enquiry should also be applied to the performance of parks.

Councils and committees need to know whether what is being done in their name is good or bad. They would be able to do this better if agendas were not so often crowded with matters that ought to be left to paid functionaries. Officials should be scolded if they introduce trivial items. Crouching behind the skirts of a committee slows up business — hides the elephant in the bush.

The council has to see that the service as a whole is heading in the right direction, satisfying its customers and providing the what they want. It needs to know that all the elements are working well together. They may have gone out to tender separately. For example in a park the management of the cricket pitches, bowling greens, and other games facilities, the entertainment programme, the grounds maintenance contract, the restaurant, and the park attendants may all be answerable to separate contractors and even to more than one client. Even saints would fall out.

The work is not an end in itself. It has a larger aim. Together its elements have to attract and please the public and provide for their recreation in attractive surroundings.

To understand the effectiveness of a service managers require regular financial and management information; details of costs; the number of users; the length of their visits; what they thought about what they found; the amount they spent; the menus offered in the restaurants and so on. The contractor is the main source of this information, others include customer surveys, and local authorities. One of the gains of tendering is that the aims of the service are now expressed clearly in writing sometimes for the first time. It is much easier to quantify and compare output and costs and to match these with the stated objectives.

It is easy to say how many people use a swimming pool. They pay to get in and the statistics are obtained as a matter of course and are audited. It is hard to get an accurate figure for a park. Admission is free and the cost of getting reliable facts may be higher than any gain from using them. It is easier to get information about parts of the park: the numbers using a bowling green; paying to see an entertainment; the takings at a beer garden; income from a restaurant; occupancy rates of caravan sites. Collectively they give a picture of the whole.

Customers should also be asked 'What was it like?' Their experience can be measured. *Job* (38.7) says 'the morning stars sang together and all the sons of God shouted for joy'. That is the target. The pleasure obtained from visiting a park is graded down from that.

Assessments might also weigh the cost of not providing a park, whether vandalism would rise, industry go elsewhere, tourists choose another destination.

The results should be compared with the targets and estimates that were set at the beginning of the financial year, the experience of previous years, the results from other authorities and the private sector, and the success of rival attractions including other parks.

Managers should be free to experiment and make changes on their own initiative, to attract more customers and make visits more enjoyable. The *Apocrypha* says 'Observe the opportunity' (4.20). It may be that the hours of opening are wrong for the flow of trade; the price structure may need revising to get more business and greater income. Incentives may be needed like cheaper rates for block of tickets. The pick up points for horse and trap rides may need changing to get more trade. Every level of management should be required to review its own performance and introduce or to suggest improvements. To do this each requires information presented in a way that is easy to use and understand. It is possible to have too much detail. Facts need condensing into graphs and charts.

Cost control

The client just like the contractor has a problem of cost management. The contractor has to work within the prices he quoted when tendering although these may be subject to revision to allow for inflation which is normally done once a year and then only after the first year. Cost control requires regular, up-to-date, accurate information about expenditure and how, on what, and where it was incurred.

Contractors have to ensure that income covers all expenditure. They have to strike a balance between monitoring too little and missing important trends and variations; and control in excessive detail which is expensive, time consuming and of dubious use. They may monitor costs against a schedule of rate, but most prices are averages so individual jobs are bound to vary, and review a sample of jobs continuously. Key measures to consider in cost control are labour productivity, and the consumption of materials. The contractor has to ensure that all the work he does is paid promptly and at the appropriate rate. Where there is no quoted rate the contractor or his representative must have the information necessary to offer a profitable price.

Client officers are concerned with the overall contract price and have to make sure that the estimates which the local authority approved are not exceeded. This is comparatively easy when only the work stipulated in the contract is involved. It becomes more complex where there are variations. They have to ensure the price quoted has been costed on a similar basis to the original tender and that there are sufficient funds to pay for the new work. The system must ensure that only jobs that have been done satisfactorily are paid for.

Several kinds of computer software have been developed to make sure that these requirements can be met but information has to be interpreted astutely and the data fed to the computer must be correct and up-to-date. *Caveat emptor!* In the hands of competent management, computer systems are useful tools. They assist in monitoring and analysing trends as well as in routine scheduling and job control. However computerising a bad manual system run by weak managers magnifies its faults. Before embarking on such a project managers should be clear what they want from the system and the benefits they expect to get.

In buying a packaged system the client or contractor should look for a supplier who understands local authority parks management and can communicate intelligibly with managers who are not necessarily computer literate themselves. The better companies usually have horticulturalists as employees or consultants and often close links with a local authority or other public body. Avoid a modified DLO package. There are many similarities in the functions but there are also significant differences.

Capital employed

Local authorities are expected to get a return on the capital they employ in the business. The amount is set by the Secretary of State and at the time of writing is five per cent. DSO's have to make sure that they do not use more than the minimum they need. Surplus plant equipment buildings and stocks should be got rid of. If more is needed in an emergency it can be hired. Leasing equipment also reduces the capital employed and it allows new, better, more efficient items to be introduced into the business more quickly. Expensive plant should be put to the maximum work and to do this it may be necessary to work shifts. Depots should be examined critically. Many DSOs will have inherited too many. They should be returned to the client or sold.

Overheads

One of the regular grumbles of local authority service departments was the level of central departmental overheads. This was so even before competition. They arise from departments like law and administration, personnel, finance, architectural services, and that myriad of costs that cannot be allocated directly to a particular service. The DSO should not pay for services that it does not require and it should be free to shop around for those that it does. Client departments should consider doing this as well.

Service level agreements are now often established between the DSO and the central departments providing services such as personnel and payroll management. Under these the service the DSO is to receive is specified and valued. No deviation occurs except with the consent of both parties. This ensures that the DSO is aware of its central charges in advance, can negotiate about them, and can budget more accurately.

Management buy-outs

The term management buy-out is now well known and there have been many examples in commerce in recent years in many countries. The name is given to the situation in which the managers of a concern buy the business from its owners. The purchase may or may not be accompanied by some form of employee share ownership scheme which can range from small shareholdings by the staff to full scale employee ownership of the company. Buy-outs have already taken place in some authorities. Some have succeeded — some have failed.

The managers may be encouraged to offer for the business by the owners themselves who may want to get rid of an under-performing or unwanted asset. They may want to buy it because of their own assessment of the potential of the business and a perception that they could run it better if free from a querulous proprietorial gaze and its accompanying restraints. They may have been encouraged by outside investors looking for a new enterprise in which to put their money. Recreation management and catering are obvious targets but the possibility also exists in grounds maintenance DSOs.

DSOs in order to function well have to become unlike conventional local authority departments: they may sit uneasily in the system. They are largely independent as employers and managers and do what they are told only so long as they are paid for it. Some of their pay may come from profits. They have many of the characteristics of commercial companies. If they are profitable and well managed with appropriate depots and plant and have a number of long contracts they have an obvious value. These also offer a secure base from which to launch into other ventures or make new bids elsewhere. Capital hungry local authorities may be willing to sell them. A privatising government may make them.

There is no obligation on the authority to sell a business to its managers or staff. The asset belongs to the public and if it is to be sold at all the best return has to be obtained for it. There is a market among existing concerns who want to expand, or companies in other fields who may want access to a new one. Expect a close scrutiny by auditors, the opposition, the press, Pro Bono Publico and Disgusted, whatever arrangements are made.

There are many considerations, ethical, practical, financial. The managers have to consider the long term profitability of the business; the opportunities for expanding it; the availability of finance and their ability to service the debt; the security and the length of the contract in their home base; the true value of the assets and goodwill they are buying. They do have advantages.

They know the business better than anyone else. They may know how to improve the profits but be unable to do so under local government control. They may think they can introduce leaner, frugal, tougher management or invest more in new more productive plant, or sell off unwanted assets profitably. They may see the opportunity for trading more widely than is permitted to a local authority department. They may simply be seduced by the idea of being their own boss or the availability of finance.

Some of these are good reasons others are not. Managers or employees thinking about buying a DSO should take a long hard-headed look at future profits and the chances of increasing them. There will be no local authority to underwrite bad judgement.

For the local authority there is the problem of who will eventually own the company if it is later sold, or taken over, or goes bankrupt. There may be problems of conflict of interest when officials planning to buy the company are still running it as employees. The doubt will always be present if not expressed, as to why the business can be managed so much better by the same people simply because they have moved from the public to the private sector and why the greater efficiencies and bigger profits that they now envisage were not made before. There are problems of getting a true value for the assets that are to be sold and of judging the right price for the goodwill.

5 Marketing

Marketing is one of the most important skills of the manager. Ability to use it affects public attitudes about the department and the view taken by members of the council. It should be used to proselytise and inform and advertise; to ensure that the best service is always available to the public and to fill the parks with people. Marketing is intended to manipulate human responses. Parks managers should use the techniques. They have a duty to be evangelists and advocates and propagandists and to do their work with style and panache and flair and élan.

Marketing is an age old idea. It started the day that the first cave dweller wanted to dispose of something he did not want. Christ himself gave a tutorial on the subject when he took a whip to the merchants in the temple. He chased them out. He was teaching that marketing should be appropriate both as to time and place. In spite of the sophisticated language in which some of these ancient concepts are now described all park managers use some of them to promote their wares and should consider them all. The most important premise is that customers come first.

What visitors want and respond to matters more than anything else in managing a park. Everything should be subordinate to it. If they admire floral bedding it should be provided; if they want places to sit these should be made where most people will use them; if they want garden advice it should be available; if they want entertainments these should be obtained in forms that appeal to as wide a range of tastes as possible; if they want to lie down or picnic on the grass the lawns should be maintained in such a way that they are convenient and pleasant to use for the purpose. Visitors to a park should be honoured guests whose needs are considered and provided for systematically.

The easiest and cheapest way of finding what people want is by observation. That is why even the most senior managers should visit the places they control not only during normal working hours when use may be at a comparatively low ebb but also when most other people are at leisure, at the weekend, during public holidays or in the evenings. Parks are busiest then.

Managing a park is a full time job. Regular observation will soon show what it is that the public admire; what interests them; which aspects of the service are failing; what should be changed. When facilities have become outdated they should be removed. The limitations of the method are its subjectivity and its failure to show whether innovations will succeed or to suggest what these might be, nor does it show why people who do not visit a park, absent themselves. Apply, Einstein's dictum 'imagination is more important than knowledge' remember the words of *Kings I* ii.7 'Behold the half was not told me'.If charges are made for a particular facility the takings provide a guide by which to judge its success or failure. But most parks and most of the things they contain are free so the information is limited in its application. It is necessary to consult the public to fill the gap in information. Consultation can be done by direct enquiry through surveys of existing customers or by listening to groups and organisations who use the park. It may be done by means of door to door surveys throughout a neighbourhood, or in a wider area by asking the local press and radio to invite views and suggestions.

Public meetings can also be used to elicit opinions or enlist support but they are notoriously ill attended unless a topic is controversial and they do not necessarily produce a wide spread of views. They are also sometimes manipulated by outsiders or dominated by particular pressure groups. The results need interpreting with caution.

Scientifically conducted opinion polls or consumer surveys may also be used if the issue is important enough to justify the expense. Some of the information they yield may also be available from existing nationally available statistics. In Britain for instance these are obtainable from the Government Statistical Service who carry out regular surveys on a variety of topics or from the results of the census. These also allow trends to be ascertained whereas the opinion poll is a kind of snapshot, offering a view of the moment only. Any politician approaching an election will declare that the scene is likely to change, even a week being a long time.

In asking people what they want in a park it should be borne in mind that the response can only reflect individual experience. A child asked what it would like to have in a playground for example will not cite the use of inflatable bouncing equipment unless he happens to have seen it or has the vision to perceive that it can be used outside a fairground. Yet if it is introduced it is likely to prove the most attractive item of all. Even detailed surveys therefore need to be used as a guide and should not become a limitation.

There is a profoundly obscure piece of jargon in the vocabulary of marketing professionals. It is to the effect that marketing is 'an integrated management function'. Every decision that is made in every section of the department or, for that matter, in every department of a local authority should be to the advantage of customers or at least it should result from considering their interest. That extends from routine processes like letting an allotment or a football pitch right through to major decisions for example as to whether to provide an outdoor ice rink and deciding its location.

The customer should be considered deliberately and systematically at all levels in the organisation — not just at senior ones. The first contact that most people have with a parks department, by whatever name it is known, is with gardeners and attendants, telephone operators, receptionists, counter assistants and clerks. Their attitude colours and illumines the customers view of the whole organisation.

Marketing affects such matters as quality control, price levels, discounts, whether admission to events is to be free or at a charge, advertising, promotions, publicity, the choice of a logo, the development of a house style in printed documents, it might extend to the colour chosen for vehicles and even buildings. It is concerned with public relations, the use of uniforms for staff or identifying badges, staff training in customer care, the range of facilities that are provided, decisions about the displays and attractions, notices, signs, pamphlets and books, the way that things are explained or interpreted to the public and the extent to which this is done. It affects decisions when annual estimates are prepared and when tender documents are drawn up. It affects both the client and the contractor.

The environment in which a parks service operates changes from time to time by way of organisational upheaval. Compulsory tendering and the subsequent internal organisation changes it brought about is only a recent example. Since all political parties are at present considering the structure of local government in Britain and in some cases the introduction of regional and de-volved government there may be further profound changes in the offing. It is the very moment to be a management consultant. Market considerations can be lost in the turmoil. They thus need particular and systematic attention.

There are changes in more fundamental ways as well. Demographic shifts in the community affect the nature and age of the customer. Increased leisure time, greater wealth, a desire for higher standards, changes in tastes (for instance in recent years there has been a shift from team games to individual sports) affect what the customer wants.

Promotions

Marketing a park should focus on some distinctive characteristic that distinguishes it from other competing choices for using leisure time. My own city of Aberdeen in the past marketed itself on a reputation for meanness with such jokes as 'The Aberdonian that installed double glazing so that his children could not hear the ice cream van'. A park might market itself because of a major conservatory or a rose mountain or poems inscribed onto the paving stones on the paths.

Giving things away is one of the best marketing ploys. At one hotel I used recently every visitor was given a ball-point pen. It was not altruism. It was inscribed with the hotel phone number and address. Australian guests pinned badges onto everything that moved in the town and on to some things that did not. One of them had taken a sack full of golden kangaroos to distribute. They offer another lesson. The best image is one that everyone can recognise. Simple, direct, needing no descriptive text.

When I last brought an airline ticket I got a travel bag that turned me into a walking advertisement for the airline concerned whose name was on its side. They gave me a wallet for my tickets with their name and logo. It was made so bulky by items of publicity that if I had put it in my pocket I would have been mistaken for a female impersonator. I will almost certainly get a calendar from them next year, because following up the customer with a second or even a third approach is a good marketing idea. There is no reason why parks should not do the same.

Sheraton Hotels have a universal symbol for themselves. It is a capital 'S' surrounded by a laurel wreath, the ancient mark of a triumph. It appears on everything even their bath towels. There is no such logo for a park which everyone can recognise everywhere in every town or in any country. In each bedroom there is a directory giving details and information of all the other Sheraton hotels in the world. If you enter a park you will rarely find a sign advertising another park even one in the same system, let alone in a neighbouring authority. Still less would it tell of a park in The Hague or Houston, Paris or Berlin. Yet all parks have a common purpose and they are not generally competitors with one another.

Marketing starts at the reception desk in the best hotels. You can see how it is done and test its effect by your own reaction. The receptionist looks you in the eye, gives you full attention, smiles, uses your name. If you have a problem it is taken over, its burden is lifted from you. The duty manager would do the same, and would also touch you on the arm since human contact is a powerful means of communication in itself, it conveys sympathy and fellowship more effectively than any other gesture. Their own names are worn on their lapels so that customers can see and know who they are speaking too and if they care can also reciprocate the courtesy of using the name. The parks staff and manager should learn the lessons. They are rarely spontaneous reactions. Do not doubt that they are the product of training and regular reminders. In one post office that I had occasion, to use there was a big sign which said 'It's fun to be nice'. The message unfortunately only faced the visitors. Even then it gave an advantage. Amiability begets friendliness. *Proverbs* 15.1 says 'the soft answer turneth away wrath'.

Parks managers have the advantage that they have at their disposal a powerful marketing tool that is individual to them. They can fill cities with flowers and trees and green spaces everybody will notice and so long as the parks are not allowed to become dull by comparison the public will be drawn to visit them as well.

Exhibitions and open days

Departments can participate in exhibitions on a variety of topics from Ideal Homes to Hobbies. Organisers will usually give room to a parks department so as to obtain a wide spread of stands or simply to fill space with an organisation that would be unlikely to buy it. They may also want help in kind like floral decorations but before venturing down this route the true cost should be balanced against any likely gain.

The things that attracted your own attention to an exhibit and caused you to remember it are the things that should be introduced to your own. The public respond to eccentricity: they like quizzes and competition and they like to win prizes. If the exhibit attracts someone of importance such as a potential sponsor there should be the facility of offering hospitality. The message of the stand should be simple and clear rather like a three dimensional poster. The staff should be friendly and bright and to ensure that this quality does not flag through fatigue they should be given regular breaks and intervals for refreshment.

It is possible to arrange an exhibition for example to encourage sports participation or to focus on some other aspect of the department's work. Local clubs would be offered space usually free. It is also possible to sell stand space to commercial groups appropriate to the occasion but this calls for great persistence and a tough skin. Not many people have the gift of selling space to exhibitors. Home grown exhibitions are not always a triumphant success because the budget may not run to making 'shell' stands which give an air of uniformity and professionalism. There may not even be enough money to advertise widely enough among the public. Sufficient publicity is crucial. It is difficult enough to attract even those who already have an interest in the topic and getting the uncommitted to attend requires formidable exertion. Only the most popular exhibitions can afford the barrier of an entrance charge and even they shower the world with free invitations to ensure that a good enough audience is present. Exhibitors have reason to complain if they have no customers.

On a smaller and less formal scale park buildings and conservatories or even the park itself can be used to display a wide range of exhibits ranging from art or sculpture, perhaps with a sculptor in residence, to explanatory matter about the park itself or the district. The same rules apply. Makeshift or botched arrangements do more harm than good. The details, which offer plenty of scope for error, should be gone through meticulously. Publicity should be ensured through a series of news stories. Someone prominent and likely to attract press coverage should be asked to perform an opening ceremony.

The alternative is to take the exhibit to where people are already present in large numbers perhaps in a central pedestrian street or a shopping centre. The opportunity should always be taken to support local flower shows for example.

National flower shows offer an important way of reaching a larger public but the venture should only be undertaken after the event has been studied and it is certain that the necessary standards can be reached by the material and by the staff. If not, there is a case for training and for a quality audit. A bad exhibit can do a lot of harm though a good one does disproportionate good. Three dimensional carpet bedding on a series of themes sometimes topical, sometimes literary, were featured at the famous Chelsea flower show by the Torbay Parks department over a period of years. They made the department and the district famous not just in the horticultural world but through national press and television coverage throughout the country as well. There is no doubt that their successes also did them great good in their home town.

Additional interest can be created by an open day. Even places which are normally open to the public can attract bigger attendances than usual by the device, though in this case it is necessary to give a sense of occasion by having extra staff on hand to answer questions arranging a series of small exhibits providing extra entertainment and so on.

Places that are not normally open attract attention because of the novelty of obtaining admission at all, but if they can be opened for a day without problems the question should be asked as to whether they might not be open all the time. Central nurseries fall into this category.

Ambush marketing

Ambush marketing is a new term but not a new idea. It involves attaching a promotion to a great event that is a major focus of interest and public attention. The world cup is an example though there are many lesser ones. It is a term applied to the exploitation of an occasion and the interest that it arouses without sponsoring it or buying the rights to it. Advertisers may for instance attach their promotion to some special aspect of the event for instance getting participating players to be seen drinking milk or driving a car to a world cup destination. It may be no more than a vague implied association like displaying an advertising slogan on a football. The people who have to obtain sponsorship are concerned in case existing sponsors resort to the same tactic themselves on future occasions. They could then reap many though not all the advantages they now get from actual sponsorship without incurring the expense of being a sponsor.

The same possibilities are open to a parks manager as well. It has long been recognised that there is an upsurge in public interest in playing tennis during and immediately after the Wimbledon tournament and similar boosts to participation occur in cricket after a successful test match or in football after the world cup. The same is true of a range of other events. The phenomenon is recognised but it is not often exploited. It should be. At the very least by using the flood of interest to promote the activity within the park or even more directly by getting famous participants in the event to visit the park to plant a tree, to give coaching advice, sign autographs or to open a facility related to the sport concerned.

Nostalgia marketing

Greensboro in North Carolina is the home of Vicks Vapour Rub. It was invented there. Its pugnacious smell filled the nostrils of my childhood. When I resort to its powerful efficacy today my mind flicks back forty years. Nostalgia is on the marketing man's preferred list of human foibles. It should also be on the Parks manager's shopping list. It might involve using old fashioned flowers like stocks, sweet peas, and sweet williams (no reason to use older inferior varieties of them though); or introducing horses for transport within a park system; or inviting visitors to wear Victorian dress for a special occasion; or having a grandmothers day; or rolling eggs down the slopes at Easter; or marking Hop Scotch on the pavements, introducing a street organ, or a steam engine, employing a punch and judy show; or arranging a heavy horse show in the park. There are scores of ways to take a corner of the market in nostalgia.

Novelty

Horace in the *Odes* says 'Mix some brief folly in your wisdom'. It is a recommendation that has appeared from time to time since. Robert Burns wrote 'Thou greybeard, old Wisdom, mayst boast of thy treasures..... Give me with young folly to live..... I grant thee thy calm blooded time settled pleasures..... But folly has raptures to give'. Thomas Hood in his poem *To Minerva* says much the same 'Then Pallas, take away thine owl..... And let us have a lark instead'. I repeat the advice here. Stodgy parks and worn out ideas do not attract any one for long or persuade people to go back or take their visitors or give a recommendation to others — word of mouth is the most formidable marketing tool of all.

I introduced the idea of a talking cactus a few years ago. It was for use at the Glasgow Garden festival. It told the most appalling jokes, thus: 'How do you make gold soup? By boiling eighteen carrots!' 'I agreed with the groan that every one uttered who heard the joke but it elicited other jokes of the same species from children mostly, but also from older people who are less inhibited about talking to plants than the rest of us. It also gave seditious advice to Glaswegians about visiting Aberdeen. It was one of the centres of attention. It was folly marketing.

In the park itself there should be other lark notes, interesting fountains, eccentric sculptures, frogs that blow bubbles at passing children, a giant signing spider on which children can climb triggering music as they do, a Hornchestra across which anyone can scamper and which plays trumpet notes as they find the right pressure point or break the right beam. Silly impractical ideas? Not at all. They are lark notes and at one place or another I introduced all of them during my own career as a park manager and made them work.

Even the Victorians used follies. How else can one explain the carpet bed! That old device should not be disdained. It can be used as a valuable promotional and advertising vehicle preferably drawing attention to some other aspect of the park concerned or another park in the system rather than to some remote worthy good cause or longeval organisation.

The written word

It is possible to get a clue as to what constitutes good marketing language by listening to good speakers. They use language that is appropriate for the subject, the sonorous phrase for the matter of grave importance, concrete terms in preference to the abstract. In illustration consider the term 'greenhouse effect'. It suggests something real. It provides a ready made headline, it is shorthand for a complex idea. Until it was invented the problem though it existed passed the public by.

Park publicity and for that matter everything from forms and routine letters right through to reports and press releases should be written in simple direct language. It is not easy to do but to appreciate its importance it is only necessary to observe the great users of English or for that matter to note what is memorable when politicians or commentators speak. The most famous phrase from the Falklands war was 'I counted them all out and I counted them all back'. In recent American elections the words that reached everybody were 'Where's the beef?' and 'Read my lips. No new taxes', and 'You're no Jack Kennedy, Senator'. These are sentences containing a single idea expressed in as few words as possible that and producing a picture in the mind.

Simple sentences assist lucidity. Long ones are harder to keep clear. Mark Twain said of a good writer 'At times he may indulge himself with a long sentence, but he will make sure that there are no folds in it, no vaguenesses, no parenthetical interruptions of its view as a whole; when he has done with it, it won't be a sea serpent with half its arches under the water; it will be a torch light procession'.

St Paul in his letter to the *Corinthians* (ch 14 v 2) said 'For he that speaketh in an unknown tongue speaketh not unto men ... for no man understandeth him; howbeit, in the spirit, he speaketh mysteries', and again in verse 4: 'He that speaketh in an unknown tongue edifieth himself.....' with the implication that he edifies no one else. Avoid jargon. It can only understood accurately by a few people who also use it. To everybody else it is an unknown tongue. Local Government uses a great deal of jargon that it takes for granted, horticulture uses even more but plain words have to be found if the public is to understand what is meant. Avoid tautology, people who say service delivery when they mean service are guilty of it. Avoid surplus words. If a sentence makes the same sense without a word or phrase cut it out. Very is a case in point.

If you listen to a modern pop song you will find that it consists of a simple short melody that is repeated several times over though if the musicians are specially skilled they may vary the key. Repetition pays in marketing as well and especially in that aspect of it that concerns advertising. It is easy to observe the principles for they are exploited all around us in the commercial advertisements seeking to sell every commodity from washing powder to holidays abroad. Parks and the things they contain can be marketed using exactly the same basic idea. A repeated slogan a recurring colour theme, a simple message reinforced at every opportunity.

Advertising

Advertising costs money. It is all too easy to spend more on it than is justified by the rate of return. In a park it will usually be limited to advertising particular events. In this case its effectiveness can be judged to some extent by attendances and the experience applied to future occasions. It is the area of the budget that is most likely to be cut when estimates and costs are considered and even in commercial organisations it is a notorious area of disagreement.

There is great difficulty in deciding how much should be spent because it is impossible to know in advance how effective a particular form of advertising will be. The classic quotation on the subject is by Lord Leverhulme who said, 'I know that half my advertising budget is wasted, the trouble is that I don't know which half'. In a local government department there is a second snag.

Advertising may seem to be optional in an organisation that is unused to it except for such things as jobs and local government elections. As a result it is more usually the case that events are insufficiently advertised. This is a mistake since on the day the success of any activity in a park is judged by the number of people who are present. If it is held in virtual secrecy it is not worth spending money on.

Budget proposals should clearly say what the proposed advertising is expected to achieve. The result can then be measured against the aspiration. Advertising should be considered in just the same light as any other investment and should be judged in the same way.

To whatever extent advertising is done however there will always be someone who claims never to have seen it. They will usually say in addition that they would have attended the event had they but known it was taking place. *Mon oeil!*

It can take several forms. These include the use of posters, direct mail, pamphlets given out in a street, door to door deliveries, press, television or radio advertising, banners across a street, placards in buses, a 'What's On' programme of daily events. There are also less usual advertisements like the use of an airship, or a small aircraft with a streamer behind, a decorated float or even the once commonplace sandwich board. They should be chosen with reference to their likely effectiveness and their appropriateness to the event being promoted. There may also be the matter of municipal seemliness!

Paying for an advertisement allows the exact form of the message to be chosen. There are some legislative provisions which affect what may be done. These are the *Indecent Advertisement Act 1889, Misrepresentation Act 1967, Sex Discrimination Act 1975,* and the *Trades Description Acts of 1968* and *1972* as well as legislation concerning equal opportunities and more recently laws which limit local government advertising intended to prevent councils from using public money to promote a political point of view.

In addition to these constraints others are applied to Radio and television advertising. At present the regulatory body is the Independent Broadcasting Authority IBA but this is to be replaced under current legislation. Its rules are set out in a useful pamphlet called *The IBA Code of Advertising Standards and Practice.* It deals with such matters as the use of children in advertising; appeals to fear and superstition; the denigration of other products; and inertia selling (that is sending goods without the authority of the recipient which if not returned are deemed to have been purchased). They can insist on compliance with their code and no doubt the successor bodies will embrace similar rules.

The British Code of Advertising Practice is the other main regulatory device though it is voluntary and depends on the co-operation of agents publishers and the advertisers themselves. It is administered by the Advertising Standards Authority who are based in central London. It is an independent body set up by the advertising business but there is an independent chairman and the majority of its members are free from involvement in advertising. The council investigates complaints; publishes reports giving the result of its investigations; and monitors advertising in a more general way. It makes an important point when it says that the essence of good advertising is that 'All advertisements should be legal, decent, honest and truthful. All advertisements should be prepared with a sense of responsibility both to the consumer and to society. All advertisements should conform to the principles of fair competition as generally accepted in business.'

Advertisements can be placed direct and if this is done advantage should be taken of discounts which are often available for regular advertisements or for a series. Most towns have an advertising agency and it is often helpful to use their services. They should certainly be approached to ascertain what they offer. Most of them work on commission from the newspaper or television station concerned. They thus involve no direct cost to the advertiser.

There are advantages in using them. They can set out the advertisements; advise where they should appear; prepare a campaign;
advise about the content; and ensure that all legal requirements
are met. They will check to see that the advertisements actually
appear in the manner that was instructed though this does not
absolve the client from the requirement of vigilance, and they will
negotiate money back or a rerun of the advertisement in the event
of a failure or a mistake.

Other services are subject to a payment by the client for
example an agency can arrange art work; have printing blocks
made; prepare tapes for radio and video for television advertisement. These can increase the costs of an advertising campaign
sometimes substantially, and should be remembered when estimates are prepared.

Posters

Posters should tell a simple message that will catch the eye and
register easily. The exception is when they are in places like tube
or railway stations where people have enough time to read them
in detail and indeed may be glad of the distraction or in a library
where they can stand and read at leisure. In other cases the poster
should aim at giving a short, direct, pithy message told in few
words or simple pictures or both together.

Most departments have places where posters can be displayed
without charge. Even in these locations small posters are easier to
display. If they are to be offered to shops or pubs or restaurants
they must be small. If they are too big shopkeepers will be reluctant to display them though they may take them as the easiest way
of disposing of the request. Larger posters require advertising
hoardings. These cost money, the amount varying with the length
of time involved, the size of the poster, and the location of the
hoarding. The art work on large posters is the most important
factor in their success it is worth going to the expense of employing a top commercial artist to prepare it. An advertising agency
will make the arrangements.

Graffiti can be a problem on posters and everyone will know of
examples. It can make a message ridiculous by subtly changing the
wording or by augmenting an illustration. Designing a poster so
that it cannot be changed in meaning by short unsolicited editorial
additions is an important skill. Putting it out of reach of them is
another.

All advertisements should be removed as soon as they are out of
date and the staff concerned should be told of this as often as is
necessary to make the reaction automatic.

Fly posting means placing a poster where it has not been autho-rised to be and where it is probably not wanted. It alienates most people especially those most directly concerned including other departments of the local authority. It should never be done.

Direct mail

Junk mail does little harm except to the blood pressure of the recipient and the weight of the rubbish bin but junk fax has the exasperating effect of using the paper not of the sender but of the recipient. Keep friends by leaving the technique to others. Before it is decided to advertise by means of a circular the first question to ask is why so much of this kind of correspondence is dumped without even a glance. It is necessary to study your own personal reaction and to assess what quality in a circular persuades you to read it. Often it is because it does not resemble junk mail at all. It may be personally addressed for example. I found myself reading a circular letter yesterday because it was or at least appeared to have been hand written. The main problem is to tease the readers into looking at the subject matter before the document is jettisoned.

Address lists can be obtained from many sources. Some organisations sell copies of their membership lists. Election regis-ters and other public documents also provide names and addresses for circulation. Every time you give your name and address to participate in a competition for a prize you are contri-buting it to an address list. Parks departments can easily get to know sections of their own customers by this means. Computer programmes will assemble lists into the order of their post codes arranged in sequence. If this is done the Post Office will offer discounts if the number of items is big enough thus reducing the expense which even with this device is high.

Publicity

Publicity is an important aspect of marketing. Letting people know about an event or a facility is one of the daily problems for park managers. In larger local authorities there may be a full time press officer with whom there should be constant liaison and indeed the parks, open spaces and recreation services the local authority pro-vides are among the most valuable vehicles for obtaining favourable publicity for the council. They are generally attractive without usually being contentious. The public relations staff can also head off bad publicity as well.

It is rare for departments to have anyone of their own, specifically designated as press or public relations officers, though some of the skills are deployed by marketing or promotions staff. In any case it should figure among the direct concerns of the manager.

There is a large technical content in the work, apart from the question of imaginative presentation or novel ideas and of course judgement. The techniques involve finding out how the local press, radio, and television operate; discovering what will interest each of them; finding out their deadlines. In respect of other publicity it may involve learning about type faces; paper weight; quality; and sizes; and even rudimentary knowledge of the way books and pamphlets are put together and the possibilities of desktop publishing.

Television, radio both local and national, newspapers and magazines are nowadays collectively known as the media. They are the best means of reaching a large number of people at the same time and giving an identical message to each. The best way of using them is to obtain news coverage or editorial comment or to participate in providing a longer feature.

In some cases comments should only be made by the chairman of the appropriate committee or the leader of the council or even the civic head be it mayor, chairman or provost. It is a matter of judgement as to who it should be, and it also varies with local practice. It is a potential minefield and newly arrived officials should take care to understand the local rules even though they are usually unwritten.

Politicians need publicity, or feel that they do, which is much the same thing, and become tetchy or worse if their thunder is stolen by an official. The feeling is especially strong as elections approach. As a matter of general principal it is reasonable for an official to comment upon matters of detail and the implementation of council policy and to deal with complaints when these are made publicly but it should be a matter for the elected representative to speak about policy or deal with controversial questions.

Officials should not comment to the press about items on committee agendas before these are discussed though the press may well invite comment. It is a trap for the unwary. Even when they quote from an official's report as they are certainly entitled to do resentment is sometimes stirred.

The media can be approached in a number of ways. The easiest of all is by way of a phone call and an informal chat. It works best when people know one another and without wishing to appear cynical all parks managers should get to know the reporters and photographers, cameramen and editorial staff of all the local media. It allows initiatives to be taken in the easiest and quickest way. However this familiarity should not lull the manager into complacency. The press are not there as publicity agents for the park. They have a job of their own to do and their prime purpose is to sell newspapers even though this may sometimes be allied to crusading zeal and a concern for what they see as the public good. At root however they are commercial organisations with a commodity to sell.

They will only trouble to report something that is interesting to their readers and they may also wish to stir a little or a lot of controversy to help in the process. This should make the manager wary and sometimes cautious even though he is also friendly. In dealing with the press it is necessary to nurse bruises in silence. Complaints do little good and ruin relationships. Most stories are dealt with in their early stages by reporters some of whom may be only starting out on their careers. The manager or director has to be prepared to deal with quite different levels of background information and to deal patiently with questions that may seem very elementary. The individual reporters nonetheless have a high degree of freedom in the line they take.

If the story is a news item the reporter will have been given the work by a news editor who will allocate the press release or the letter or give information about the phone call which first drew the story to attention. When the story is finished it will pass through the hands of a sub editor who will correct it where necessary or edit it to suit the space available or adapt it to the style of the paper. He will also determine its importance relative to the other items that have become available and on the basis of this judgement he will give the story its position in the paper and place it on the page. He will also give it captions and a headline. Television and radio stations have a similar process varied only by the nature of the medium.

The other most frequently used way of passing information is through the vehicle of the press release. This allows a lot of people to be given the same information at the same time. Everyone likely to be interested should be told, even the national papers and television stations if the item is of particular interest.

A matter need not be of earth shaking significance to catch the eye of the national press and television. John Clyde the Director of Parks in Arbroath some years ago noticed that a family of rabbits that had made a nest up a tree. He hit the jackpot with this bit of soft news. Newspaper and television reporters beat a track to his door. (As an aside he stood in the council election following his retirement and beat his former chairman to get a place on the town council. That also took a few headlines.) Human interest stories or ones about animals always catch attention.

In my own case the most widespread coverage that I obtained for an initiative was when I suggested to the City Council that they should bring back working heavy horses to replace a motor vehicle. Aberdeen at the time was being billed as the oil capital of Europe and was in the throes of a major oil boom. The contrast between the proposal and the circumstances of the place created major attention although nostalgia and affection for cart horses also motivated the coverage. Both the BBC and ITV took the story and used it in their main news bulletins throughout the day and the various national newspapers gave it space as well. It had the further merit of offering the chance of good pictures and everyone was invited to the first outing of the horses. Naturally they also focused on human interest and took pictures of children feeding the horses, they wanted to know a little about the history of the driver and they were interested in the reaction of members of the public. It offers a variety of lessons. The main one is that managers should ask themselves what it is that will interest the public. This is also what will interest the media.

Press releases should be concise and to the point, but they should contain enough information to allow an editor to decide whether the item is of interest or has the potential of being made interesting. They should state their purpose in a clear succinct opening sentence so that the news editor can determine its importance at a glance. They should contain as many facts as possible to make life easier for the reporter. Information about any individuals who are involved should also be given. Most news stories are based on human interest of some kind or other. Some comment may also be included but it should be limited in extent unless it is an opinion attributed to a named individual who may then be quoted. If the press are interested the reporter will search out further comment.

A press release should give the name and phone number of the person to whom further enquiries are to be made. If the manager is not to deal with these direct the person who is to answer them should make sure thy know all about the subject. If the invitation is to an opening or a ceremony of some sort the release should clearly state the place, date, and time. The names of any notables that are to be present should be given if necessary explaining who they are and why they are there if it is not self evident. Every effort should be made provide the opportunity for interesting photographs. The release can also be supplemented by a phone call to make sure the matter has got to the right person.

Sometimes a press release has to be sent out well ahead of the event. In such a case it may be 'embargoed'. That is to say the person issuing it says when it can be published and asks the media to wait till then before using it. This is a well accepted practice and although it is voluntary it is usually observed. To avoid accident the words embargoed until the date concerned should be large and unmistakably clear.

The most elaborate method of talking to the media is through a press conference. Invitations should contain the same sort of preliminary information as might be in a press release. The difference is that reporters are able to ask questions systematically in a formal setting. It should also be borne in mind that the reporters who come are by way of being invited guests and should be offered appropriate hospitality which will of course vary with the time of day and the length of the conference. They should be provided with as much written information as possible giving specific details. This makes their job easier. Reporters are like the rest of us and respond more favourably if a job is made easy to do.

It is also important to remember that news gets old and stale very quickly. It has its moment and when that is passed it dies. Just as newspapers will not use old stories unless there is a new angle to them so park managers should not trouble to purvey them. Press conferences sometimes fail as well as succeed.

Newspapers, television and radio news programmes and magazines all work to strict deadlines and in order to cooperate best with them it is desirable to find out what these are. For example if it is desired that a story should figure in every edition of an evening paper it should be in the hands of the press well before 10.30 in the morning. If it reaches them later than this it may only get into the last one or two editions, its coverage will diminish and fewer people will read it. All other newspapers have deadlines as well even those that are only published once a week. The same is true of television, radio and magazines.

Parks' staff have one piece of good fortune. Part of their work involves horticulture which is the most popular hobby in the country. There are scores of gardening writers as a result most of them publishing a weekly newspaper article as well as writing for specialist magazines. I do this myself and I know how hungry a regular column is for new material. The writers are always on the look-out for facts and information and even snippets of gossip. They should be approached directly for their support and help and supplied with press releases and information just like the rest of the media.

Reporters have a difficult job to do and often have to sift information obtained from many sources. Their work is edited by others. They work under pressure of time. Naturally there are sometimes errors or a story may take a line different from the one that was anticipated. It is no use complaining about matters like these. The complaint in any case is likely to alienate the staff of the paper so that when they are next asked to help, they may be unwilling to take the trouble. If however there is a grievance on a matter of genuine importance then a complaint can be made to the editor and if that does not bring about a redress then there are other complaint mechanisms. In an extreme case this might mean a letter to the owners of the paper or to the Press Council.

The problem of dealing effectively with complaints against the press was the subject of the *Calcutt Report* published in June 1990. It sets out the problem and suggests among other things the establishment of what it calls a press complaints commission. The Press Council gave a rather tart response to the effect that it was an independent body itself not attached to Government patronage and likely to carry on its activities no matter what the committee said. Press freedom is precious but the Home Secretary in speaking to the report in the House of Commons in June 1990 said that unless the press installed effective voluntary mechanisms to prevent abuses then legislation would be introduced to install a statutory system.

Talks

Many local organisations meet regularly some of them every week. They have a greedy appetite for speakers. Parks, open spaces, flower displays, natural history, recreation, are welcomed as topics by club secretaries anxiously seeking an interesting subject and a willing speaker. Women's Guilds and Institutes, church guilds, Rotary, Probus, and business clubs, Round Tables, Ladies Circles, Inner Wheels, all need speakers from time to time. The list of possible organisations is very considerable.Their requests should be accommodated. In this way active elements of the community can be contacted and their goodwill, even their support, can be enlisted. All members of the staff should be trained to give talks so that the burden of presentation can be shared.

Invitations arise spontaneously but they can also be solicited by contact with the secretaries of the organisations concerned. Addresses can be obtained from the library or the Citizens' Advice Bureau. Some national organisations furnish a list of local secretaries.

Visual displays are usually welcome and they can make speaking easier. The best of them help to avoid boredom in the audience. They need handling with care however and they are not an unmixed blessing. They range from the straight-forward use and discussion of samples for instance of plants, right through to multi projector slide shows, audio visual displays, videos and films. Speakers should always be prepared for something to go wrong and should not rely totally on the efficiency of equipment. The simple slide show is the easiest to handle.

If slides are used they should be in a logical sequence and be relevant to the subject matter. They should not be repetitive or duplicate one another without good reason. They should be run through beforehand and put the right way round and the proper way up. Once in place the top should be put onto the carousel so that no one can scatter the slides to the four winds when adjusting the position of the equipment. I speak with feeling. Slides are not worth using if they only show words or if the room cannot be darkened sufficiently without a lot of fuss or if they are not of the best quality.

The projector should be checked before use the lens should be cleaned if necessary, the lamp tested and the remote control equipment plugged in. It is best not to stand near a projector when showing the slides. The best position is at the front from where the audience can be seen, their reactions assessed and the speaker heard most easily. The speaker should know his slides well enough not to have to turn to look at them.

Overhead projectors reek of self importance. They are beloved of management consultants. They give an air of portent to the banal. They are often used to list the headings to which the speaker is talking. In this role they add nothing. They may also be used to display charts of figures. Occasionally these may indeed be useful but if so they should be printed in advance and handed round before or after a speech not displayed ineffectually during it. When used badly they are a hindrance and a distraction. In the worst cases the charts may be illegible because their writing is too small for a large hall.

I have seen overhead projectors used well to show cartoons illustrative of the subject matter of the talk. This demands a double skill — a witty pen and a deft hand at changing the transparencies whilst also talking. Unless you can deploy both these my advice is to leave overhead projectors to management consultants.

More elaborate equipment has a greater risk of breakdown. The more complex it becomes the more likely that sooner or later the speaker will be left to ad lib. Slide projector and tape link ups are possible. They require little intervention on the part of the speaker once the system has been set up and started but offer no possibility of interaction with the audience and so eliminate the main benefit of having a speaker and audience together. The advantage is that a completely standard presentation can be made and that a consistent point of view without gratuitous nuances or overtones is put to each of a succession of audiences. Making the tape requires skilful speaker to avoid the very real risks of sounding stilted and ill at ease and very amateurish. Coordination with the slide projector is achieved by the introduction of an electronic pulse onto the tape. This cannot be heard by the audience. Good amplifying and loudspeaking equipment is essential.

Projectors can be combined together to get a variety of effects for instance fading one slide into another, superimposing pictures on top of one another and so on. It calls for professional skills and the risks of something going wrong are high.

The least troublesome way of all is to address the audience direct. The talk should be prepared in advance and be of the right length. We have all suffered from speakers who had too much to say. All talks are better for some humour but the great skill is to get the balance right as between this and the serious content. It will vary with the nature of the occasion.

It is usually best to speak from notes but these should not be read verbatim. They are more of a guide. It is desirable to look at the audience as much as possible and to make eye contact. This not only helps in the process of communication it also gives a guide to the reaction if any and allows the speaker to adjust.

In all cases it is desirable to arrive in good time. This gives the opportunity to view the arrangement of the room adjust the height and angle of the microphone, and find out how to switch it on without a lot of fuss. It allows the chairperson to find out how you wish to be introduced and it gives time to set up any equipment.

The speaker must make sure that it is possible for everyone in the room to hear him without straining and one of the important preliminary skills is voice projection. It doesn't matter how good the talk if no one can hear it. A microphone should be used if one is available. It should be kept at the right distance from the mouth though this differs with the type and for the maximum effect it is desirable to speak straight at it though some are more sensitive and allow some movement of the head without a major variation in sound. This should be checked in advance. Modern systems use hidden equipment that makes a whole lectern or table into a microphone. These are easier still but beware of the *sotto voce* conversation to a neighbour which can reach everyone in the audience. Sometimes tiny radio microphones are supplied. They should be attached to the clothing about the middle of the chest and tried out in advance. If there is anything as sophisticated as this there will usually be a technician at hand to give assistance.

After dinner speaking is another skill. It is not an appropriate medium for conveying a long earnest message though some serious matter is necessary. This could be a brief thought or two on a subject appropriate to the company or attention might be drawn to a proposal or an idea floated. The basic intention however is to entertain.

The best speeches are those that draw their humour from the circumstances of the moment of the occasion and are so particular to them that they cannot be transplanted and used elsewhere. But this is an ideal that is not often attained. The principal after dinner guest ought not to speak for more than twenty minutes and the lesser ones for much less. It is best to err on the side of brevity.

6 Risk management

There are always risks. They are present in every human activity. Good management tries to minimise them and limit their effect, hence the term risk management. Some of the problems are dealt in discussing children's play grounds where safety surfaces, bank slides and careful choice of equipment are all forms of risk management. The health and safety legislation which now exists in many states is another example.

Poisonous plants

Every now and again there are scares about poisonous plants, Deadly nightshade was the British vegetational *bête noire* a generation ago. It has been replaced in the national hate list by Giant Hogweed. Many ornamental plants are poisonous including familiar ones like Clematis, Aconite, Delphinium, Foxglove, Monkshood, Rhododendron, Rhus, Yew. Not many of them are likely to tempt anyone's palate so they can be grown with reasonable confidence though not near cattle or grazing animals.

In some cases poisonous fruit looks attractive and children in particular may be tempted to try it. Plants like this should not be used in parks and children's playgrounds. They include the fruit of the familiar Skimmia japonica though in this particular case the problem can be avoided by using only male plants, Daphne, and Laburnum, Some weeds like deadly nightshade also have poisonous fruit and should be suppressed when they appear.

Some plants contain skin irritants. In Britain Giant Hogweed has acquired great notoriety though it is not so long ago that it was esteemed as a handsome foliage plant. It can cause a severe allergic rash and swelling if it is touched often enough and should be kept out of public places. There are plenty of others ranging from stinging nettles to the familiar pot plant Primula obconica. Staff that regularly handle Sunflowers, Poinsettia, Primula, Humea, Daffodils, Ivy, and Chrysanthemums should use protective gloves and keep their arms covered. Not everybody is affected but there is no telling in advance.

Vandalism

The first gardeners were the four daughters of Hesperus, the evening star. They cultivated golden apples in a garden near Agadir which was guarded by a dragon that never slept. No park security has ever been as vigilant since. Theft, vandalism and graffiti are still a source of nuisance in nearly every park system and are made worse by press reports based on the vituperations of the well intended bursting into spluttering indignation at the sight of a broken tree, a camera and a reporter's note book.

It is necessary to get vandalism into proportion. It is not a new problem. It has been known to every urban society since history began. The very name is taken from a 4th and 5th century tribe who invaded Western Europe and which was associated with wilful, barbarous, wanton destruction. It does not betoken an abrupt deterioration in modern standards of behaviour. All urban societies have experienced it. Moreover most building in most areas are not damaged most of the time and nor is most private property. That is not to take a complacent view. Vandalism is disfiguring and depressing. In some localities it is prevalent and the cost of vandalism anywhere is an unnecessary drain on scarce resources.

Occasional damage to pavilions, shelters, fountains, conservatories, lights, public lavatories, young trees, park buildings and benches occurs in most areas. Some say that it costs local authorities in Britain a billion pounds each year. Any figure should be regarded as suspect, few local authorities are able to isolate all the costs, and aggravation exaggerates. Most minor damage is anticipated already and is corrected by staff as they see it. Damage that stems from legitimate though robust use can sometimes be placed in the wrong category.

Not all damage is deliberate and probably not much is premeditated. Some is the result of children experimenting or trying their strength or playing on or with objects too weak to take the strain; some may be caused by a drunk wending his way home after the last bus has gone and finding *divertissement* by snapping the street trees en route; some may be the result of wear and tear, or the outcome of bad design. Some of course is wanton and systematic.

The incidence of vandalism varies but surveys have shown it is most prevalent in large industrial conurbations but within these may occur in one locality and not another. It is least frequent in rural areas. Damage tends to be directed at public rather than private property and to things that seem to belong to no one. It is worst in large impersonal estates and is less in small ones where people tend to know their neighbour. Research in Europe shows that it is less in places where there are interesting streets in which people linger and worst in desolate out of the way places with little to give pleasure or command respect and through which adults hurry.

It is less where there is diversity and more where there is monolithic development out of scale with the human form. These may seem statements of the obvious but in spite of their self-evidence planners, architects and even park designers continue to create situations which appear to favour vandalism.

It is often suggested that the number of children in a given area is a factor. It has even been quantified, more than thirty children per acre of development and vandalism grows. Why this should be so has not been explained and nor is it consistent though larger families may offer less parental supervision; there may be overcrowding within the home; the play space may be insufficient for the numbers; and there may be none for the robust games of older children with consequent friction between them and adults.

These conditions steal self esteem from the young. Damage and aggression follow. Consider the words of Dr John Simon. In the *City Medical Report 1849* he said 'Who can wonder that the laws of society should at times be forgotten by those whom the eye of society habitually overlooks and who the heart of society often appears to discard'. It is hard for a visitor not to feel heart-sick and depressed by even a casual visit to some areas; how much worse it is to live in them.

It cannot be a surprise that a failed, inadequate or degenerate environment is attacked by those who have to face it every day. It is a widespread though empirical observation that vandalism is reduced when these places are made more diverse, interesting, varied.

Vandalism can be mitigated by a number of practical steps as well as by the grander ones of environmental and social improvement. The most important quality to deploy in facing an outbreak of damage is silence. That will half the length of any newspaper report and relegate it to an out of the way page or may make it hardly worth using. All staff should be instructed accordingly, contractor and client alike. Vandals are encouraged by publicity and may feel impelled to take up the challenge of an apoplectic park keeper threatening dire penalties if he happens to catch them when they return. They know the risk is negligible.

There is also the phenomenon of copy cat vandalism. Well publicised damage in one place will suggest the existing possibility to others elsewhere. For the same reasons reports listing vandalism and its costs are to be deprecated. They should not be put forward spontaneously no matter what the sense of outrage. They inevitably, generate press and media comment and a sense of helpless impotence. There is nothing to gain from them.

Damage should be restored and made good immediately so that the park or open space or street resumes its normal appearance at once giving no opportunity to crow about what has been done or to show it to admiring peers. There is then less chance of it being seen and copied, a reduced risk of the citizen feeling imperilled and insecure, there will be only muted claims that urban civilisation is coming to an end and civic pride will be unabated.

The next step is to consider the immediate reasons for the damage, and to design it away. Vandals are lazy like every one else. They are more likely to attack soft targets and less likely to tackle tougher ones that take more effort to damage and need more time.

Seats and items of park and street furniture should be robust wherever they are located, they should be anchored securely into place, litter bins should be firmly attached to a strong base,they should be emptied regularly and if they contain an inner liner it should be locked into place. Coping stones on walls should be firmly fastened and they can be made in long heavy sections or cast *in situ*. Walls should be kept pointed and in good repair so that bricks or stones cannot be prised out of them. Glass should be armour plated or replaced with heavy duty polycarbonate or butyrate sheeting.

Notices carrying lists of prohibitions are rarely necessary and are easy targets. Avoid them. They are intrusive, expensive, difficult to maintain, and ineffective. The police sometimes say that they cannot intervene to stop a nuisance unless there is a notice to prohibit the activity. Do not believe it. If there is a genuine nuisance they have every authority to act against it and if there is no nuisance they should not be called.

Notices that are intended to inform are another matter but even these need locating with care so that they fit into the landscape not intrude on it. They are no less subject to vandalism and should be made of tough durable materials. If possible they should be based at the edge of a shrub border where their feet can be protected by spiny shrubs, or have their backs to a wall so that they are harder to damage. Wording should be unambiguous so as to not attract waggish additions. Notice boards should be maintained regularly so that they never look as if they are the neglected leftovers of an earlier endeavour. If fronted, the glass should either be plate or clear strong polycarbonate. Out of date posters should be removed as soon as their life span has ended.

The fittings in lavatories should be tough. Pipes and conduits should be out of sight, embedded in the walls, covered with plas-

ter, mechanisms should be concealed, projecting pieces minimised, the walls should be tiled so they are hard to scratch and
easy to clean. Light fittings should be robust, recessed, and covered with armour plated glass.

Externally down spouts should be embedded into the walls,
external lighting should be out of reach and made of tough resistant materials. Lever handles on doors should be replaced with
strong conventional doorknobs. Flat roofs should be avoided whatever the architect may say about his design integrity and there
should be wide projections at the eaves to make it hard to get onto
the roof. Nuts and bolts should have self locking devices which
prevent equipment being dismantled without the proper key. Light
deters vandalism and consideration should be given to flood-
lighting vulnerable buildings or installing lights that are activated by
movement or sound.

If shrubs are used in difficult places though not where children
play they should be self protecting; prickly roses, spiny barberries,
gorse, thorns, holly. Or they should be quick growing and robust
so that they recover quickly if they are damaged.

Flowers should be so numerous that even the most assiduous
vandals hardly know where to start and cannot make a noticeable
impact even if they do. Flowers should be planted on the same
principle that motivated the seed sowing of farmers, sow a handful
for the birds, it then does not matter if some are taken. Standards
of maintenance should be high, neglect stimulates vandals. Multistemmed trees or close planted thickets though not appropriate
everywhere are harder to attack than standard trees with a single
vulnerable stem.

Tree guards are a deterrent and even though expensive are
worth the price in vulnerable areas. They should be fastened to a
strong stake at the level of the lowest branches of the crown so
that the most vulnerable part of the stem is protected even though
it means leaving part at the base exposed. Heavy stock should be
chosen even though it is more expensive. If damage occurs the
tree should be replanted at once even if it means using a container
grown plant.

Fire can be a weapon of the vandal. Timber should be treated to
increase fire resistance. In extreme cases it may be necessary to
replace wooden items with steel. Safety surfaces should also be
flame resistant.

Fences should be avoided on the whole unless they stop children running onto a nearby street or are essential to protect a
vulnerable area. If they are not of architectural merit the presumption should be against them. They are expensive to erect and
maintain. Existing ones should be considered for removal. All

fences are sometimes subject to vandalism but chainlink fences are easy to damage and are often unzipped. Ranch type fencing should be avoided unless it is desired to provide a climbing frame. Chestnut pale fencing and other temporary fencing should be removed as soon as its job is done. It sags after it has been up for a time and looks unsightly as well as becoming a target for vandals.

Supervision should be at its most vigilant in the spring when children burst into the open air and expel exuberant energy and in the autumn when the onset of darker evenings causes another surge in damage to occur. Supervision should not be aggressive though at times it has to be firm. Not every one has the gift of controlling and regulating the mischief of children and youths without causing aggravation and confrontation. Staff should be changed until the right ones are in place. A bad attendant does more harm than good.

Perseverance is needed. Clear away signs of damage quickly, replace broken seats and trees at once, repair buildings and structures immediately.

Civic pride is the best watchman of all. Everything should be done to stimulate it through publicity, and getting people of prestige to associate with the efforts of the department, members of football teams, actors from the theatre, television personalities, pop groups, anyone in fact who has a claim on the esteem of those who might be inclined to vandalism. Not only will it deter the vandal it will help to restore that other ancient sanction against misbehaviour, neighbourly disapproval.

Everyone should be involved in tree and bulb planting, schools, colleges, youth and community organisations, any one living in the neighbourhood. Public planting programmes need assistance from contractors. This can be specified, but they also need active cooperation, pleasant supervision, friendly instruction, sympathetic advice and willing help which cannot. Publicity and goodwill should be directed towards contractors and their staff, it will persuade them of the value of the work. The client has to bear in mind Samuel Butler's words 'He that complies against his will is of his own opinion still'.

Graffiti

Writing graffiti is also an age old human pastime and the name was first applied to the words and pictures scratched on the walls of Pompeii and the other cities of the Roman Empire. It has been given a modern impetus, greater visibility, and made much more fun, by aerosol paints and felt pens. It attracts as much or more attention as physical damage and can be just as disfiguring. Even so it is not a major nuisance everywhere and getting rid of it immediately improves the situation anywhere.

Graffiti should be cleaned off uncomplainingly and unfailingly every morning and all evidence of it removed. It is nearly always unsightly, repels the public and it multiplies if left. Of course graffiti can also be entertaining and sometimes special graffiti walls have been provided to accommodate it in the hope of limiting its spread and providing a focus of interest. Beware! Graffiti, its outrageous witticisms and extravagant designs, is addictive.

Erase graffiti before anyone can see it, keep up these efforts indefinitely. Use materials that can be cleaned easily or apply coatings that can be cleaned by chemicals, hot water or steam without damage to the surface below, lacquer finishes are less satisfactory because they can become patchy and unattractive if they are subject to repeated graffiti and cleaning. Vandals are prone to discouragement too.

Litter

Litter breeds. There should be enough well placed litter baskets in each park and they should be emptied regularly. Litter that is scattered should be cleared as soon as it appears — leaving it begets more. The penalties for casting litter are now severe and there should be a willingness to apply them and secure publicity for doing so. There is a problem of education and to help with this the assistance of the Tidy Britain Group and its Regional Directors should be enlisted. They can draw on wide experience.

The group was responsible for a programme of research that led to some of the provisions in Part 4 of the *1990 Environmental Protection Act* and the associated code of practice, which relate to litter. They found that smoking materials constituted as much as thirty per cent of all the litter thrown in British streets. Even a casual glance will show the same to be true in a park. The items are not individually very conspicuous, cigarette ends, packages, match boxes and spent matches, but they are shed in large amounts.

The research found that sixty per cent more litter is dropped on already dirty surfaces than on those that are clean. Any park will illustrate the truth of this observation. Tender documents should ensure that litter is collected promptly not left to attract more. They should set the target that parks should be clean all the time, rather than stipulating frequencies of cleaning, 'if it isn't dirty', say the group, 'don't clean it'.

Litter bins should be adequate and emptied regularly. They advise that a busy street requires a 200 litre litter bin every six metres. Park access paths and the approaches to the major attractions should be just as busy.

They also unearthed the truth that there is a connection between the amount of litter and the way refuse is collected. You bet! And what is worse for the manager — a fair proportion of it finishes in the shrubs or flowers or roses or on the grass beside the street. The park manager has more than a passing interest in the standard of street sweeping and rubbish collection and should grumble if they are done badly.

Campaigns to stop litter do not have a long effect. They need repeating. In some communities like Mansfield in Nottinghamshire remarkable reductions in the problem have occurred as a result of programmes of litter collection involving the Guide and Scout organisations. They form cheerful enthusiastic teams to clear litter in the evenings. They are rewarded by a cola at a famous hamburger store at the end of their shift. The volume of litter is now a fraction of the amount they had to gather when they started their efforts. The streets of the town centre are noticeably clean even on a busy day. Persistence pays.

Dogs

Even after a century of vexation the protagonists in the dog debate are still snapping at the ankles of the parks manager. Legislation about dogs appeared in the *Town Police Clauses Act 1847*. This makes it an offence to allow any unmuzzled or ferocious dog to attack or menace any person or animal. The *Dogs Act 1871* allows magistrates to order the destruction or control of dangerous dogs.

The *Dogs Act 1906* empowers the police to seize detain and dispose of stray dogs. The *Control of Dogs Order 1930* requires dogs to wear identity discs in public places and allows local authority to make curfew regulations to control dogs. The *Guard Dogs Act 1975* requires the supervision of guard dogs. *Civic Government (Scotland) Act 1982* makes it an offence to allow a dog to foul certain public places, including parks if there are notices about it, and increases the power of local authorities to deal with strays.

The *Dangerous Dogs Act 1989* allows courts to order owners to keep dogs under control or to have them destroyed. The *1990 Environment Protection Act* requires dogs to wear identity discs be kept under control and obliges local authorities to deal with strays and appoint dog wardens for the purpose. The legislation has danced in a circle. All these worthy laws are extremely difficult to enforce. The problem is unabated.

In Britain alone there are 6,800,000 dogs. Their owners find companionship, fun, security, exercise, affection and uncritical loyalty from keeping them. Some of these dogs are allowed to stray and most of them are still permitted to foul open spaces and paths. This is a major source of bitter complaint to parks staff who have to face irate complainants. Sometimes dogs, not vicious but simply energetic and excited, frighten people using the parks. Occasionally dogs are dangerous and bite.

There is periodic concern about Toxicara canis an unpleasant creature also called common round worm of dogs. The adults live and mate in the intestine of dogs. Some of the eggs are passed in the faeces and it is through these that the pest is spread. After two or three weeks, depending on environmental conditions, the larvae develop within the eggs. Adult dogs are resistant but if they are swallowed by a puppy at this stage the larvae hatch, enter the blood stream, lodge in the liver and the lungs growing all the time, and eventually migrate to the trachea. They are then swallowed again and find home sweet home in the intestine. They become adults and if both male and female are present they breed and the cycle starts again. Worms can infect a puppy in the womb if the mother is infected.

The number of dogs with the worm is not known but research has shown that it can be as high as twenty in a hundred among strays though less in the population as a whole.

Humans are affected in two ways. They may be infested in which case antibodies develop though the worms never get beyond the larval stage. One or two healthy adults in every hundred have the antibodies and were thus infested at some time. Disease can occur but is rare and in Britain there are only two cases a year in every million people. There are two disorders. One causes breathing problems allergic reactions and inflammation of the liver and perhaps other troubles too. The other produces lesions in the eye, and in severe cases, blindness. They are difficult to treat. Prevention is important.

Anyone who has touched a dog should wash before handling food.

Dogs should be treated against worms as a routine. In the park or open space dog faeces should be removed and disposed of — not left around where the eggs can develop and cause trouble. There are of course aesthetic reasons for clearing up as well. Dog owners should be provided with the means of doing so, it is their responsibility and they should be penalised if they neglect it. Special bins are now available and should be installed, and equipment for emptying them mechanically should be provided.

Campaigns should be promoted to try to get owners to clear up after their dogs and keep them under control. Not only do romping dogs damage flower beds and borders, they also cause alarm. Unfortunately it is hard to see whom a loose dog brought with it. Owners even when identified are not always receptive to the idea that their dog may be mischievous or its faeces objectionable. Park attendants frequently suffer abuse and sometimes threats when they remonstrate. Even the dogs turn nasty.

Notices do no good and are widely ignored by owners and used by dogs as territorial marking points. Dog toilets are often advocated but they require more discipline than the members of the canine world usually vouchsafe and they must be cleaned and disinfected regularly. If they contain sand they may attract small children looking for somewhere to play. A system of dog wardens like the one now obligatory for British local authorities seems the best available solution. Their tasks are to collect strays to inform and educate the public, and to do their best to resolve a difficult and divisive problem.

Sport risks

All sport contains a degree of risk. Even superficially amiable croquet, a game based, like politics on frustrating the ambitions of others, equips its participants with formidable weaponry. Broken limbs are one of the hazards of football. Other field games break noses, ankles, arms, legs, cheekbones. All fields should be provided with first aid equipment and managers should seek the cooperation of the voluntary first aid associations. Attendants should be instructed in first aid. Precautions like a phone to summon an ambulance and a list of the numbers of hospitals and doctors are minimum requirements.

Playing surfaces should be kept in the best condition. When pitches are dangerous because of frozen, iron hard, slippery ground the games should be cancelled by the management not left to the referees who will be under great pressure from team officials and players to let the matches take place. Pitches that are too wet should also be declared unplayable not because of risk to the players who would probably only be mired but because of the chance of untold damage to the pitch.

Hockey is best played on an artificial surface which is guaranteed to run true. In the near future it is likely to be a requirement that first division games to take place on these surfaces. Cricket wickets in the general games area of a park should be given an artificial surface if the club will agree to play on it. The alternative is turf that becomes marked, scored and pitted by other uses. Erratic surfaces are dangerous. Cricket in a park looks splendid but can be dangerous if the ball can reach a playground, picnic area or even the paths where people are likely to be walking. Plenty of space should be left for games if possible. Tree planting helps to reduce the risk and provides a better setting for the games.

Some sports are capable of being a nuisance if pursued in the wrong locations. *The Control of Pollution Act 1974* allows the Secretaries of State to approve codes of practice seeking to minimise noise. Motorised sports and gun sports are the most obvious examples of those with a high capacity to generate unwanted noise but the incessant whine of a model aircraft, or worse a squadron of them, has an unparalleled aggravation quotient. The Sports Council produced reports in 1990 one on providing for motor sports and the other about motorised water sports. The Clay Pigeon Shooting Association is consulting with the Department of the Environment to produce a code for their sport. A code on model aircraft was produced in 1982.

Managers with suitable locations within their bailiwick are also likely to encounter requests for other air sports, parascending, gliding, hang gliding, and flying microlight aircraft. Watch out. Some air sports generate cattle stampedes that would have tested the resolution of John Wayne. The British Aviation Authority should be consulted as a matter of course in case there are restrictions on the use of air space, so should the Sports Council and the governing bodies of the sports concerned, so of course should the public.

Golf played casually on open space is particularly dangerous. Park golfers have an uncertain control over the distance of their shots and less over the direction. Golf practice in some areas is a plague. The distant park and its patrons are gratuitously pelted with golf balls. Stopping it can be even more perilous. Attendants who approach golfers to ask them to go elsewhere sometimes feel themselves deeply threatened and sometimes they are. The best way of ending this dangerous nuisance is to make ground available for golf driving preferably in the form of a range or in larger communities more than one. Along with that should go tree planting schemes to break up the large barren prairie playing fields where practice golfers believe they can find an El Dorado.

The space will look a great deal better for the vegetation. It need not inhibit football though it may reduce the number of pitches.

Security

Attendants who handle cash are at risk especially on isolated sites like the starters box or professionals shop on a golf course. The amounts should be reduced by encouraging the use of season tickets, if necessary by giving a price advantage, and by introducing a system of advance booking and payment at a central computerised box office. There should be regular secure collection of the cash so that the attendant is never left with a large sum.

Credit cards and cheques cards should be accepted at golf courses and restaurants where the payments are comparatively large. The police crime prevention officer should be invited to inspect all premises and advise on securing them and on the safety of the staff that use them. The problem is that of the contractor but the client has an interest in any losses and in the reputation of the facility.

Pay day used also to be a time of peril when often large sums were carried round departments. It is inexcusable today. Cashless pay using credit transfers removes not only the problems of security but also the time wasted whilst waiting for pay to arrive and the risk of loss or pilfering which started as soon as it had been distributed. It took competitive tendering to speed the process and even now not all authorities nor all contractors have introduced it. Their reasons sound meritorous even egalitarian but they have little relationship with modern attitudes, nor do they recognise with what quite excessive ease money can be withdrawn from a bank.

Undesirables

I first heard this slightly old fashioned term when I was an apprentice in a park in Nottingham. The foreman was eyeing a man, for such it usually is, loitering near a playground.

'Now there's an undesirable' is the expurgated nub of what he said. He amplified his character assessment with words that are on the Longman disapproved list and which in any case this book has voluntarily abjured. The action he took is still appropriate. He went across and spoke with courtesy using neither threat nor accusation. He merely passed the time of day. In doing so he let the man know he had been seen and was observed.

'Now watch' he said as he returned to me. The man made off. We never saw him again. It is an unfortunate fact that occasionally undesirables do gravitate towards parks. It is sometimes difficult to distinguish between them and people there for legitimate reasons, and tact and care are necessary in making an approach. Staff should be vigilant and if suspicious should call the police. If there is an attendant the responsibility is clear. DSO or contractors staff should be asked to cooperate.

Glue sniffers, drug takers, drunks, are further occasional visitors and although they usually isolate themselves they can get the park a bad reputation and are sometimes the source of damage. The problem requires sympathetic understanding but determined staff and the cooperation of the police and social work departments. The primary concern of managers must be the safety and convenience of the public and the reputation of the park.

Harmful chemicals

Pesticides, that is to say chemicals which kill insect and other pests and diseases, weeds, algae, moss, and worms need handling with care. There should be a presumption against using them in deference to broader environmental concerns and the alternatives should always be examined first. The work of applying them is a matter for the contractor but the way they are to be used and handled should be stipulated precisely in the specification. The judgement as to when they should be used is a matter for the client.

In Britain the *Food and Environment Protection Act 1985* introduced strict rules and safeguards about the use of chemicals. People employed to apply them must be qualified to do so and have a certificate to say that they have been assessed and are competent. They should be over eighteen years old. The staff that handle chemicals must have appropriate protective clothing and should be required to use it. They should have ready access to a place to wash themselves. The materials must be stored securely and must be transported safely from the store to the site.

The storekeeper must hold a certificate and the store has to be approved and registered as well. The amount stored should be limited to 300 litres of liquid chemical or 100 kilograms of dry chemical or if both are stored the total amount should not exceed 300 units. The equipment used to apply chemicals should be maintained carefully and should be more leak proof than the British Cabinet.

At every stage the materials should be handled with care to avoid spillage or accident. If a spray is to be used it should be applied when there is no chance of wind carrying it onto esteemed plants nearby. If a green house is fumigated the doors should be locked afterwards and notices put on the doors.

It is essential to ensure that streams, ponds and lakes are not polluted. Containers should be disposed of only on licensed tips or incinerators. The makers instructions should be followed meticulously . Before spraying chemicals the Act requires that the public is warned and that neighbours are told about it in advance. Spraying should not be done near playgrounds when children are likely to be about nor in school grounds during term time.

Insurance

A variety of risks arise for local authorities and their employees. They are normally insured though in some cases the cost may persuade the council that it is cheaper to carry the risk itself.

Public liability insurance covers bodily injury or disease contracted by third parties but in order to found a successful claim it is necessary to prove negligence on the part of the council or its employees. Events that give rise to special risks for example a bonfire and firework display should generally be notified to the insurer. Any group organising an activity in a park should be required to take out this kind of insurance policy and should demonstrate they have done so before their event is allowed to go ahead.

A personal accident policy is also usual for staff. It could cover such matters as the risk of an accident arising at work, or injury, disablement or death as a result from a violent assault suffered in the course of or as a result of the employment . Staff may also be covered for loss or damage to personal effects whilst they are at work, though employees are expected to exercise reasonable care of their property. Fidelity insurance is usual for staff handling money or having the opportunity to defraud the council.

Sometimes employees are protected from claims of libel and slander that arise from the pursuit of their duties for the council. Money is often insured for example to refund the council if the takings at a golf course are lost or stolen. Fire insurance protects both building and contents.

Livestock on model farms and zoos, or horses can be protected and it may be difficult to get money to replace them through any other route. Vehicle insurance is a standard provision but it should extend to ponies and traps, landaus, steam engines, street organs, mobile playgrounds, mobile changing rooms, portable theatres, and other equipment that a park might have, in addition to conventional vehicles. Insurance should also cover employees who use their cars for occasional business purposes. Marine insurance may be needed if there are canoes, rowing boats, sailing dinghies, sail boards, or if playleaders take parties on adventure courses, or if other water or marine sports are encouraged.

7 Catering and recreation management

Most larger parks provide for sports of various kinds. It is the best place for them so long as there is adequate room for all the other elements that ought to be there as well. In a park the scale of the space they require can be balanced by woods and trees and when the sport is not taking place it becomes available for general use. The sports help to broaden the range of interests and may bring additional people into the parks. There is continuous pressure for more facilities and this is even helpful to the manager so long as casual users wanting informal or passive recreation are not disadvantaged. They have no organised lobby to support them.

High quality sport attracts spectators. It serves the double purpose of recreation and entertainment. My unfulfilled hope was to see an outdoor skating rink in a park in the UK. The roller skating rink in a park at Middlesbrough used to be a major focus of life; and at Cologne the outdoor ice rink seethes with bright faced cheerful humanity and is surrounded by parents, visitors, friends and the curious. It is as good as a pipe band. It gives delight.

Local authorities provide the majority of sports facilities. Collectively in Britain they manage nearly 2000 indoor centres many of them modern and the product of the 1970s and 80s. Some of these are in parks or playing fields or are close enough to affect the way they are used. There may be joint programmes and coaching schemes.

In addition there are thousands of bowling greens, tennis courts, football pitches, hundreds of municipal golf courses, park restaurants and kiosks; and a host of other facilities such as running tracks, cycling tracks, boating lakes, outdoor swimming pools, artificial ski slopes, trampolines, mazes, crazy golf and so on. They are all affected by the requirement to go out to tender.

The only facilities that are exempt are those used exclusively by educational institutions for substantial amounts of time even though they are also available to the public under an arrangement for joint use. Even these will be affected by the greater autonomy now being given to individual schools.

In England 35 per cent of sport and recreation management including marketing and promotion must be put to tender by January 1992, a further 35 per cent by the August of that year, and the remainder by January 1993. The tenders are to be in four to six year periods. There are modified versions of this programme in Scotland and Wales.

Some of the organisational considerations that affect grounds maintenance apply to this branch of the service, so do some of the rules. A minimum of three tenders from outside contractors must be considered if enough people are interested. If not, all those that announce their interest must be given the chance to put in a bid. If other local authorities bid they must be extra to the number. They do not reduce the number of outside contractors that have to be involved. The same caveat applies as for grounds maintenance.

The leisure management Direct Service Organisation

The local authority has to decide whether it wants to have a bid from its own department at all. In order to compete effectively the DSO will have to negotiate local variations of national agreements in particular those which relate to paid overtime and increased pay for what have been considered to be unsocial hours. Expect that phrase to disappear from municipal vocabularies. Contractors are unlikely to pay extra at weekend and on public holidays. Leisure facilities like the parks themselves are open for long hours and every day of the year. The difference in costs from this cause alone will be decisive. The number of staff employed may have to be reduced to increase the chance of winning.

The DSO may want to shorten lines of communication in its own structure and get rid of surplus tiers of management. It may have to get rid of outdated bonus schemes and consider profit sharing and other incentives for its staff. The greater use of part time and seasonal staff may have to be considered; coaches may have to pay their way; the sports development officers that burgeoned during the 80s may have to dislodged onto the client. It will have to look more critically at its other costs and overheads and at charges that are imposed on it from elsewhere in the system. It may even seek smaller more economical offices. It should be allowed to shed bureaucratic constraints which stop management decisions being taken quickly without doing much to increase accountability.

The DSO has to gear up its marketing for competition; renew arrangements for caring for its customers; plan ways of increasing the income and attendances; make sure that it has the same ability as the competition to vary prices for admission so as to encourage business; to charge higher rates to get the most from peak time use; and to make the client pay for concessions intended for social purposes like free admission for the disabled, the old, the unemployed, and the young. It will have to increase the speed with which it can produce management information especially about income and spending and it may have to consider the introduction of new systems to do this. It will not be enough to lumber behind the treasurers department.

Some of the changes may breach long standing local government traditions. So be it. The council for its part should set up a committee or board which can manage all the DSOs so that it acquires enough experience and *chutzpah* to assert the need for change; to judge what is suggested; and put forward ideas of its own.

Some authorities previously chose not to manage recreational facilities themselves or decided to abandon doing so. They instead appointed outside independent contractors voluntarily. It is partly as a result of this that firms of contractors already exist. They are sure to try to expand, new ones will form and firms in related businesses like hotel management will see the chance to diversify, others may be attracted from abroad. Management buy-outs will also be proposed. The value of the work that will be put to tender nationally is high.

The client

It is necessary to decide whether to separate the client and contractor into different departments and if so whether to leave them as specialists or to combine them with others. The same considerations apply as in other services that have gone to tender. The independence of the client from the contractor should be evident in whatever structure is chosen. If it is not, there will be pressure over a period from auditors and competitors to bring the separation about.

The Council through the client has to define the policy of the service; plan ways of developing or adapting it as needs change; decide for which groups it is mainly provided; consider the prices at which it is offered and the level of subsidy if any that is appropriate or profit that is desired. It should ensure that the amount of use is satisfactory; determine the minimum hours of opening; outline the programmes of coaching and promotional events and the policy which underlies them; stipulate the minimum periods during which the public is to have unimpeded access free from club, tournament or competition use; and decide what extra uses are to be encouraged or permitted: for instance the number of gala days that football fields can be used without special permission being obtained through the client.

It will be necessary to say whether any activities are to be prohibited, for example the authority may not want to allow go-kart racing on its running track; to explain the council policy about sponsorship it may dislike sponsorship by tobacco companies.

A mechanism may be needed to regulate sub letting and allocating income that may result for example from a physiotherapist setting up a practice in the premises; or freelance coaches paying for time in a facility; or even a specialist shop asking to have an outlet for example on a golf course or attached to a restaurant. The client also has to decide whether and to what extent elite sportsmen and women are to receive special consideration and on what terms.

The client must then recommend the best form of contract for the interest of the public and the local authority; advertisements have to be placed; short lists drawn up from the contractors who come forward; tenders invited from the selected companies; the offers judged; the contract awarded, started up, managed and the outcome monitored.

Some work for example maintaining putting and bowling greens, golf courses, croquet lawns, tennis courts and football, hockey and cricket pitches may already be included in grounds maintenance contracts. Disputes can be expected between contractors if they are responsible for different parts of what are essentially the same function.

Many situations of disagreement can arise for instance when the contractor managing a golf course or a football pitch is denied income because the ground maintenance contractor has failed to keep the facility fit for use or has closed it because play would damage a water-logged surface. Building cleaning and catering may also be involved. There is a strong case for making the recreational management contractor responsible for all the roles. This is permissible under Section2 (5) of the Act.

Forms of tender

The facilities can be offered area by area. This has been usual in grounds maintenance. They may be offered in groups of similar facilities for example all the football and other outdoor games pitches might be put together. Making very big tenders of disparate facilities almost certainly exposes the authority to the risk of successful claims of unfair competition.

Catering and sport and leisure management present perhaps greater difficulties in specification even than grounds maintenance since the fundamental approaches can differ widely. The contractor will be responsible for wage costs; interior decoration and repairs to the fittings of buildings; replacement of equipment; bills for heat, light, fuel rates, and water. These are the normal responsibilities of tenants. The client will pay loan charges and keep up the exterior of buildings, which are the the normal duties of landlords. From that point on the potential permutations are numerous.

It may be decided simply to offer the facility as a franchise for which the contractor would put in an offer. There may be conditions attached for example stipulating minimum hours of opening, explaining the expected quality, the range of services and standards of maintenance.

The arrangement gives a great deal of freedom to the contractor. For this reason it is likely to yield the best financial return for the authority. Franchising might be appropriate for a park restaurant or tea room and indeed many are already treated in this way. It is also suitable for golf courses. The most favourable offer is then accepted considering both its value and the quality of the service proposed. This gives the contractor maximum freedom and the greatest fleetness of foot with which to respond to changing fashions. It gives an powerful incentive to develop programmes and increase income and public use. It removes nearly all responsibility from the client whose only residual concern is to see that the obligations of the lease are fulfilled and that information is available that can be used when the arrangement is ending and new offers have to be invited.

The authority may ask for contractors to do the work in return for a management fee. The local authority would then be left to bear the costs of the enterprise and would get all the income. This will probably prove a bad deal for the authority and a cause for celebration for the contractor. It is the recreation management equivalent of day rates in grounds maintenance.

Much of the income in recreation depends on marketing skill and the zeal with which new opportunities are seized or developed. Economy of operation depends on the contractor's vigilance and business sense. A simple management fee gives no incentive either to keep down costs or boost income. Even DSOs will perform badly in the circumstance.

There will be various other arrangements with a variety of details. Some may involve fixed subsidies; price control to make sure that no one is priced out of the facility; provisions for sharing surpluses. Other profit and loss sharing arrangements will emerge.

The sums are complex. There is a high risk of failure if they are not right. The main point is to put the contractor or the DSO in the position of having to develop the service; attract customers; bear the cost of failure and operate economically. Any arrangement that offers less will be expensive.

Contractors need the fullest information in order to tender including a statement of the aims of the service; records of past performance and attendances; actual prices; the pricing policy; the hours of opening; the income and spending in enough detail for sensible judgements and projections to be made; records of fuel consumption, rates and all the other details of the business. They should be encouraged to inspect the facility. The contractor has to be left to make judgements on the facts that are available or which can be adduced. If the assessment is wrong the business will fail. In such a case expect a vigorous search for alibis and a lively spat in the press.

The DSO will have all the information already and failure to make it openly available to competitors would be probably construed as unfair competition. In the long term the public interest is in obtaining an efficient friendly high quality service at a reasonable price not in who provides it.

Catering

Catering contracts are formed on the basis of the same considerations that apply to sports and leisure management though the timetable was different at the outset. As with the other services the authority only has to go to tender if it wants its own staff to get a chance to do the work. Many authorities put their catering out to outside contractors in any case and the legislation does not cut across these arrangements. Indeed franchising or leasing buildings in this way whether to an outside caterer or to the DSO after competition is an option that should be considered. It gives the caterer an incentive to invest in the facility, develop the trade, and requires the minimum supervision.

Franchises to sell ice cream from vans should still be advertised and allocated on the basis of the highest tender. Standards of cleanliness are the concern of the environmental health authorities and it can be left to the trader to make advantage of the trade when it exists.

Catering for open air events or in park cafés is heavily dependent on the weather. The manager has to be quick to adapt to changes in the business, sending staff home as soon as it is clear they are not wanted and having the power to get extra staff quickly in the case of an unexpected flow of trade. Local authority terms and conditions of employment including long periods of minimum call out during which wages have to be paid whether there was work or not acted against the commercial interests of this kind of business and have been modified or dropped altogether, so have conditions about higher pay for weekend work.

The DSO or contractor must be free to introduce new menus and lines of stock; vary prices; invest in marketing and promotional work; improve the decor and furnishing; look for special events and bookings; and in general develop the trade over the full period of the contract. Tenders should be framed to encourage this approach.

The reason for catering at all in a park should not be forgotten it is one of the park attractions persuading people to go there; encouraging them to stay longer; allowing families to go as a group without the need to leave someone behind to prepare a meal at home; helping to persuade people to return in future.

Some local authorities took over this form of catering because commercial caterers sometimes ignored these wider interests. If the terms of the lease allowed it they opened only at the peak times and sometimes remained stubbornly closed on days when rain was forecast or the weather was cold even though the interest of the park as a whole was to have the facility open. The tender documents must clarify the minimum hours of opening and the level of service. Once the contract has been awarded then the client must see that the requirement is observed.

Choosing a contractor

In ground maintenance the choice of a contractor is relatively easy. If the specifications are clear and the quality assured the cheapest will normally be acceptable. In recreation and catering the best may not be so obvious.

The council has to satisfy itself that the contractor has the resources and the ability to do the work and the finances to withstand periods when income may fluctuate. It has to be sure that in preparing estimates of income the contractor was not influenced by unjustified optimism about attendances and the possibility of increasing them. It has to be satisfied about the quality of the management.

Bidders should be interviewed and given the chance to make a presentation of their proposals. They should then be subject to questioning and discussion in order to probe their suitability. It is time consuming but essential work which should not be skimped or hurried. After that the council has to decide not only which of the competitors offers the best sustainable financial return; is capable of managing the facility over the full period of the contract; and has the will and resources to do so no matter what emergencies or crises arise, but also which is most likely to meet the other targets and provide a vigorous, well marketed, friendly service.

There is no need to explain the potential for complaints about unfair competition in these arrangements. Full records should be kept of meetings. The whole process of deciding to whom the contract should go should be documented. Even if there is no complaint the auditors will no doubt wish to make sure that the best offer was accepted. Local authorities may well take the precaution of inviting an outside independent advisor or assessor to be present to express an opinion and confirm that the contract was awarded fairly and on reasonable grounds.

Contract failure

Contractors can fail, be dismissed, or wish to be relieved of their contracts if things do not work as expected. If this happens abruptly serious problems can arise because the public expects, and commercial considerations require, facilities to be available all the time. They should not be closed because of an hiatus when the management has to change. Contractors should be required to furnish a performance bond so that the extra costs which arise from a failure can be recovered. Client departments should have contingency plans ready. There is not always much warning.

Contractors should be required to give regular operating information to the client whatever form of tender has been chosen. This is needed to measure success of the venture and to ensure that the client is being treated honourably under the terms of the contract. It can also be used to guide potential competitors when future bids have to be invited either through contract failure or at the end of a contract period.

In the case of new facilities that have not been previously open to the public, the risks for contractors are greater because they cannot rely on past experience as a guide to future performance. In buildings the cost of heating can only be estimated and the figure may be far from the mark. The rateable value may be unknown. The income can only be guessed and even the most experienced managers can produce estimates that are wildly wrong. If the contractor fails to get his calculations right he may want to renegotiate the tender or the authority may have to face tendering all over again. The client should be ready.

Supervision

Once the contract has been placed the client has to be sure that its conditions are fulfilled. There should be a regular programme of visits. The client should be satisfied that the facility is operated safely; the property is kept to the desired standard and that the assets of the business are not allowed to deteriorate through defective or skimped maintenance; that facilities are open when they should be; that the public is getting the service that was asked for; and that the chance of improvements are taken as they arise. The income and the expenditure should be examined and recorded to make sure that the local authority is being given its proper return. Both the internal and external auditors will be involved.

Complaints going direct to the client should be investigated and followed up. The record of those received by the contractor should be examined. They offer a glimpse of public reaction. The client may also wish to commission or undertake consumer surveys to ascertain the level of satisfaction and to find what the public wants so that the service can be adapted or developed accordingly.

Meetings with contractors help to develop ideas and iron out differences. Unfriendly letters do not help relationships, and smaller matters can be dealt with verbally. But if there is serious doubt about a contractor then copies of written correspondence may be essential to act as evidence in the event of a dispute or if the contract is terminated. Minutes should be kept of meetings and agreed by both parties.

Quality control is crucial to the success of tenders. Managing a leisure provision or catering is largely a matter of attracting customers and responding to them, giving them satisfactory goods or services and trying to get them to return. The contractor will therefore be much concerned with these and other aspects of marketing.

Unlike grounds maintenance in which the client bears the brunt of complaints many of those arising in catering and recreation management will be put direct to the contractor's representative sometimes by angry or exasperated customers. Like other complaints they should be dealt with promptly but they should be noted and the records made available, unbowdlerised, to the client. They are a valuable guide to the quality of the service.

Community management

There has been a trend in recent years to introduce various arrangements for community groups to manage facilities like bowling greens and this may remove them from the effects of the legislation depending on the arrangements involved. There are positive gains including a potentially more fluent response to the needs of users and the chance to harness and use the talent and leisure time that exists in all communities. There are risks.

The group may become exclusive and self perpetuating and deter outsiders who may want to arrive as casual users. Before embarking on such a course it is essential to decide what the service is meant to do, for whom it is mainly intended and then to enshrine conditions in the lease that protect these interests.

Golf courses

Golf courses are a special case. They can make trading profits if they are properly managed and if the green fees are set at realistic levels, despite muscular pressure to keep them low. There is a national shortage and the Royal and Ancient at St Andrews published a survey in 1990 that said a further seven hundred new courses were required in England, Wales and Northern Ireland before the year 2,000. In the South East of England there is only one course for every 40,000 people compared with one for every 12,000 in Scotland.

Some municipal sources are integral parts of larger public parks for example at Wollaton Park in Nottingham. Besides providing for the sport itself they are usually attractive pieces of landscape grading from the wilder parts of the rough, woodland or dune to the highly managed turf of the greens.

Arrangements often exist already for managing municipal courses through independent golf professionals who take the green fees which are fixed by the council, handle the cash, and give information. Their recompense is usually based on a combination of a free or subsidised shop and a retaining fee. The Professional Golfers Association recommend minimum fees. The arrangement is convenient and economical and is probably the best way of managing the facility. It is common on private as well as public courses. There are many local variations on the arrangements.

Under the legislation the task of marketing the facility is also subject to tender. Minor adjustments to the contracts of golf professionals should be negotiated, if necessary, so that this is included in them as well. The professional has a substantial interest in seeing that the course is marketed and promoted to the best effect. Income depends on it.

Most club houses are managed by the clubs concerned and are often the property of the club even though they may stand on land that has been leased. In this case, they are not subject to the legislation but if the club house is operated by the local authority the catering and the cleaning will have to go to tender.

Sometimes the resident club has been given the management of the course or this may be considered as an alternative to exposing it to competition but the only case for providing public courses is to ensure the freest use by members of the public arriving for a game casually. Clubs naturally set their members interests first, it is the reason they exist and it should not be a source of surprise or complaint, but this may militate against the needs of the ordinary member of the public, the casual player and the beginner.

Even on the best managed public course, where the clubs associated with them are kept at arms length the visitor is all too often barred by medal competitions, tournaments, or local manipulation of the booking system. If they want to be the managers of the course, or to take out a franchise on it, then the club or clubs concerned should be allowed or even encouraged to bid along with any one else, but then they should be subject to the full conditions of the contract including these which protect public access, and these should remain unabated despite special pleading.

Complaints

The client side has to deal with the steady flow of complaints that all councils receive. They should deal with them promptly and efficiently and they should make sure that contractors do so when the responsibility rests with them. It does not matter to the public that a particular problem is the contractors fault or responsibility. The complainant should not even be made aware of it still less redirected to the contractor. To most people the local authority appears as a unity and is of no interest to them as to where the blame for a fault happens to rest. Complaints should be monitored and recorded. They may indicate that the contractor is failing to do the job he is paid for.

Complaints about catering or recreational facilities tend to be made at the time the problem occurs. In these cases the contractor's representative will get them first. It should be required of them that they deal with complaints promptly and sympathetically, keep a record of them and the action taken; and make the information available to the client.

There always was a temptation to pass the complainant on and a contract increases the opportunity for doing so. But the practice is a bad one and eventually brings the local authority into disrepute. Indeed it is the perception that local authority staff are unwilling to make responsibility for dealing with problems and are apt to shunt the client from one functionary to another that has contributed in part to it's public disesteem and thus its comparative weakness in the face of sometimes hostile legislation and adverse ministerial and media comment. In Britain this has stemmed from all political parties from time to time. It is not only the local authority client that looks for a scapegoat.

Entertainments

Recent research in Central Park New York showed that eighty per cent of the people going there simply wanted to escape from the city for a while and indeed one of Olmstead's ideas in designing it was to provide a green refuge. Central Park is a special case because it is surrounded by a packed city which provides it with an estimated 14 million visits a year. Even then it has a variety of attractions: playgrounds, a zoo, entertainments.

Entertainment programmes are crucial to most successful parks. They provide extra interest that brings people back. They offer variety and change. One effect of the National Garden Festivals and theme parks, has been to illustrate how a continuous programme of varied often small scale entertainment has been able to encourage frequent return visits. The same can be true of a park. The only limit is imagination.

The programme may act as a vehicle for some of the hundreds of voluntary interest groups and organisations which every larger community contains. It may offer a chance to exhibit, recruit, provide displays or perform. It may even be a means of fund raising most obviously when a band or poetry group or team of dancers or a magic circle stages a performance in return for a fee.

Tin rattling, badge selling collectors have no place in a park. All approaches and there are likely to be many, should be rejected. Once started there is no natural stopping point, all communities contain scores of organisations who will want to raise money this way. Visitors should be relaxed and at ease not repeatedly importuned for cash. If a charity comes forward and asks to make a collection say 'no' but offer alternatives which do help the park: a sponsored planting scheme; donkey derby; a stall at a firework display; face painting; a gala; busking; balloon racing; an art and craft market; a talent show; a flower show; hunting easter eggs.

These groups, like the park events themselves, should be covered by public liability insurance. Taking this out should be a condition of using the park. The cost is not large and the cover should be substantial.

Organising an entertainment programme has two elements: the leap of imagination that produces a new event or the skill that welds old attractions into a new programme; and thereafter attention to detail.

The programme should know its purpose. This might be to entertain people who are there anyway so they find extra interest and are persuaded to return; to draw in new customers; to cater for a particular age group; to even out the peaks of attendance. The interests of the public or of special groups have to be assessed. A string quartet for instance appeals to a special group of people but it may also attract others. The park gains because of a new group of visitors and because regular customers may discover a new interest.

Other peoples programmes should be examined to avoid a clash or allow a joint promotion. Novelty either of the promotion itself or the venue should be considered. What interests the public at the moment should be studied. Unless this is done the programme will lag behind public taste and seem old fashioned, tainting the park with the same imputation.

Size is important and attracts the public. For example a busking festival may crowd the park with new customers but a single busker would only entertain people there anyway.

Then more question have to be asked. Is the event intended to be free or are charges to be made? A charge has to be high enough to be worth getting but not so high as to kill the trade. Is it intended to recover all the cost? If so can a private promoter take it on, thus removing the risk from the council? Making a charge increases the costs of a promotion. Can it be sponsored?

Is the event only to attract people from the locality or does it have wider significance? International events like the world bowls championship or the world pipe band championships present special circumstances. They need a major organisational effort, involve years of planning and are usually organised by the national body concerned with the council in a supporting though a crucial role. Before the council is asked to extend an invitation a lot of preliminary work is required including assessing whether the event is feasible in the location; whether there are enough resources to support it; whether more can be provided; and whether the benefits are worth the cost.

This must be followed up with a major effort to sell the venue to the organisers. They will probably have several competing bids. After that years of work ensue; work in liaison committees; setting up the detailed organisation for the event; helping to find sponsors; marketing it so that the town gets maximum advantage from tourism and publicity; preparing the venues. The success of the occasion will also depend on getting a thousand details exactly right. After the first imaginative leap all events big and small depend for success on skillful attentive administration.

A budget has to be prepared for every event except the smallest. It should show the spending which is easy to work out and income which is not . The estimate should include every item. The job should be thought through, the spending listed systematically, and every item priced. It is no different from working out a tender. Do not miss an iota. It will be too late to add it later.

To these costs should be added the overheads like phone bills, an allocation of administration, stationery. The income can be guessed from previous experience from seeing how similar events have fared, from a customer survey if the occasion is important or costly. There is no science to assist. Take a pessimistic view. Whole companies have foundered through optimism.

Once the cost is known the next task is to find the money. If the item is planned well in advance it will find its place in the programme of entertainments and be considered along with all the others. If you love it treat it this way. Tucked obscurely in a long programme perhaps not even identified separately it will pass untroubled into the budget and later into reality. If the item is of abnormal importance and involves a major commitment it should be made the topic of a separate report clearly explaining the issues and the costs. It should have been fully discussed with colleagues. The careful advocate might have an informal chat with individual councillors and several with the chairman of the committee.

The rest is detail: fixing the dates, times, prices, values; negotiating fees or appearance money; booking artistes or acts; circulating competitors; finding sponsors, following up an initial approach with a phone call if there was not a swift acceptance; gathering the staff, training them if necessary; marketing; advertising; printing and distributing posters, pamphlets, tickets, banners, getting publicity; arranging seating, fencing, car parking, sign posting; assembling the equipment down to the least item; catering, getting a licence if alcohol is to be sold in premises that are not licensed already or out of the hours for which the licence applies; getting a first aid team to attend; liaising with the police; providing toilets, litter bins, litter clearance, catering for visiting

VIPs and sponsors; providing a public address system, a place for lost children; arranging the opening ceremony; getting the participants or performers on parade: meticulously addressing every particular.

8 Children's playgrounds

Children learn through play. They acquire social skills: make friends — sometimes foes — related to others; manage them; make judgements; enforce decisions; abide by the sometimes complex rules of the games they play; find fellowship. Play teaches them the possibilities and the limitations of their physique; allows the development of new skills; gives confidence; contributes to healthy growth; increases muscular strength. It allows children to use and develop their imagination. It gives the chance of role playing and helps to develop self esteem. It is an essential part of their education.

Not all playgrounds work well and some offer little or nothing to children hoping to find fun, delight, and excitement. Surveys and simple observation, show that children play less in playgrounds than in streets and informal play areas they find for themselves. *Zecharia*'s vision of Jerusalem (Ch.8 v.5) in the penultimate book of the Old Testament was '..... the streets of the city shall be full of boys and girls playing.....' He saw nothing incompatible with this and his earlier idea that the streets would also be full of old people.

Children play everywhere not just in places that adults designate for the purpose. They are moreover anxious to start so that a playground that is even only a few minutes away may be impractical. Children also need places for solitary activities and for quietness and reflection.

Parks and urban areas should contain places where children can play spontaneously. The equipped play area is not a substitute. At its best it is a supplement. Children are very capable of organising themselves and need the space, environment and freedom to do so. One of the reasons for wild places and woods in parks in to allow tree climbing, den building, hide and seek, to let children exercise their imaginations, and find and organise their own enjoyment. Parks offer varied play venues but these need to be identified for what they are and protected from other developments or from zealous tidying up.

The best play item that ever appeared in any park under my management was a large fallen tree. It had to be moved eventually but while it was there it was the star attraction. It was the subject of complaints from the public and councillors who thought that it was bad management to leave it and who felt that it was untidy. It was also a source of noise because of the swarms of children it attracted. The health and safety officer, ever cautious, threatened dire consequences if it were left. At no point was a child injured when playing on it. It was moved when it became the site of fires which did indeed make it unsafe. Managers are always under pressure to sanitize the environment tidying away the best playgrounds in the process.

In spite of all the evidence that can be obtained by watching how, where, and at what, children play given an unrestricted choice, there is constant pressure to provide formal play equipment and communities feel cheated if they do not have a playground. As a result most local authorities provide scores of playgrounds and bigger authorities may have hundreds. Understanding how they are managed is part of everyday work.

Playgrounds allow a child's instincts to swing, climb and slide to find their safest outlets. In a park they may be important enough to be one of the major attractions not only for the children of the neighbourhood but also as the focus for family outings. Their significance is undoubted but they are only one of the series of answers to a complex problem.

Look around! You will certainly find playgrounds that have died or that never lived. Many contain little more than a swing or two, a slide, a climbing frame and a roundabout or its equivalent. Little wonder that they are often deserted. After the initial surge of use the pleasure of such places is soon exhausted. The problem for a playground designer is to ensure that a child can find a constantly renewed challenge and stimulus in what is provided. That may mean looking beyond the equipment commonly available for purchase.

Types of playground

Categorising playgrounds into types is rather theoretical. The best ones provide wide opportunity. Understanding how children play is a help in developing play facilities that meet their needs and many psychologists, including such eminent figures as Freud, have made studies which relate to it. The subject is complex but children require places for physical play involving movements such as jumping, sliding, playing ball, swinging. They need the opportunity for solitary play sometimes using materials like sand or water; they need space for games involving others in large as well as small groups; and they can take advantage of equipment which allows them to cooperate as, for example, is required in order to use the traditional see-saw. They should be given the chance to interact with the environment for example by climbing trees, gathering conkers, damming streams; and they should be afforded conditions which allow them to role play and use their imagination. The playground, its equipment and supervision can make a contribution to all of this and should be able to accommodate the different types of play that occur as the child grows older.

Equipped playgrounds

The playground that is the most commonly sought after by parents is the familiar one containing several kinds of manufactured equipment. Sometimes these areas are supervised and occasionally this takes the form of a play leadership scheme. The question of locating, designing, furnishing and managing this kind of play facility is one of the most frequent that occurs.

Location

Finding a location for a new playground is a troublesome matter. If it is a success the playground will generate noise and whilst that produced by very young children may be just tolerable the more boisterous play of older children is often characterised by shouting, raucous laughter, argument and bad language. It is not easy for adults to accept. Playgrounds designed for older children or which are likely to attract them, should be built well away from houses. An adequate buffer space is essential. A park is probably the best place.

Play space should be within easy distance of the children it is meant for and it should be safe to reach. Small children will not readily go to play, unaccompanied, beyond 150 metres of their homes and ought not to have to cross a busy road to do so. Even older children are unlikely to use a playground that is more than 500 metres away. The distribution of play spaces is thus important as well as their sizes.

For reasons of safety, playgrounds should be away from main roads and railway lines and at a remove from canals and rivers. There should be services nearby so as to permit drainage and also water and sewerage if toilets are to be built either at the outset or later. Drinking fountains are often omitted because they are frequently the subject of damage and are as often used for squirting other children as for drinking, but if a play area is a success, children may use it for long periods and get thirsty and playing with water is part of the fun. Electricity may be needed for the most elaborate schemes — a playground done halfheartedly is quite likely to be a flop.

The site should be big enough to accommodate a range of activity without mutual interference. It should have the space to permit children of different age groups to keep apart. They play in different ways as they develop and it is desirable to separate the more robust older child from vulnerable younger ones.

The site should be well drained or capable of being made so; it should be visible so that casual supervision is possible and malefactors are deterred from loitering in the vicinity; it should if possible have an interesting topography with varying levels so that equipment like bank slides can find a natural place. The site should be sheltered or have enough space for tree planting. Children enjoy playing in woods among shrubs or in streams and if these features exist near the site, they should be viewed as part of the play area and be managed for the purpose.

The amount of space needed is the subject of periodic discussion and various standards have been proposed. There are also ideas about the frequency with which playgrounds should occur. The problem of stating minimum requirements is that they all too soon become maxima and can at best make only general stipulations about the nature of the space or its location. They are inevitably silent on such important local considerations as topography; the shape and size of individual sites; the nature of the ground; the existence of natural resources; the micro climate, aspect and aesthetics. They do however offer a useful general guide when new developments are taking place or when an existing open space has to be protected from building.

The most widely used reference in Britain is the National Playing Field Association standard which not only stipulates the area of play space for use by children but also the area they feel appropriate for other age groups. Most planning authorities also have standards which they incorporate into development plans and into the conditions that are applied when new housing developments are proposed.

The National Playing Field target is between 1.6 and 1.8 hectares for every thousand people, for pitches, courts and other games facilities intended for use by adults and youths; and between 0.6 and 0.8 hectares for children. Of this they recommend that 0.2 to 0.3 hectares is used for equipped playgrounds and 0.4 to 0.5 hectares for casual or informal play.

Other standards have been proposed from time to time including suggestions about the space needed for each individual dwelling. An example follows:

Overall 15 sq metres per dwelling divided into —
Casual or informal play space 10 sq metres per dwelling
Formal play space with equipment 5 sq metres per dwelling

The formal play space is further sub divided as follows:
Play space for toddlers 25 per cent (within 50 metres of home.)
Play space for 5 to 12 year olds; 75 per cent (within 400 metres of home)

There are also minimum sizes suggested for each individual play area. These are as follows:
For toddlers 100 sq metres
For 5 to 12 year olds 500 sq metres.

Sometimes standards are expressed in relation to "child bed spaces" and 3 sq metres for each of these was chosen both by the Department of the Environment and the Scottish Office in the 1970s in suggesting the space that should be made available in housing schemes. The Parker Morris report which did so much to influence housing standards in the same era also addressed the problem of play space and suggested that between 2.2 and 2.8 sq metres should be provided for each person on an estate.

There are also differing views about the role of private gardens and their effect on play provision but though these are of great value they do not meet the needs of all kinds of play nor are they suited to the social play of older children.

The park manager should speak to the planning department for the district to try to influence the standards that they stipulate to developers and should certainly comment when consultations about local and structure plans take place. Most standards are insufficient and if they had been applied by our Victorian predecessors would not have been enough to provide the heritage of public parks that exists in most older urban areas let alone the network of play and amenity spaces for which they are intended. Nor do they allow for sufficient buffering space between a play area and neighbouring homes. Without this the desire of older people including parents, for peace and quiet is incompatible with the necessity which children have of letting off steam and playing sometimes noisily together. The consequence for the park manager is a steady flow of intractable complaints especially in the Spring in Britain, when children are suddenly released into the open air by the lighter evenings and the better weather.

Layout

Playgrounds should be designed planned and managed with the customer in mind. It is difficult for a manager to cast his mind back to infancy or childhood or even youth — it may be far away and out of reach, but everyone concerned with play should make a deliberate effort. What would have interested me at that age? is the first question to be asked. Where would I have chosen to play? What would I have found to be fun? What would have brought me back time and time again?

The topography of a site is important. The area used to erect the equipment and for the safety zone around it should be flat and kickabout areas should be level otherwise slopes and variations in level add to the interest of the space and make it more suitable for imaginative and informal play as well as for sledging in Winter. They also permit slides to be placed on banks without the need to construct artificial mounds to accommodate them. They allow the playground to grow naturally from the landscape of which it forms part.

All too often natural changes in level are removed during developments. Not only is this expensive but it may create drainage problems as well as reducing the potential of the area for play. On naturally flat sites an artificial mound may be needed on which to locate a slide but it should be big enough to be interesting and have various angles of slope so that it fits into the landscape and does not look like an upturned basin as many do. It should be built up in layers using sub soil, each layer being consolidated to minimise sinking. Even then it is desirable to leave it for a period of six months or so to allow further settlement to occur before the slide is put in place. Slopes with an angle of greater than 1 in 2 present formidable maintenance problems and may suffer from erosion.

Play areas should be planted with trees to give a sense of enclosure, to resolve the conflict of scale between the playground and its surroundings, and for shelter. Shrubs are difficult to keep in a play area and hard to establish as they naturally attract children and provide a useful venue for some kinds of play. Any trees and shrubs that exist should be retained if possible. New plantations will need to be protected by a fence until they are established, only vigorous species capable of growing and regenerating despite tough use should be chosen and they should be planted close together. Plants which have poisonous leaves or fruit or which carry thorns or prickles should be avoided, there are plenty of others to choose from.

The disposition of equipment on the site will depend on the choice of items and their varying safety and space requirements. Items intended for different age groups should be kept as far apart as possible. There should be a range of challenges for the child but these should be within the normal capacity of the age group concerned and should be capable of accomplishment without frustration or danger. It should also be possible for a child to opt out of difficult situations without humiliation. Subject to these points the equipment should be grouped so that it appears as part of a design. It should not be scattered randomly across the site or be placed so far apart that it looks lonely and inhospitable. As much thought should go into the appearance of playgrounds as into any other aspect of the aesthetics of landscape.

Play areas should be designed to provide a series of social spaces in which children of different age groups can gather and play free from conflict with other groups or individuals. The size of the spaces should vary since children sometimes wish to play on their own and then need small intimate areas of defensible space. At others, they may form part of a large group for example when playing football or rounders in which case a large preferably grassy space should be provided. The spaces can be defined by trees or contours or by groups of seats or equipment which also help the small child to orientate itself and get its bearings especially in larger parks and playgrounds. The spaces should be visible from one another so that children can choose the place they prefer easily. Visibility improves supervision and positively deters the person who may "be up to no good" and who might otherwise be tempted to linger where children play.

Paths should be wide enough for wheelchairs and should be free from steps. They should have durable non-slip surfaces, they need drainage and support at the edges by kerbs. They are an expensive part of the design and need planning with care and economy. They should not cross activity areas or lead a child across the front of a swing or chute.

Paths also have a play value, observe for example their use for skate boards, cycling, chasing games, and for wheeled toys. Sometimes these uses may be in conflict with one another and thought needs giving to this. The best remedy for cycling, roller skating and skateboarding on paths is to provide more interesting places elsewhere for children to play with these items. Prohibition is always ineffective.

Real life objects like railway carriages and engines can make a play space interesting but only if they are adapted for a variety of uses — climbing, crawling, sliding, hiding, running, jumping, and playing games of make-believe not necessarily directly related to the object itself. In general play items that are too realistic limit and hamper children's play and soon fall out of regular use. The child's imagination is versatile and play objects should allow it to be exercised. Only adults seek realism.

Playgrounds should be designed for use all the year round and should be equipped with this in mind. Shelter against rain is much to be desired and should always be considered even if it is only obtained by crouching under picnic tables or other equipment. Buildings are often subject to damage in playgrounds and should be robust. If shelters and toilets are provided then it is best if the playground is fully supervised at least during the school holidays and at weekends. The additional use of the shelter for indoor play should also be considered and discussed with voluntary groups who might be interested in helping with its management. A facility might also be considered for parents so as to encourage them to accompany their children. Playgrounds can act as social gathering grounds for mothers who are all too often isolated in the home when their children are young.

Selecting equipment

Climbing frames

Climbing apparatus does not often hold a child's attention for long. Children prefer to interact with equipment, that is why swings are so popular with all age groups and hold their place no matter what the fashion of the moment. Climbing frames are popular with designers nonetheless. The better apparatus is that which is made specifically for the particular location and therefore adapted to the features of the site.

Climbing equipment should provide a challenge otherwise it will be completely deserted. It should however be limited in height, always have a soft surface beneath it and be free from rough edges, jutting pieces and narrow angles in which a child might trap a limb. The rungs which a child has to grip during climbing must not be so big that small hands are unable to hold them safely. Wood is the best material because it reacts more slowly than metal to changes in temperature which can make frames made of tubular steel unpleasant to grip. Wood should be weatherproof and free from splinters. The heads of bolts used in construction should be sunk below the surface of the woodwork.

There should be space around the equipment to allow a child to jump down onto a resilient surface. If ready made equipment is to be bought it is a good idea to see it in use somewhere so as to be sure that it is attractive to children.

Climbing nets should also be considered. They are more challenging and call for the development of difficult skills of balance as well as strength and daring. Rope is easily damaged by cutting or burning and it also gets frayed and worn in use so it should be rigorously inspected and replaced whenever necessary.

Swings

Children of all ages like to swing and indeed the instinct to do so is still present in the adult. There are many competing designs with varying lengths of swing and different seats and fittings. They are subjected to considerable stresses when in use and should be made to the highest standards. Home made or improvised swings are attractive to children but should not be used in publicly provided facilities. Swings are one of the most frequent causes of accident even without the risk of equipment failure.

Swing heights should vary so as to interest a range of age groups and provide a variety of movements; longer more daring arcs in the higher swings; quicker shorter ones in the smaller. Very high swings should not be installed because they unduly increase the risk of accidents from falling, the risk of misuse is great and a child on a swing is at the mercy of those who push it.

Swing seats also give rise to injuries, even empty seats if they are heavy and hard can deliver a severe blow when they are left to swing loose. Seats should not have sharp edges nor be made of hard materials. The best are light flexible seats which must nonetheless give adequate support for the user.

Slides

Free standing slides can still be purchased but despite the safety features which minimise the chance of accidents caused by normal use, they offer many opportunities for misuse including, most commonly, climbing up the sliding surface and horseplay on the steps. If a child is high above the ground even though this may be padded, the impact from a fall can cause serious injury.

Slides are sometimes part of larger composite structures but even on these a fall is still very likely to result in an injury. The most important safety problem is to minimise the risk of falling at the point that a child moves from the relative security of the platform onto the sliding surface. Enclosed platforms and guard rails should be used where appropriate but these must be so designed that they do not augment the already considerable possibilities for mischief. Spiral slides which of course cannot work on a bank should only be erected over a safety surface.

Bank or contour slides which are parallel with the surface of a slope are much to be preferred to any other kind, accidents from misuse can still occur but the consequences are likely to be much less severe. The angle of slope is important and if this is not sufficient the ride will be too tame and will soon loose its interest. Thirty degrees is about the minimum for a bank slide. It is also the maximum slope recommended in the standards of some countries. The angle can vary along the length of a long slide and should be less as the lower end is approached so that the user gradually loses impetus. Slides including those intended for use on banks can be purchased with waves in the surface. Changes in level should be gradual to avoid the risk of spinal injury which can result from the severe jolt which occurs when an abrupt change is encountered at speed.

The width of the sliding surface can vary. Wide ones may permit several children to go down together or allow an adult to slide down with a small child between the legs but a child on such slide has no easy means of reducing speed and small children may have difficulty in remaining upright.

Even bank slides ought to have side rails or walls which should be high enough to prevent an accidental fall. The recommended height varies depending on the standards of the particular country but it is better to err on the side of safety. It makes little or no difference to the pleasure of the ride.

Accidents also occur at the foot of slides where a child that has arrived, but not got out of the way, can be hit by the following one. The design should permit an easy quick exit to be made.

The sliding surface itself can take a number of forms but joints should overlap so that foreign bodies like glass cannot be introduced and caused to project from them. If this particular sadism sounds unlikely, then look around. In hot countries steel slides may be uncomfortable to use but in temperate regions they are probably the best simply because they are the most durable. Slides made of plastic are also available but they can be damaged or destroyed by arson which in some areas is a major problem even affecting plastic swing seats and fittings on climbing frames. High density polythene slides are more durable.

Whirling equipment

This is a popular range of equipment which very often appears on the shopping lists of adults wanting a playground in their area. It includes whirling platforms, merry go rounds and their sub species.

The equipment can cause injuries if not properly installed and carefully maintained. Children can get trapped beneath it when it is in motion or can get their hands in the moving parts if these become exposed through neglected maintenance. Accidents also occur if children try to get off whilst the item is still being pushed by others, and smaller children can be terrorised by older ones whirling the equipment at excessive speed. The remedy is careful installation, scrupulous maintenance, a willingness to change and renew older equipment and the use of smaller diameter items and ones with dampers to keep the speed down and slow and stop the movement when pushing itself stops.

Rocking equipment

In recent years the spring mounted animal made of plastic or metal has made its appearance and is popular with toddlers for whom it is intended but it is also attractive to older children. It should be robust. The springs however should not be so strong and stiff that small children are unable to rock the equipment. See-saws require children to co-operate together in order to play. They should be designed so that the children do not hit the ground nor should it be possible to have a foot crushed beneath the descending plank. See-saws should be inspected and replaced promptly if they become unsafe.

Consultation

The most important step in designing a playground and in choosing the equipment is to consult the children themselves. They should be asked to contribute ideas about the design and content of the playground and comment on any suggestions that are being considered. There is a limit to the usefulness of this approach. The suggestions can only be drawn from the child's own experience. It takes a major imaginative leap to suggest something new and the result of formal consultation is not often a vivid new idea.

It should be followed up by getting the designer to work with groups of children talking over and evaluating suggestions and encouraging new ideas and initiatives to evolve from discussion. There are other advantages. Consultation brings contact with local schools. It helps to show which items of equipment and types of play are popular at the moment and which are not. It helps to focus attention on the playground. In the longer run it may reduce the level of vandalism. Is is an exercise in practical civics.

The reward for an entry into a playground design competition need not be large or expensive, it might run to a certificate, a badge, a reception at the town hall or council chamber at which cola and crisps can be dispensed, and an invitation to open the playground once it was built or redeveloped. It brings children into benign contact with the Council early in their lives. Local government all too often seems remote.

Safety

First a caveat: if playgrounds become too bland and dull for example under the influence of the Health and Safety at Work Act or through total reliance on standardised equipment children will certainly look elsewhere for challenge. That is not to say that safety is a secondary consideration. On the contrary. Safety has to come first, but play areas also have to be good enough to attract customers and for them interest and diversity and excitement are priorities.

There are no soundly based systematically produced statistics on playground accidents and in any case many incidents are never reported. From time to time there are surveys based on the records of hospital casualty departments. Untrustworthy and alarming figures are sometimes extrapolated from the very limited factual information that can be obtained.

Serious injuries can arise if a child falls from an item of high equipment like a climbing frame or a slide especially if there is a hard unprotected surface beneath. Injury is likely to occur if a child is struck by moving equipment for example a swing seat or if it runs into a projection. Trapping or crushing can occur if whirling equipment is badly installed or has become defective or if a child can get its finger or hand into a moving part or even into the links of a swing chain. It is quite wrong to assume that a child or for that matter even an adult will always behave sensibly or be aware of danger. The most frequent injuries are minor ones — scratches, bruises, cuts, grazes — but they should be taken seriously and their causes eliminated wherever possible. Playgrounds should offer a challenge not a risk.

Good design can forestall some accidents. The height of equipment can be limited to a maximum of 2.5 metres from the ground though many prefer the European recommendation of a maximum of 2 metres. Slides should be used which run with the contours of the ground so that a child is never elevated far above the surface. Not only are such slides safer they can also be longer and more exiting. Equipment should be oriented so that a child approaching moving items is not momentarily blinded by the setting sun.

Safety zones around equipment should be adequate. They should be 1.2 metres as a minimum around static equipment and 1.8 metres from any moving parts. The safety zones should not overlap with one another nor should they accommodate circulation space. (Two children passing in opposite directions require a width of 1.2 metres.) Items of equipment that are too widely spread however are less attractive than those that are grouped together and which can be seen to relate to one another.

The layout of a playground can also affect its safety. Sliding and climbing equipment should not interfere with play in sand; swings should be located at the side of the space and away from the natural routes through or across the site, these 'desire' lines should also avoid climbing equipment from which children may be tempted to jump.

Barriers can be placed so as to prevent a child from accidentally running into the path of a swing and entrances should be placed away from swings. Swing seats should be made of impact absorbing materials such as rubber straps even though these are more vulnerable to vandalism. Some rubber protected metal seats are as heavy as a cosh and are capable of delivering a blow of just the same severity.

Protective handrails of a minimum height of one metre should guard high platforms on climbing equipment and flank stairs or steps. Protruding beams which a child could run into should be removed, bolts nuts and screws should be countersunk. Surfaces should be smooth to avoid grazes or splinters. Swing chains should have small links so that a child cannot insert its finger. Concrete foundations should not protrude above the ground surface where they might form a trip and may cause serious injury if a child falls on them. New equipment should be erected strictly in accordance with the makers instructions and checked independently before it is put into use. Worn out or irredeemably defective equipment should be removed and replaced with something better. These are common sense precautions but you would be surprised how often they are neglected.

Some once common items have been considered dangerous for a number of years now because of high accident records. They can still occasionally be found in older playgrounds. They should be replaced. The items concerned are plank and boat swings, ocean waves also called witches hats and old rocking horses not made in accordance with BS 5696. In addition to these, managers should look askance at slides which elevate a child far above the surface of the ground whether or not there is safety surface below. Tunnels below ground level, which were once popular, should be avoided not only because they can be claustrophobic but also because they are so vulnerable to misuse. Any equipment which involves a child going into a confined space should be restricted to supervised playgrounds.

The management of the area also has an important part to play in safety. Staff should know at least the rudiments of first aid. They should be capable of recognising and dealing with an emergency; have equipment to deal with minor injuries; have access to a telephone or radio for emergency calls.

Not all injuries arise from accidents. Children sometimes fight or throw stones or urge a smaller or weaker child into danger. The supervisor must be alert to these risks. Danger to children may also come from adults. Parents and those obviously interested should be encouraged to use and visit playgrounds with their children but park staff are sometimes aware of lurking and surreptitious adults in the vicinity of places where children play. In such a case the police should be called, their appearance usually resolves the problem without the need for further intervention.

Legislative requirements

There are various laws which require the operators of playgrounds to ensure that the places they offer for use are safe for the purpose. There is also a profound moral responsibility. A further set of demands may be made by the insurance company asked to provide third party cover against accident or injury.

The following are the principal Acts of Parliament which affect playground safety in Britain.

The *Health and Safety at Work Act 1974* as amended in 1980 imposes criminal penalties for negligence and requires managers to ensure that the places they look after are safe not only for employees but also for anyone that visits or uses them. It is a very wide ranging piece of legislation and has profoundly affected the way local authorities regard children's playgrounds and has resulted in the virtual disappearance of the adventure playground which sometimes involved children in improvising equipment of their own and using potentially dangerous tools.

It is very desirable to have a written safety policy so that everyone concerned is clear about their responsibilities and there should be systems of inspection to ensure that the rules are followed. To avoid liability under the act it is necessary to ensure that the equipment provided is safe to use; is kept in good repair; is regularly inspected and maintained; is properly supervised; and that accidents which can be foreseen are forestalled. Surfaces should also be in good repair and free from dangerous materials like broken glass.

The *Occupiers Liability Act 1957* as amended in 1984 requires the person occupying premises to make sure that lawful visitors are kept reasonably safe when using them. In respect of a playground intended to attract children the obligation is greater since a child is less aware of risks than an adult, is likely to be less careful, and is more vulnerable. The use of notices seeking to limit liability is permitted under the Act but in practice do not remove the obligation of care, because they must be read understood and agreed to by everybody involved. Notices intended to limit liability are also cut at by the *Unfair Contract Terms Act 1977*. This prevents a contract from excluding liability for negligence. There is equivalent legislation affecting Scotland, and it finds its parallel in many other countries in the world.

Playground managers building their own equipment may also be affected by consumer legislation which imposes duties on manufacturers.

Standard specifications

Various countries have standards for play equipment and work is in hand to produce a standard that can be applied in all the countries of the European Community.

The British Standard Specification that affects play equipment for permanent installation out of doors is BS 5696. The original standard was published in 1979 and it has been amended since.

The German standards DIN (or Deutsche Norm) 7926 and DIN 18034 are also used. They differ from the British Standard in that they not only take into account safety and the resistance to wear of the products and materials but also require that the play value of the item is not lost by taking too extreme a view of the other factors. Three cheers for them! The German TUV standards of the German Technical Testing Institute, are even more rigorous and involve testing equipment and the parts that it comprises to destruction They are also likely to become more prominent.

These Standards and any European ones that emerge will be come increasingly important as manufacturers become more international. It is already possible to buy British, American, European and more recently Australian equipment in many countries besides the ones of their origin.

Safety surfaces

The surface of playgrounds has always been a vexed question. Grass is the one that is most sympathetic, though hard enough to anyone falling onto it from a height. The village playground that I patronised in my youth had grass beneath the equipment but it is not practical for playgrounds that are even moderately well used. Grass is soon reduced to mud — slippery, soon eroded and highly productive of parental complaints as children return home pleasurably caked with it. The search for alternatives still continues.

The standard municipal surface was tar macadam or sometimes even concrete both of them hard unsympathetic materials very likely to cause injury to anyone falling onto them. Smooth hard surfaces are indeed the best for access so that physically disabled children or those in wheelchairs or parents with prams or push chairs or burdened with small children can reach the equipment safely and conveniently. Hot rolled asphalt is an expensive surface but it has a long life and a smooth surface so it is less likely to cause abrasions to those who fall on it. It is hard of course but is much to be preferred for pathways than tar macadam or concrete.

Any equipment from which a child might fall from a height should have a resilient surface beneath and around it and the latest amendment to BS 5696 says that this should be provided whenever a fall of 600 millimetres or more is possible. What the material should be depends on the circumstances of the site and the type of equipment concerned. Because the market in safety surface is a vigorous and expanding there are many competing materials available already and it is likely that more will be introduced. There are three main types: tiles of various designs; materials that are applied when wet and allowed to set once in place; and loose materials like bark and sand. There is no reason why all three types should not appear together on the same play area.

Wetpour surfaces and tiles are costly. The first question to be asked is whether the equipment for which they are proposed is worth the expense. Some of it may be old and have too short a future to justify the cost. In such a case the item should be replaced by a new piece with a life equal to that expected from the surface. In some cases equipment may be failed and unpopular, or repetitive offering only the same play experience as other things on the site. This too should be considered for replacement.

The major cost of providing surfacing for the whole of a playground system should be the catalyst for an assessment of the quality and effectiveness of each of the playgrounds. Some playgrounds may even be in the wrong place and the opportunity might be taken to relocate them. Eliminating a playground altogether produces more than a little aggravated opposition and few areas are so well endowed with play space or equipment that they can afford to lose either completely.

There are several competing makes of rubber tile of various designs intended to increase resiliency. The problem is that they are quite likely to attract vandals and this can materially shorten their life or even terminate it in infancy. They should only be considered where the risk of damage is slight and even then resistance to vandalism should be a major consideration when choosing a particular make. Resilient surfaces can be poured into place and these are harder though not impossible to damage. They require expert installation. The expense of both types can be daunting.

Loose fill materials appear on the face of it to be cheaper but they must be laid to a sufficient depth to be effective. This should not be less than 300 millimetres and may mean expensive excavation. The materials also get scattered and frequently need sweeping up. A proportion is lost as time goes by and has to be replaced. They can also be troublesome to keep clean especially where broken glass in a problem, or on sites where dogs or cats can get access. Thus, even where these materials are proposed, the equipment should be appraised first.

The loose materials that are most suitable for use under equipment are sand and bark. Sand should have a minimum particle size of three millimetres though it is preferable that it should be smaller. The particular risk of using sand is that children may be attracted to play in it and thus find themselves in danger of injury if a child falls or jumps onto them. An alternative and more inviting sand play area elsewhere in the playground helps to reduce the risk.

Pulverised bark and wood chips can also be used but they can get soggy when wet and are sometimes set alight when dry. Both bark and wood chips vary in their suitability and tests should be made before using a particular source of supply on a large scale. The best grade of bark is pulverised to a size of between 20 and 50 millimetres. It should be stacked for a few weeks before use so the loose fibres rot away. This reduces the risk of its being set alight. Both materials can make broken glass difficult to retrieve and other steps may be needed to reduce the occurrence of glass for example by negotiation with neighbouring shops to use returnable bottles where possible. Dogs, cats and for that matter children themselves can foul both sand and bark. Whichever material is used it will require cleaning and disinfecting regularly and should be changed completely once a year, or more frequently if necessary.

Whatever material is chosen it must be capable of absorbing an impact of the maximum likely severity: BS 7188 refers to this. Manufacturers should state the height of the fall for which the surface is effective. It goes without saying that this should be adequate for the equipment concerned. Not only the surface immediately beneath the item but also the immediately surrounding area should be protected. In the case of climbing equipment the area should be at least 1.75 metres beyond the extent of the equipment, in the case of swings it should extend by this amount beyond the reach of the swing when fully extended. This is a minimum and a wider spread may well be justified particularly on items of equipment which offer several functions to the user.

Inspection and repair

Regular inspection of playgrounds is essential and it should be done by trained staff. The frequency of inspection will depend on the nature of the playground and its popularity which is affected by the time of the year, the day of week, the location the range of equipment and the number and the age of children in the neighbourhood.

It is desirable that each site is checked every day including weekends and particular vigilance is necessary during school holidays and at other busy times. If a playground is particularly busy or has varied equipment with moving parts hourly checks may be necessary The busiest and most frequented playgrounds may justify the employment of a full time attendant or better still play leader, during the busy parts of the year. Supplementary visits by technical or senior supervisory staff should take place once a month. In addition to these an annual inspection and report by an independent specialist should be made.

Repairs should be carried out immediately they are needed. Damage and graffiti should be dealt with at once. Publicity about vandalism should be avoided. Anguished public complaints about deliberate damage simply suggest the possibility to others and are quite likely to result in an outbreak of copy-cat vandalism.

Records should be kept scrupulously so that if necessary they can be referred to if a claim is made, they should also be sufficient to form the basis of a judgement about the success of the playground and the equipment it contains, and suggest changes that may be needed to make it safer or less prone to damage. They should record the date and time of the visit; the name of the inspector who should sign the form; they should record whether or not the equipment is in good safe working order; and what action has been taken to remedy any defects. A full record should also be kept of accidents and complaints, and of the response to them.

Staff training can be done under the scheme developed by the National Playing Fields Association or through the Local Government Training Board. Use should also be made of the Local Authority's own Health and Safety officers.

Insurance should always be considered for playgrounds since if an injury occurs for which the authority is liable, compensation can be high. The insurance practices of the particular local authority will determine the nature and the value of the insurance cover and managers may have little or even no influence on it though they will soon find themselves in the front line in the event of a claim. In places where voluntary workers or groups are involved in managing or supervising playgrounds a different circumstance arises and the insurance company should be told of the arrangement and adequate cover ensured. New playgrounds or those which introduce new possible hazards should also be notified to the company.

Fences

The only justification for a fence round a playground is to keep out dogs especially if there is sand, either as a surface or in a sand pit, they will certainly foul any they can reach. Fences have a role if they stop children running straight out onto an adjacent road or into the path of moving equipment, or to stop a ball from escaping where kick about games are to be encouraged but in no case should railings with spikes be used.

In general children's play should be left uncaged. Children do not always play long at the same thing and given the chance they will move quickly from one game and location to another. Fences impede this natural pattern and there can be little case for them in a park which should be free from traffic; in which dogs should be controlled; and where chasing a ball across the grass is part of the fun. Some definition to the area can be given by tree planting and this will also give a sense of enclosure.

Seats

Seats should be provided not only to encourage parents to visit play areas and parks with their children and to provide them with comfortable places to sit and chat but also because children also sit and play on and around seats, indeed one of the most frequent complaints that managers encounter stems from older children congregating around seats especially in the evenings and often making noise there though the real cause for complaint probably occurs when they are silent. In play spaces meant for small children toddler sized seats are needed as well as big ones for parents.

There are many makes of seat but all too few are designed with any deference to the eccentricities of human anatomy. Before selecting a seat, sit on it. If it is intolerable after ten minutes choose another design. Then try to smash it. If it breaks find one that is more robust.

Once a suitable location has been found the legs of the seat should be firmly anchored by getting a blacksmith to fit metal attachments which can be fixed in concrete. The surrounds of the seat should be laid with slabs or covered with some other durable surface otherwise it will erode as the seat is used and normal wear and tear takes place.

Alternatives

Even when they have been installed playgrounds need adjusting to suit changing tastes and adapting to the shifting demography of an area as children grow older; become teenagers, then adults; and later on are replaced by a new generation when the cycle starts all over again. A playground is nearly always seen as a permanent solution to a fixed problem. It is nothing of the kind. The problem keeps changing and so must the response.

The usual demand from parents and indeed the usual reaction from a local authority is to build a playground with fixed equipment when the need for play provision becomes apparent. This is not the only answer. Indeed in view of its high cost and inflexibility it should be only one of several solutions canvassed. The problem is that parents feel cheated by any other response and for the local councillor that may mean a loss of votes.

Portable playgrounds

Portable playgrounds should be considered. They have several advantages. They can be removed at night and so need never become a nuisance to the neighbours by attracting noisy teenagers after dark; they are virtually immune to vandalism; they are flexible and the equipment can be changed often; they can be moved from site to site; they are supervised and though this is an expense it may still be less than funding the loan charges and supervision for a playground costing £30,000–£40,000. They require transport but there are purpose made trailers available or these can be designed and made for the particular sites.

Play busses can also be used. Bus companies periodically dispose of vehicles that are no longer fit for passenger service but are still suitable for conversion as play vehicles. They can be surprisingly cheap to buy but beware, the tyres are sometimes not part of the deal and may have to be purchased in a separate transaction. Any kind of games equipment can be used but it should be changed as time goes by. It can follow the trend of the moment.

Play fashions change, there was a time when no child seemed happy without a hula hoop. Skateboards, roller skates, BMX tracks, swing ball, mountain bikes, frisbees, pogo sticks, have all come and for the most part gone. Some like old pop songs, have even enjoyed a second manifestation. Portable playgrounds can provide not only these items as they come and go, but also the more enduringly popular items like swings and slides. They can also be used for mobile discos but the sound travels surprising distances and the play leader must be strong minded enough to resist demands for ear blasting emissions of sound which will bring whole neighbourhoods into the angry streets there to clamour for blood.

Consideration can be given to small electric coin operated cars, trampolines, or if a space can be found that is big enough to swallow the noise go-karts for older children and youths. There is no reason why fairgrounds should have all the fun.

Adventure playgrounds

The Adventure Playground which offered a variety of materials, and tools for building dens, houses, play equipment, or simply for messing around with, suffered a body blow when the Health and Safety legislation made its appearance. In terms of public parks it is possible to write of them in the past tense. Local authorities were the main suppliers either through their own departments or through surrogates who sometimes used land, materials and money provided by the authority. They offered the kind of play possible to a child growing up with a private garden and understanding parents but which is generally not available to the child living in a heavily populated urban area.

They required sensitive skilled supervision for success. There were wide variations in the quality of this and as a result some adventure playgrounds were triumphantly successful and others were flops. They were not lovely to look at having an air of anarchic disorder and as a result were difficult to site. Sometimes they were put in places that were already ugly and desolate so children were inclined to go elsewhere. They did however have powerful articulate proselytisers and most local authorities were under pressure to provide them.

The need of this type of play has not disappeared though by and large the possibility of it being provided by the estab-lishment of publicly managed adventure playgrounds has gone. A more relaxed view of the way children use the spaces around them helps to offset some of the loss that may have been sustained. A greater tolerance of play activity in woodland; in larger established shrub borders; or in streams in parks; or in wild areas, allowing a child to mark out its pitch in chalk on a path or bounce a ball against a wall are examples of how sensitive park management allows children to find opportunity to play without highly organised play spaces or leadership schemes. Parents also have a role and the adventure playground sometimes duplicated activities which could have been accommodated in the home and or in the garden or yard.

Children's farms

Children like to play with animals, look after them, handle them, feed them or even just watch them. These interests can be met by providing farms, zoos, aviaries or the so called pets corners. These can be used to keep ponies, horses, birds and rare or interesting breeds of domestic and farm animals. They have been a familiar part of the attractions in parks for generations in many countries. They can be extended to include pony and trap rides, donkey rides or rides on the backs of heavy horses.

They are dependent for their success on intelligent knowledgeable supervision by staff capable of imparting both knowledge and an understanding and love of animals not only to children but also to other visitors. Good intentions are not enough.

Animals are not toys or exhibits and it is essential that their interests are protected and that the conditions in which they are kept are appropriate and suitable. Animals fish and birds must have sufficient space and the temptation to overcrowd them to generate a livelier interested has to be resisted. Most departments will be able to provide plenty of room, if necessary by using more than one site.

There will be vigilant querulous eyes focused on this kind of provision and complaints for alleged or real neglect are likely to be immediate, vehement, articulate, impassioned, numerous, coordinated, well publicised, skillfully orchestrated, and competently directed.

Animals and birds are expensive to keep and feed. They require attention seven days a week and every day of the year. They generate unexpected and sometimes large vets' bills. In the case of sheep, cattle, pigs, and poultry they produce some income through normal farming practice, and horses and ponies do so through paid rides and hires, and through the breeding and eventual sale of stock.

Kick-a-bout games

Sooner or later boys in most countries will want to play soccer. If provision is not made for this where the games can take place without nuisance to neighbours, it will occur in unsuitable places. Prohibition by notice board or supervisor will not stop it or at best will do so only temporarily. In new developments space for casual games of football should be provided from the outset even though to start with the children may be too young to use it. It cannot be introduced afterwards. The co-operation of planners is necessary to ensure that adequate provision is made. It is often omitted partly through failures of understanding, partly because of economic pressures on space. Kick-a-bout areas need not be full size soccer pitches indeed if they are, their intended patrons will be displaced by older youths or even adults but they should be big enough to allow for energetic use and have the normal space for over runs at the ends and sides.

They can be made of grass in most British conditions but must be of a more durable surface in countries where grass is a difficult surface to keep because of drought or wherever the use is so intense that grass cannot survive. One alternative is to surface them with shale. This needs regular watering, raking and rolling to keep it fit for use. Concentrated wear is no problem so fixed goal posts or walls which act as goals can be installed. The alternatives are artificial surfaces such as are used for full scale games. There are several kinds and the range is increasing but they are still costly.

Kick-a-bout areas can be fenced to keep the ball within bounds but fences must be high to be effective so they are expensive and they can be intrusive and even ugly. They are only justified where the surface itself permits continuous use.

Inflatable equipment

Inflatable equipment should be considered. A lot of this is now available. It suits all ages. It can take the form of bouncing equipment made into various shapes some of them appealing to the adult rather than the child. It can also take the form of inflatable tunnels which can be explored and which give various lighting and colour effects. Both types can be associated with music.

They can be made in the department using nylon reinforced PVC. It is desirable to use fire retarding material to the standard of BS 119/3120

Inflatable items need anchoring when used in the open air and there have been accidents when they have been overturned in strong winds. Adequate sturdy anchorage points should be provided. There should be sides of sufficient height to prevent small children from slipping off. A top can also be made so that they can continue in use even during rain.

There are several competing manufacturers and a wide range of different designs. In choosing the advice of children should be sought. Their choice will often differ from an adults and it is what attracts them that counts.

Inflatable equipment is highly vulnerable to damage for example it can be punctured or slashed easily though damage can of course be quite quickly repaired again. It thus needs constant capable adult supervision to control the large number of children who are likely to be attracted. The equipment also has to be stored securely at night.

Inflation can be provided by a small portable generator and air pump. There is thus no limitation as to where it can be set up. In fact a programme of appearances can be drawn up and the equipment moved from one place to another. Inflatable equipment greatly enriches the play opportunity and if not provided all the time then it should certainly be considered for use during holidays and at weekends.

Play sculpture

In order to make the playgrounds that were in my care more interesting and individual and to extend their interest I had the idea twenty years ago of making wooden play sculptures. At first I looked for a wood carver but no such person existed within reach. Then I realised that it was not carvings but sculptures I was looking for. It did not take long to see that the best people to make them were the sculpture students from the college of Art.

Later on we found that any art student with an aptitude for working in three dimensions would do as well. The main need was to find those who could look at things through children's eyes and make something that would appeal to them. If the use of students is impossible for some reason then consideration should be given to employing a 'sculptor in residence' working all the year round preferably with the support of an Arts Council Grant or sponsorship. The work can be done in a place where it can be watched by the public and act as another of the park attractions.

The sculptures make unusual things to climb on or are used as seats. They are also interesting to look at. The ones that we produced were mainly of animals and items from children's stories but abstract shapes can also be fun and it is easy to work to a theme.

The wood used should be a hardwood — preferably oak. Often suitable wood is available from the felled trees that are available in nearly all departments from time to time. It is a matter of looking out for it and leaving it to one side where it can cure. Beech is easy to carve and is often readily available in good sized pieces but it does not last long out of doors even when treated with preservative. If wood is not available from the department's own resources it can probably be obtained from the Forestry Commission or from a private estate. Fibre glass can also used but there is a warmer quality about natural material.

It is desirable to find a shed in which to do the work so as to make sure that it is not interrupted by bad weather but it can take place out of doors in any secure area. An electricity supply is necessary so as to permit the use of small items of machinery which greatly improves productivity. Each employee should be able to produce up to four items depending on their size and complexity during the course of a summer vacation. If the idea is pursued over a number of years a considerable addition to the range of interest in the playgrounds can be brought about by this means alone.

Once made the items need securely anchoring onto a concrete base into which they should be fixed by means of metal attachments.

Maintenance consists of keeping the sculptures clean, scrubbing them down, and oiling them in winter. They should not be covered with varnish as this blisters in the open or wears unevenly and soon looks scabrous and unattractive. Any damage can be repaired with plastic wood. If names are carved on them these can be sandpapered or planed away. They should not be left otherwise more will follow.

Sand

Ask a child to list its favourite materials and sooner or later the name sand will appear. It is easy to provide in a park or playground but hard to keep. It gets scattered during the normal course of play; it is sometimes thrown around deliberately; it attracts dogs and cats who foul it; broken glass can be difficult to remove; it has to be cleaned and disinfected regularly; and every now and then it must be replaced — the old soiled and blackened sand carted away and new fresh sand put in its place. However its value for creative play and its popularity more than compensate for the cost and trouble of keeping it in good order.

Sand can be used on sand tables or in sand pits dug into the ground. The contents of sand tables are very likely to be scattered and are troublesome to put back. They are best confined to supervised playgrounds. Sand pits can be in unsupervised play areas but they need regular inspection and attention throughout the period they are in use.

In the British climate the pits are best placed where they receive full sun and rain to purify the sand. In warmer countries shelter and shade are desirable to protect the child as it plays. The pit or pits need not be rectangular and indeed they should be designed so that they are an attractive feature of the landscape of the play area. Since they are likely to attract children up to seven or eight years old they should be located where they are easily seen and supervised. They should have places near them for parents to sit. It is best if they are at a distance from other equipment so that children are not tempted to run through them on their way from one piece of equipment to another.

Sand soon becomes sour and unpleasant if it is waterlogged so sand pits require good drainage. There should be an outlet to a drain, the base should be made of open porous material, for example crushed aggregate to the depth of a foot at least and this in turn should be covered with paving slabs with open joints to allow water to escape into the sub-stratum. The firm base allows the sand to be changed without too much difficulty and stops excavations extending into the foundations of the pit.

The depth of sand should be up to 400 millimetres to give plenty of scope for digging. The sand surface should be a little below the neighbouring ground levels to permit the scatterings to be swept back easily. The space should be big enough to accommodate the likely number of children, without interference with the play of their neighbours. It can be made more interesting by subdivision into more intimate spaces by low dividing walls; places to sit; raised platforms for moulding the sand; and variations in level. These produce a series of inviting sub divisions and recognise that at its best playing with sand is a creative activity often solitary or done in small groups. They also protect the child from interference from others who might trample over or even destroy what it has made. Sand pits should not be close to buildings into which the sand will migrate attached to the feet of children. If dogs are likely to be a nuisance the area can be fenced or covered at night with a mesh.

There should be a nearby water supply because most of the sand should be kept moist for moulding for which it must be capable of holding its shape. Sand is very variable and the right texture is essential, it should have a range of particle size down from a maximum of 1.5 millimetres. It should be free of clay and contaminants. It is desirable to try sand from several local sources so as to find the best for the purpose.

Water

Water like sand presents problems of hygiene as well as safety and is expensive to provide and keep to high standards in a playground but children enjoy playing in it and it should always be considered especially in supervised areas.

Children play in water in several ways they splash, paddle, attempt to swim; chase and threaten one another; jump across streams. But they may also wish to use it in more thoughtful ways to sail boats or rafts; to race sticks under bridges; to dam or divert the flow and pools should be designed to encourage all these kinds of play.

Water is a danger and even shallow water can cause accidents. There should be careful supervision at all popular times. The depth of water should be limited and be capable of being controlled by means of overflows. Parents should be encouraged to accompany their children through the provision of seats and sheltered places in which to sit and watch.

If there is a stream on the site it should be harnessed. It must have a reliable flow of clean water and not be liable to pollution. The water should be regularly inspected and analysed. Since it cannot be treated without causing pollution lower down the pool should be closed immediately there is anything wrong until the problem has been dealt with or has passed. Cooperation with riparian owners upstream will help to minimise any chances of pollution.

In the playground the stream can feed a series of pools of different depths though each should be shallow enough for use by children of all ages and abilities, the stream can pass under bridges be narrowed down here and there so that it can be dammed, broadened out to form pools and used in ways that permit a variety of play activities along the whole of its passage through the park. It should also be viewed and treated as part of the general landscape and will then be as interesting to adults to watch as it is to children to use.

The floor of the stream will need to be of a firm hard nonslip material that is comfortable for bare feet but which is easy to keep clean. The banks should be gently shelved and any abrupt changes in level should be eased out. It should be possible to drain the system for cleaning especially to permit removal of broken glass and the water level can be regulated by a series of dams and overflows.

If there is a stream in the park my advice is to adapt it in these ways so that children can play in it. There will be plenty of doubting voices and a chorus of Jeremiahs to point out the risks and dangers but treated imaginatively a stream is capable of providing the best kind of play facility and it can be augmented by sprays and fountains and the kind of artificial water feature that modern leisure pools offer. Why should their patrons have all the fun?

Children are also attracted to play in fountains or even swim in ornamental pools. They are often shooed away by self righteous adults but they are unlikely to do harm and should be allowed to play unhindered.

Artificial paddling pools are expensive features to provide and maintain but they are fun for children and are likely to attract large numbers on warm days even in the British climate and a few even on cold ones. In warmer countries they are even better value. The designer should go and look at the most recent examples of leisure swimming pools and starting from the ideas that are to be seen there explore all the ways of introducing water into the play area. This might include sprays, fountains, water jets, waterfalls, rippling cascades, water tables at varying heights for use by disabled children and others who may not want to go right into the water.

The ponds should be designed with inlets, islands, peninsulas, sandy beaches. The rectangular paddling pool is a dead duck. The design should be as exiting as the water itself.

The base of paddling pools should slope gently to a maximum depth of 30 centimetres or so and should also fall gently towards the drain outlets. Too deep and the risk becomes excessive, and the smallest children will feel intimidated. The water should be changed regularly, at busy times at least once a day, and provision should be made to chlorinate it. Electric pumps can be used to keep the water moving and to operate water features. Drains should be adequate for emptying the pools quickly and so should the water supply for filling them again.

Entertainments

Entertainers can be employed to add diversity to playgrounds and parks especially during the long summer holidays when children can often be at a loose end. Entertainers can travel from site to site on a prearranged and advertised programme and the best ones are capable of attracting and holding the attention of large audiences of parents as well as children and passersby. Most theatrical agents have lists of appropriate artistes. It is desirable for the manager to vet them beforehand so that they can be arranged in an interesting and varied programme and to judge their quality and suitability. They must however be able to interest children not just the adult observer.

Readings by staff of the children's libraries can also be a success in playgrounds during holidays but should be part of a programme so that they build up a regular clientele. They should be well advertised through the schools before they break up; in the local press; on local radio and by pamphlets and posters. As with all such events they do best if they take place where potential customers are likely to be present anyway.

Play leadership

Children will play perfectly well by themselves and are best left to do so but in long holiday periods are often glad of other things to do. In playgrounds the role of the attendant should be more than custodial and can extend to making games equipment available. There is also a proper place for a sympathetic adult.

Play leadership at its best it is a stimulus to the use of parks and playgrounds. It requires trained staff who among other skills learn not to intrude on and interrupt the spontaneous play which takes place all the time; or try to substitute in its place competitions between parks games that are esteemed by adults or television companies, or organised sports of various kinds. These well meaning endeavours may rob children of one of the benefits of play — that of organising games for themselves.

A skilful playleader can provide materials and equipment for games, drawing, modelling; encourage drama, plays and productions; lay the foundations for a study and love of nature; act as a catalyst and arbitrator and referee; and extend the range of activities for children beyond the limitation of things they can organise for themselves. Sometimes children simply require the approval of a sympathetic adult or reassurance after a fall or a disagreement. No one who has seen a group of children intense at drawing or painting in a park under the eye of an unobtrusive adult can doubt that playleadership has a role but it is that of enabling not organising.

Disabled children

Just as the general environment should be designed to permit the freest possible use by disabled people so should play areas. They should be free from obstacles which might exclude or deter them. There should be smooth surfaced paths over which a wheelchair can move easily; ramps rather than stairs; alternative routes that are free from obstructions. There should be handrails for guidance and protective barriers on the approach to swings to assist the blind or partially sighted who can also respond to changes in the texture of surfaces. Some equipment may need grab bars to allow children to get out of wheelchairs.

Designers should place themselves in the position of the users. Playgrounds should be convenient and accessible for everyone. Disablement can take many forms and is not always accompanied by a wheel chair. Disabled children require the same challenges and respond to the same stimuli as others and should be given access to the same range of equipment. Disabled parents should also have unimpeded access.

Organisations

Many countries have organisations which promote play or some aspect of it. In Britain the following are among the main groups. They can provide information and help the park manager in other ways. They also act as pressure groups. Sometimes the pressure may be exerted against the manager who must then use his judgement because worthy good intention however stridently expressed should not be confused with infallibility. Most of the groups have local branches that can be valuable for consultation or which may put forward suggestions of their own.

The Sports Council is concerned with a wide range of interests but it did take over the responsibilities of the short lived Play Board. It has a regional organisation and is a useful source of advice and commentary as well as giving grants for some projects.

The Fair Play for Children Campaign has the main aim of making children's play provision a higher priority than it is at present. It is made up for the most part of voluntary organisations concerned with children's play though there are also individual members. They have a number of publications and are concerned with children of all age groups.

The National Playing Fields Association aims to encourage the provision of recreational facilities for all but specialises in the needs of children and young people. Some of its former role is now undertaken by the Sports Council. It provides technical advice and information and has a variety of publications. It gives grants, but these tend to be small. There is a regional organisation.

The Pre-School Playgroups Association was formed with the idea of helping mothers to form their own play groups but its interests have expanded to include many aspects of living with small children. It has a number of publications and has local branches and area organisers in many areas.

There are many organisations concerned with handicapped children and adults and their advice should be sought when particular difficulties are encountered or are anticipated.

9 Native plants and animals in parks

Parks are often subject to contradictory pressures. One concerns tidiness. Neatly mown grass in often esteemed by the public. Failure to mow it begets complaints. There is a contrary pressure. It is to allow more wildlife into parks. The easiest step is to encourage wild flowers, and this requires a more relaxed system of maintenance which includes leaving the grass uncut for parts of the year. The question that must be answered is: which treatment will produce the highest level of public use, enjoyment and advantage?

Public interest in wild life has revived in recent years together with the environment at large. Specific interest is generated by the wildlife programmes that are prominent on television. The loss of wildlife habitats in the countryside has become the subject of concern. Schemes of restoring derelict land have drastically changed areas once occupied by wild flowers, trees, mammals and birds and these have been inadvertently driven out. Ecological groups have entered the political arena in many countries forcing all the other parties to adopt some of their concerns and incorporate them in their manifestoes or into legislation.

Parks departments have always been active in nature conservation but they respond to shifting public priorities, so the wildlife issue now gets more prominence than at any time in recent years. Like everyone, managers respond to the beauty of wild flowers and recognise that wild plants and animals enrich parks and open spaces aesthetically and add to their recreational value. Landscapes of native plants can be cheaper and easier to keep and are apt to be more robust and stable. The pressure to favour native plants as against exotic ones is not new. William Robinson complained as long ago as 1870 in his book *The Wild Garden*, 'The passion for exotics is now so universal that our own finest plants are never grown'.

There are two principal means by which local authorities can cater for the interest in the subject. One is to establish local nature reserves or better still to cooperate with others to do so. Local authorities were given the power to do this by the *National Parks and Access to the Countryside Act 1949*. There are many groups like the Nature Conservancy and its successor body, Wildlife Trust, the British Trust for Conservation Volunteers and others who will cooperate.

Local authorities are unlikely to have to search long to find advice from other interested parties. Reserves offer the chance to sustain and study flora and fauna. They may also be of interest because of their geology or features of their landscape. They have an important educational value. It is also possible to make nature trails; develop natural areas in country parks; sustain areas of broad leaved woodland with a rich undergrowth; and interpret long established plant communities.

The second way of enriching parks and green spaces is to amend the normal practices of maintaining and landscaping them so as to permit the maximum possible number of wild plants, insects, birds, and mammals to coexist with the other uses of the park or open space.

New landscape is likely to be composed of plants which are all of the same age. Comparatively few species are used. Many are clones having no genetic variation at all, and thus reacting in exactly the same way to the environment in which they are placed ageing evenly, afflicted by the same diseases and equally vulnerable to them. This kind of planting is fragile, and liable to abrupt deterioration if conditions change.

The antidote, at least in the framework planting of the larger park or landscape is to use a wide diversity of plants and regard them as a community which must be capable of sustaining and renewing itself. In designing this it is necessary to keep in mind the purpose of the planting scheme. It may be for shelter or screening or as a background for other brighter plants, it may in itself be intended for floral entertainment or decoration.

The framework planting may be meant to offer an interesting place in which children can play, or to create a series of green rooms: some with a ceiling of overhanging boughs, some open to the sky. It may be intended as a natural piece of landscape in which wild life can predominate intruded on only by children finding a place in which to make their dens.

The use of alien species or even garden varieties is perfectly compatible with this idea. The pressure to use only native plants or in some countries only endemic ones, stems in part from the assumption that communities of these are the most stable and capable of self renewal; the most propitious for the life of native birds, insects, and mammals; the most compatible with the place. Sometimes there is the merest touch of xenophobia. In wild landscapes native plants should indeed be the main choice.

In urban areas exotic ones can fit comfortably into the landscape enriching it by adding new textures, colours and forms whilst still satisfying the needs of the other components of the natural community. Compatibility and suitability — not provenance should motivate choice.

Designers should learn from natural plant communities — studying them to see how the plants relate to one another; how the balance between them shifts and adapts as time goes by; how they respond to intrusions by man. The more varied the plant community the more easily it adapts. The larger it is the more likely it will be to develop its own stable independent ecological pattern. A hectare of woodland has a high chance, a narrow shrub border in a housing scheme not much of one, useful though it might be for other reasons.

Wild animals are shy and need safe corridors along which they can travel, isolated trees or small clumps are not much use to them. They need hedgerows, shelter belts, larger woods. With these come more habitats for insects and more homes and sources of food for birds and small mammals. This biological wealth has a subtle beauty, a contrast to gardeners gaudy flowers.

Woods and shelter belts

The plants have to be chosen in accordance with time honoured horticultural principles: choosing species that suit the soil and climate; looking to see what is already flourishing in the neighbourhood; planting in groups; interlacing one kind with another to give a succession of interest and a diversity of plant associations. Plants grow best in company.

Pioneer species may be needed on sites that are being started from scratch. These are trees that settle in quickly. They are usually easy to transplant as larger specimens to give an early sense of maturity — in Britain, alder, ash, aspen, birch, willow, even sycamore and poplar. They should not all be straight nursery specimens, some should be eccentrics, twisted, bent, lopsided. Such plants may be found amongst the rejects that are never sold. They may finish life on the nursery rubbish dump or bonfire. Rescue them. Nurserymen might do well by offering an odd ball selection in their catalogues. Trees can also be planted at an angle to suggest a natural deformity, though it should never be possible justify the word 'twee' (which is derived from a sarcastic mispronunciation of 'sweet'). They can be planted in tight clumps so close that when in leaf they appear as if they were a single enormous many stemmed plant.

Establishing natural plant communities and wild life areas sometimes, though not always, means standing conventional horticultural practice on its head. The old woodland management technique of coppice also deserves reviving and has a useful part to play.

With the nurse species should go the other sylvan elements of the landscape that are sometimes difficult or slow to establish, beech, oak, scots pine, sweet chestnut. Nurse species can remain dominant to the disadvantage of their more desirable neighbours and they may need to be checked or selectively removed as time goes by. Olmstead later in life had an exasperated correspondence with the Central Park Commissioners who were reluctant to thin the trees he had planted in the wild woodland areas of the park and when they eventually did, also cleared out the ground flora as well.

Natural plant communities are highly complex. They consist of several layers not just one or two and these may be in varying stages of development on the same piece of ground. This is the principle difference between them and the conventional, ordered, managed landscape of a park. The various canopies will develop naturally in time but the urban eye resents the untidiness and apparent disorder whilst this is taking place. The problem of the manager is to accelerate a natural process that may take many years if left to itself. To do this the shrubs, small trees and herbs which it is hoped would eventually appear have to be introduced deliberately early on, smaller shade tolerant trees like holly and yew for the darker interior of the wood, trees for the margin like rowan, wild cherry, shrubs such as hazel, elder, thorn, wild roses, juniper, climbing and scrambling plants ivy, honeysuckle, wild clematis, small shrubby species like the cowberry, various herbs, the woodrush, grasses and ferns; always matching the location to the plant and its ability to grow in the eventual conditions.

Richness of species also creates a choice of lodgings for other wildlife and the perfect place for children to make dens or explore, or play hiding games. Wild woods like this are not easy for adults to use and may even become impenetrable so if they are big enough they eventually need paths and clearings and rides to permit public access.

These areas can be merged with the rest of the park or open space by flanking them with grass land that is rich in herbs and by the use of groups of trees and individual many-stemmed trees which help to grade the wild landscape into the more formal park and its play and picnic lawns. For a lesson in how this can be accomplished see the golf course with its gradations of rough flanked by fine turf on one side and possibly linear woodland or dunes on the other.

Even on a smaller scale or in an existing park with a settled design small adaptations will produce better conditions for wild life and for children who like the same sort of places. The best wildlife reserves and children's playgrounds in Duthie Park in Aberdeen are three large plantations of shrubs with a top layer of trees and an undergrowth of bushes. Where enough light gets through there is a ground cover of herbs ferns, and annual plants as well. Birds thrive, there is a family of hedgehogs and, less desirably, a colony of rabbits which eat some varieties of roses on the nearby rose mountain.

Any group of existing park trees can be under-planted with smaller trees and shrubs preferably those that provide a winter source of food for birds, rowan, holly, cotoneaster and so on. The treatment also makes a park more habitable and inviting for its human customers as well. Just as wild creatures are repelled by hostile, featureless, big spaces, so are we. There is a trace of agoraphobia in many of us.

Where the wood is large enough dead twigs, branches and of course fallen leaves should be allowed to lie and rot where they fall.

They provide a home for a range of insects and grubs which in turn provide food for badgers and hedgehogs. It is too much in a public park even in a big one to ask for large standing dead trees or even dead branches to be left to decay naturally where they are. The potential danger to the public is too great. Woodpeckers may have to look elsewhere.

Holes in trees are another matter. They provide valuable accommodation. If there are none then the introduction of a few bird boxes should be considered, they should be well out of sight. If they can be seen they will be a natural challenge to every youngster who visits the park and their life and that of any eggs they contain will be ephemeral. Places for bats to roost may also be introduced in buildings.

When a new park or large open space is to be developed the greatest effort should be made to preserve the plant communities that already exist. They may have taken generations to form. Moving them is a waste of money if they can become part of the new landscape. The design should include them. Even unpromising clumps of gorse need not be bulldozed away. They can be interplanted to provide an upper canopy and to increase the diversity.

The natural contours of sites should be left as they are if possible. They may add interest and offer a diversity of habitats. Changing them disturbs the pattern of drainage and this alone may be enough to injure bigger trees whose roots systems may not be quick enough to adapt to the change. Earth moving is the most expensive of all landscape operations and should be minimised or avoided anyway. Swampy ground can be dug a little deeper to create open water and increase the chance of other wild plants and amphibians finding a home.

Wild flowers

The term green concrete or even green desert is sometimes applied to mown sward from which plants other than grass are excluded. Sometimes the point is illustrated by photographs showing desolate empty lawns. They are misleading. A park needs such places and if it is properly managed they will be thronged with people at some part of the day or week. For them the surface is a green carpet. In any case nature resists and penalises a monoculture and few areas are as sterile as the pejorative suggests.

Many park lawns could be made more interesting and still keep their practical utility through minor changes in cultivation — increasing the range of herbs in the sward; letting the grass get longer so that they flourish there; waiting for the flowering and seeding cycle at the least of the smaller and earlier flowering plants to be completed before mowing; and avoiding the use of weed-killers and fertilisers. In response the range of plants increases. Insects, birds and animals grow in number as more sources of food become available. The park will be richer and more attractive. It may draw more visitors who may be induced to stay longer which is the point of it all.

The change in attitude to native flora is not confined to Britain. It is a widespread phenomenon. Australians have discovered the merits of their own wild plants as opposed to introductions. A visitor to Texas in Spring is quite likely to be invited to marvel at the sheets of colour provided by the Texas Bluebonnet. Some British wild flowers are in the same league of showiness as many esteemed garden plants. Bellflower, coltsfoot, cowslip, foxglove, primrose, poppy, tansy, kingscup, yarrow, are florescent swanks. For mass effect fields of buttercups and daisies are compelling enough to have found their way into the vocabulary of nursery rhymes. The bluebell woods at Kew attract thousands of Londoners to make a special trip to the gardens in the Spring.

These plants and their equivalents elsewhere in the world have a place in parks but they should be seen as an integral part of the attractions, a response to a renewed interest by the general public, part of the floral entertainment.

It is necessary to look for subtler qualities in many other wild plants. Some provide essential dietary elements for butterflies and other insects. Nettles offer sustenance for the caterpillars of no fewer than nineteen species of butterfly; chickweed, which gardeners generally hate, for twenty four; plantain which is a blight of fine turf feeds twenty eight; dandelion twenty six; and the thoroughly disliked docks and their relatives the sorrels no less than fifty two. Some native trees are a much bigger deal than herbs. The most important larders are oak, birch, poplar, aspen, willow, hawthorn, blackthorn, and to a lesser extent ash, beech, privet and hazel. Most parks already contain some of these trees. More can easily be planted.

Many once familiar plants disappeared from view when selective weed killers became widely used in agriculture and horticulture. The change occurred quickly. Within a few years after the war, plants that had been common and widespread disappeared. The rest went as farmers removed hedges, cleared ditches, drained wet land, filled ponds and pulled down trees to make their farms into food factories. Forestry practice changed as well. Conifers which eventually wipe out most of the plants that grow below them replaced the slower growing broad-leaved trees which for the most part allow a ground flora to prosper.

The loss of wild flowers impoverished us all. Country road verges were less colourful, country walks lost their sense of botanical exploration, plants of delicate beauty vanished from view. Naturally there was a reaction. The surprise is that it took so long to occur.

Park systems nearly all contain wild spaces sometimes large ones. It is misconception to suppose that these have not always existed and been valued as nature reserves. Managers can sometimes feel exasperated when highly successful planting and thoughtful management has produced an area that looks as if it is completely natural only to have it used as an example of what could be done if land was left alone.

University Park in Nottingham for example had a large area set aside for the purpose from the time it was first laid out seventy years ago — quite apart from the ribbons of wild flowers along the banks of the brook which flows through it. Cambridge has a hundred hectares of common land within its boundaries some of it close to the very heart of the city. It is in the state it has enjoyed for a millennium and is maintained by grazing as it has been in all that time, using cattle and horses. Most towns can tell a similar story.

The campaign to keep these areas and to allow new ones to develop is an old one not a new. Literature is crowded with passages drawing attention to the beauty of wild places and plants, and artists like Constable and Fragonard spent lifetimes in celebrating them. The start of what can now be seen as a modern movement to reintroduce wild flowers and natural areas deliberately was made by the Parks Departments in Glasgow and Whitley Bay in the 1960s. Its proselytisers today are not enunciating a new idea. They are in the mainstream of an old one. Aesop told a fable about a fly which sat on the axle wheel of a chariot and said 'what a dust do I raise'.

Other changes occurred about the same time. Britain felt less prosperous. The Department of Transport stopped paying local authorities to mow country verges. It was not an attempt to restore lost habitats. It was an economy measure. Wild flowers said thank you and crept back.

The Common Market came and subsidies induced ever increased agricultural production. Grain mountains grew and in spite of wellfounded Biblical evidence to the contrary were regarded as a form of sin and in so far as they were built at the expense of our own as well as wild flower habitats they were. The idea of setting aside areas without crops as a means to reduce production was introduced. It was the best scheme of wild flower restoration ever devised. Some maintenance is involved to prevent the land from becoming derelict but only so much as allows many types of wild plant to grow.

The Countryside Commission introduced an experimental premium scheme in 1988. This gives extra payments to farmers to persuade them to maintain set-aside land in the interests of wild life, landscape, and the local community. In the first year alone nearly three thousand hectares of land had been covered by the scheme. By 1990 it was possible for the commission to envisage extending the scheme to all important English landscapes where there is pressure for public access.

The extensive plantations of daffodils in Aberdeen and elsewhere help wild flowers to establish themselves in the grass.

The long period that the haulms are traditionally left to die back before mowing allows many wild flowers to enter the turf and to complete their own flowering and fruiting cycle before they are whisked away by mowing machines. They extend the otherwise limited period of floral interest. They bring delight, and restore the daisy chain.

There are perfectly good reasons for areas of mown grass however. It is a mistake to trust those who sneer at all lawns as the manifestation of the crude bad practice of a dying breed of park keeper. Wild flowers on many playing surfaces are weeds that interfere with some sports and even prevent them from being played with any reasonable level of skill. Broad leaved plants are anathema on a golf green for example though they can and should find a place in the rough.

There are some lawns which are so heavily used by the public that durability of the surface becomes an overriding consideration. Properly maintained mown grass is harder wearing than a mixture including herbs and is the toughest of all natural surfaces if the grass species are chosen correctly. It can be trampled and run over without becoming immediately unsightly. It dries more quickly after rain and can be used sooner. Air moving over it desiccates the deposits of ever more numerous dogs. Broken glass is easily visible and can be removed not left as a hidden danger. Litter is easy to clear. Some attractive species of birds feed on lawns and cannot get their food from a meadow.

A well kept lawn is still the best setting for a flower bed or a formal garden. There are perfectly sound reasons for the regular traditional upkeep of some lawns in public parks. Wild flower meadows offer floral entertainment but not every piece of turf is appropriate or suitable for the purpose.

How to get wild flowers back? The easiest way is to amend existing practices. Even a little change will sometimes make a lot of difference. Avoid weed killers which should be a last resort in any case; when possible allow plants to form and scatter their seed before they are cut down; avoid nitrogenous fertilisers because most esteemed wild flowers do best on poorer soils; leave the base of hedgerows uncut until the hedge itself in trimmed; keep hedges instead of removing them even though they need regular costly maintenance; never mow officiously in places where long vegetation is as suitable as cut grass; leave banks uncut except for a trim in the autumn to make them better for sledging later on; leave nature to take its course; and most of all protect the wild flower colonies and habitats that already exist.

Most cities have plenty of wild spaces alongside canals, rivers, streams, and railways and in many secret corners. The energy sometimes spent in tidying them would be better directed at making them more suitable for their existing inhabitants, and safer and pleasanter for the public to use.

Introducing wild flowers deliberately also has to be considered. Unless this is done, plants not already present in the neighbourhood are unlikely to reappear spontaneously and some like the much loved primrose and cowslip not at all. Establishing them is not as easy as it is sometimes made to sound. Plants fight to the death with one another for survival. The worthy use of plants not adapted to living together or unsuitable for the soil or climate is doomed to failure.

I know a place where the plant called Town Hall Clock (Adoxa moschatellina) grows, it is not an uncommon plant in Britain but is not easily found either. It has formed a tiny colony which flourishes because it is better suited to grow in that position than anything else. It has expanded just as far as the limits of its best environment, no further. Beyond them it cannot prosper and other plants take over to be replaced in their own turn when conditions subtly change again. There is no point at all in sowing its seed outside its limits however fervently we may wish to see it grow there. It will not thrive. Sooner or later it will disappear and the same is true of any other plant removed from its own best setting asked to colonise an alien one.

It is no use planting a shade loving species in a sunny meadow; nor a sun loving one in the shade of a hedge; nor a calcifuge species on a chalk down. Horses for courses. Gardening is based upon doing just that but if high horticulture is needed to get a plant to grow it cannot become naturalised. It is really no better than any other garden plant.

Wild flower meadows are not maintenance free. Meadow plants only continue to succeed if the herbage is cut down after seeding, and once more in the autumn. If this is not done they will be smothered and conditions will start to favour something else. Charles Darwin noted that land left untended gradually reverts to scrub and from that progresses to woodland in the British climate and although the species and the time taken may vary, the same is true in many parts of the world.

Trampling also kills some wild flowers especially the taller summer flowering ones like scabious, ox-eye daisy, the scottish bluebell, and knapweed and even if it does not kill them it makes them unsightly leaving crushed flattened stems to mark the nature of use to which the place has been put. The parks of my apprenticeship employed many skilful interpreters of such signs. Not all their analyses were polite!

To be sure of keeping this kind of vegetation in a busy public park it may be necessary to try to keep the public off the areas preferably by mowing grass paths through the meadow. Most people will prefer to walk along these and will voluntarily keep off the flowers. Where there is a conflict public use should be given priority over floriculture. Tougher plants like the Hawkbit will still survive.

Shade can also become a problem under trees especially those with a very dense canopy like beech or at the base of a hedge if it is allowed to grow unchecked. Even tough guys like cow parsley or shrubby plants like the blackberry can be killed by too much shade. Thinning may be needed to let in more light.

The most effective way of reintroducing wild flowers to existing turf or to woodland is to plant well established seedlings as if they were bedding plants. The techniques are familiar and well established and contain no mysteries.

The seed should be sown onto the surface of boxes or if the amount is small onto pots filled with a seed compost — that is one with plenty of sand to make sure that the soil is well drained. Water logging kills many wild flower seedlings with the exception of bog plants. Compost free from lime or chalk should be chosen for plants that only grow on acid soil.

The compost should be moist but not saturated and the old method of assessing whether it is suitable is still a good one. If it retains the imprint and shape of the hand when pressed it is wet enough if not it needs water, if the shape shatters into fragments when it is dropped it is dry enough, if not it should be left until it is.

The seeds should be sown thinly and pressed into the soil surface gently. A sprinkle of sifted soil completes the process. The container should be watered then put in a greenhouse or a cold frame until germination occurs. The young plants should be spaced out into boxes or small pots as soon as they are big enough to handle and kept in the protection of unheated glass until they have started to grow again. Transplanting causes a check to growth.

As soon they are well established they should be put outside in a sheltered place until they are big enough to fend for themselves in the park. The plants should be thoroughly hardened off so that they are acclimatised to the harsher more competitive conditions there. The aim should be to have them in place at about the time plants in the wild have reached the same stage of growth — preferably in the Spring. They should be planted in colonies in the same way that other wild plants grow.

Seed can be sown direct onto bare ground that has been lightly cultivated but it is quite likely that the choicer kinds will be smothered by their more aggressive brethren especially if the soil is too fertile. Taking away most of the top soil for use elsewhere can produce better conditions for wild flowers. Sowing direct onto existing turf is a prodigal misuse of valuable and expensive seed little of which will germinate and grow despite harrowing or scarifying the surface in an attempt to get it into contact with the soil. A better way is to kill the grass with a grass killing chemical, to cultivate the surface and only then to sow the seed.

The classic horticultural advice should be followed of sowing thinly. It is a waste of money to do otherwise and may well be counterproductive since the young plants will compete not only against the seedlings that occur naturally on any cultivated ground but also against each other.

Obtaining suitable seed is comparatively easy since the trend to reintroduce native wild herbs has allowed firms specialising in wild flowers to develop. Mixtures can be obtained for use in particular situations — wet or dry sites; shaded or exposed ones and so on. As an alternative seed can be collected and sown as soon as it is ripe.

What about people that pick the flowers? Plant extra to permit some to be gathered by those who want them without spoiling the spectacle for everybody else. Never rail to the press or on the local radio about the peculations that inevitably occur. Doing so merely suggests the possibility to everyone else.

Ponds

Ponds are an important home for wild life in parks and those that exist should be treasured not least because the persistent draining of wet land nationally has eliminated many habitats where aquatic and amphibious creatures once lived. Who would have believed a few short decades ago that the common frog could become uncommon in Britain. I did a survey of children in a park that I once managed. Fewer than 20 per cent of them had ever even seen a frog though all knew that if they kissed one it would turn into a prince. Dragonflies are also disappearing. They need water, and water plants like the spiked water milfoil, to survive and some, like the brown aeshna dragonfly, need dead wood in which to lay their eggs. Many other once common insects and mammals are in the same plight. Tidiness is death to wildlife.

Ponds should be retained not only for the habitat they provide but because they attract the public. In one park that I surveyed half the people with young children who visited it regularly did so to feed the ducks on the lake. Some older people did as well.

New ponds must be safe for the public and especially children. The point will no doubt be made that a child can drown even in a few centimetres of water and the risk should certainly be considered. The problem is that if every risk is expunged the park will become inexpressibly dull and children will go elsewhere into even more dangerous places for their adventure. Open deep water in parks should be guarded by an appropriate barrier where there is a risk of someone blundering in. This should be made of sympathetic materials not chestnut paling or chain link. It might also be made to fit into the landscape by appropriate planting. A barrier will also help to protect the fragile wetland vegetation which should be encouraged at the water's edge.

For safety reasons and to permit a wide variety of plants to grow abrupt changes in the water level should be avoided. So should a sterile hard edge to the pond except in those places where it is desired that the public should approach right to the brink. Water is part of the park entertainment and the banks should be able to provide space for large numbers of regular visitors without being destroyed or becoming degenerate. Piers promenades, viewpoints, promontories, peninsulas, places from which to feed the ducks, seats from which to enjoy the view should be the manager's first consideration. These also bring diversity of habitat.

Water areas can provide for reed beds, and a range of other plants; islands allow water birds to breed undisturbed and provide a place for amphibious mammals. Alders and willows by the water's edge help to keep the water cool and shady in summer and delay freezing in winter to the advantage of fish, their roots give stability to the bank and their fallen leaves feed some of the aquatic organisms.

Pond water is biological soup. If it is kept free from pollution it will support many living creatures, fish, newts, frogs and toads, water voles, water hens, coots, ducks, geese, dragonflies. It will provide drinking water for birds and wild animals; and it will allow a wider range of plants to grow; floating aquatics, plants that spend their lives in total immersion; and others that like to have their roots in wet soil or bog at the margins of lakes and ponds. If ponds have to be cleaned out for any reason the debris should be left on the side for a few days before removal so that some of the pond life that it contains can ease its way back into the water.

There is a lively interest in these plants as the expansion of nurseries that specialise in them suggests. They include many attractive species not only natives like marsh marigold, water forget-me-not, the flowering rush and the flag iris, but also stately introductions like the royal fern or *Gunnera manicata*. They too have a place in parks.

Management plans

Natural areas are not maintenance free indeed they need skilful, sensitive attention. A management plan can describe what should be done and can eventually express itself in specifications and tender documents. It should be available to the DSO or the contractor so that they can understand the context of the work and cooperate in its aims. In this kind of landscape development is continuous and does not stop when maintenance starts.

Local Authorities can get help in these high endeavours and they will be assailed by not a little advice some of it contradictory. Urban wildlife groups are springing up in many places and they should certainly be consulted and asked to help. The British Trust for Conservation Volunteers and similar groups are able to organise practical assistance. Most areas support local branches of national organisations concerned with wild life for example the Royal Society for the Protection of Birds, Friends of the Earth, the Nature Conservancy Council, even the World Wildlife Fund which is not concerned only with pandas and elephants. There are often naturalists clubs and groups interested in ornithology

If it does not already exist a group of friends of the park can be established. It will not arise spontaneously because people take parks for granted until they are under threat of development. Local schools should be involved so should a range of local voluntary organisations also the press, radio and television.

Interpretation

Addison refers to the ambiguity of oracles. Wild life oracles are like others. Their discoveries and ideas even their language needs explaining, their mysteries interpreting. Only then can they give instruction and information and pleasure to others, the exposition should not be confined to natural history, there is often a long human association which deserves explanation and in some of the ancient open spaces this may stretch back centuries. It deserves the effort and expense of interpretation. Local schools and museums and the appropriate departments of universities and colleges should be asked to cooperate. It is a joint effort which can bring the parks manager a range of sympathetic contacts in the community. It can involve pamphlets, posters, books, labels, explanatory signs, nature trails, guided walks, and elaborate centres. For a lesson in how this should be done study the provisions made by the National Trust. They recognise that to give the public the best return from a visit, they have to provide detailed knowledge and engender appreciation. This enriches the visitor inducing a longer more fruitful stay, and a more frequent return.

Nature trails

The buzz concept of 20 years ago was the nature trail. Trails proliferated. No large park was complete without one. They were the natural history equivalent of jogging tracks. Everybody wanted one but after the early surge of use in response to their novelty and the initial hype of the opening, they were all too often left to a handful of enthusiasts and some to desuetude.

The idea is to encourage people to take a walk from station to station in the park. At these points explanations in a guide book or better still by a guide, describe what can be seen. Signs point out features of interest. At their best nature trails are a valuable stimulus to continuous observation and awareness, at their worst they are aggravated walks.

To be worthwhile nature trails have to be nurtured, sustained by a flow of publicity, kept up to date, maintained and adapted. At their best they are valuable for getting people to explore and understand a park as well as to appreciate its story and its plants. They can also be used to direct people away from sensitive areas. They sometimes cause disappointment by raising the expectation that timid wild animals can be seen when in fact they seldom can, or referring to birds that are not often on parade either. These should be written about in general terms related to the area as a whole and intended to increase powers of observation rather than suggesting that they are likely to be found in specific spots. In these it is better to rely on trees, plants, topography, geology: features that are likely to be there when the visitor is induced to look for them. They focus on the easily missed details of a place as well as on its more obvious characteristics.

Self guided trails are the most common. They take the form of signposted routes and paths sometimes supported by maps, leaflets, or explanatory booklets. Planning them needs a great deal of skill and thought addressed to the convenience of the customers and the range of interesting things that can be seen and explained. Like the best landscape design they are the product of a careful assessment of detail and they should be worked out on the site itself.

Long trails should have alternative, easier or shorter routes, so that the user can vary the time taken and the challenge of the walk at will. Disabled people should be able to use them conveniently, not only those in wheelchairs but also the ambulant disabled. This may mean providing handrails as an aid to the old and a guide to the blind, recorded commentaries for those who cannot see to read, and easy gradients.

The path surfaces needs careful thought. They should be appropriate for the place but should be passable at all seasons, bare earth will seldom do and if the trail is a success, grass will not survive. The easiest materials to fit into a natural landscape are gravel or pulverised bark or wood chips but they need regular replenishment, and maintenance. They can be difficult for wheelchairs or push chairs and on those parts of the trail where this is the case a hard surface may have to be introduced instead.

Signs are a difficulty. They can be so discreet that they are invisible and they can be so intrusive that they are an eyesore. They have to be carefully designed for the particular location, they must be durable and weather proof and strong enough to resist vandals and souvenir hunters. The best way-markers are probably those perfected by the Forestry Commission with arrows of different colours according to the route, carved onto the chamfered surface of a simple wooden post.

Signs intended to give information are a greater problem because by nature of their function they have to be bigger. They are harder to place where they can be read easily without intruding on the scene and spoiling it. They are at risk of defacement or damage. They must be made of strong durable materials and these can be backed by a steel plate to give extra strength. If they can be placed on an existing structure so much the better, if not they should be on a strong post concreted into place and secure enough to resist dislodgement, posts are a handy test of strength to passing youngsters. The message on them needs to be informed by the art of writing a poster, simple, direct, free from jargon, clear unembellished statements of fact. Line drawings may assist clarity.

Maps should be clear and easy to refer to whilst in the open. Booklets should be informed, not loquacious companions. They should be copiously illustrated with line drawings and pictures and easily handled even on a windy day. They should refer the reader to sources of further information and to clubs and organisations active in natural and local history so that the interest that is stimulated by the trail can find a more enduring expression.

Nature trails need not be confined to parks and they can be developed to encompass a wider area. They can be used to activate a system of footpaths and stimulate agreements to create new ones, especially when these connect areas of special interest. Trails within the urban area can take a number of forms drawing attention to esteemed buildings, architecture and history. They can describe the secret natural history, lichens, mosses, algae, and explain about the birds that inhabit towns and the wild animals that have taken refuge there from an increasingly inhospitable countryside.

The Countryside Commission for Scotland at Battleby, near Perth, soon to be merged with the Nature Conservancy Council to form the Scottish Natural Heritage, has a valuable range of publications giving practical advice and design details for the accoutrements of nature trails. Even where the trail is in a town or an urban park the information and guidance that they give is of use.

Park rangers

Once a member of staff is appointed the cost of nature interpretation moves up a gear. Not only are the wages and overheads a continuing expense but an energetic appointee will develop a whole range of further demands. This is not a reason to shirk such an appointment but it is a warning. If adequate financial provision is not made at the outset frustration will surely follow.

The first task is to decide what the ranger is expected to do. The terms of reference are not only a guide to applicants they also help to clear the mind of the employer and allow the post to find its place in the pattern of others that exist. The number of rangers has increased sharply in recent years because of grants from the Countryside Commission. These emphasise the countryside rather than the urban area but the expertise they bring or develop, can have a wider use.

The basic function of most of the posts is to inform and educate the public about the countryside and its opportunities for using leisure time, also to open urban eyes to the beauty of nature. They may be in charge of the client function in some of the areas where their interests predominate for example: in maintaining country parks, woodland or nature trails; they should have the expertise to design or advise on new trails; the aptitude to guide walks, give lectures and talks, answer enquiries, cooperate with schools; they have a role as publicists and should be encouraged to work with the press and radio and television. They must also have the tact and diplomatic skill needed to harness the work of voluntary groups and individuals. They have a lesser role in surveillance and liaison with the police and the other members of the park patrol system. The posts are attractive and advertisements usually yield a big response often from older people wanting a change of direction in their careers or who wish to make a job out of their hobby.

The broader functions of countryside rangers are potentially just as useful if they are applied to the urban park. The mobile patrolmen and the individual park attendants are usually retained in the client's staff. Their traditional role is to superintend the parks and their customers. They should be encouraged to expand the horizons of their duties. When posts become vacant the job specifications should be redesigned and enlarged so that they demand a more positive active relationship with the people who go to the park. The welcoming informed host is more useful than the janitor.

Interpretation centres

Another migrant that should be encouraged to make its way from the country to the urban park is the information or, more grandly expressed, the interpretation centre. Many older parks contain buildings which could be adapted for the purpose, some are already museums but these all too often turn their back on the space which surrounds them. They should look out and explain what they see.

Museums have undergone a revolution, so should information centres. In Britain the Jorvik Museum at York, the Imperial War Museum in London, the Cabinet War Room in Whitehall, in South Kensington the Natural History Museum's various exhibits like the hall of memory and learning, the Museum of the Moving Image on the South Bank in London all use techniques which leave the usual interpretive centre not to mention the average local museum gasping in their wake. Facts and information should not be served in an indigestible pottage. The centres have to be good enough to attract visitors; lively and interesting enough to get them to stay; diverse and active enough to persuade them to return; like the park itself.

The best museums now find queues at their doors. So should centres in parks. To do so they need the same techniques. Audio visual displays, laser discs for instant access to information, for instance to help a visitor identify a plant or test knowledge, videos, film, plants that talk — hidden microphones, loudspeakers, concealed commentators. Centres should be used for drama, story telling, interaction, tests of memory, problem solving, questioning assertions, and challenging received wisdom: intellectual adventure.

They should address themselves to all the human senses, sight hearing, touch, smell, taste. They should echo with the sound of bird song, wind soughing in trees, creaking branches buffeted by gales, foxes barking. At a touch they should be able to show films of germinating seeds, hatching eggs, accelerated growth, unfolding flowers. They should simulate environments humid, dry, hot, cold, windswept. They should show how perfumes can be extracted from flowers and the scent should permeate the building once the process is complete. Fanciful? Not at all. Somewhere or other there are museums using all these ideas or something like them. The manager should go and look, garner ideas, filch them, bring them home, develop them, adapt them, use them to stimulate further enquiry and invention. Costly? Of course! So are empty buildings, spurned exhibits, unused assets, wasted resources, lost opportunities.

National plant collections

It is not only wild plants that are in retreat so are some once familiar garden plants. They may be rare or hard to grow or out of fashion or just ignored. They drop from catalogues as nurseries rationalise their stocks, limit themselves to plants that sell quickly and which are adapted to life in garden centre containers. When they are lost they go forever. In Britain the idea of national collections was born to preserve them. What has that got to do with managing a park? Plenty if the collection is interesting to the public, nothing if it is not.

A national collection attracts people to come and see it, gets publicity for the park, gives extra interest and satisfaction for the staff and, what should be the last consideration for a park does a good deed, preserves plants that might have disappeared unique genes and all, giving a passport into a specialist world.

There are now many collections and they include a formidable range of plants, some of them are in the hands of parks departments others in botanic gardens, horticultural colleges, private and National Trust gardens, and still others in nurseries and garden centres. There is still scope for more. The scheme covers not only ornamentals like magnolias, narcissus, lilacs, hollies but also fruit including gooseberries and rhubarb, and vegetables.

Some of the collections are highly specialised thus *Primula allionii* cultivars or Russell lupins or pre-1900 shrub roses, other groups of plant like Rhododendron are so big that the collections are divided. The scheme is a British one organised by the National Council for the Conservation of Plants and Gardens but it has international implications and reflects a general concern. Some plants like roses, chrysanthemums and dahlias have so many cultivars that it is not practical to conserve them all even if they were all worth the effort. The criteria for a national collection are that the species or varieties are important in the development of the plant; are genetically useful with characteristics that might be of value in the future for example in bringing back qualities of disease resistance; are aesthetically valuable or represent an important period of garden fashion; are useful for scientific research or for medicinal or commercial use or are important to mankind in other ways; or are endangered in the wild, or are rare.

Some organisations are engaged in similar work in respect of particular plants. The Food and Agriculture Organisation of the United Nations is seeking to conserve plants of economic importance with an emphasis on sustaining ancient and primitive cultivars which are genetic pools of great diversity and high potential value. The International Dendrology Society (dendrology is the study of trees), the Hardy Plant Society, the Garden History Society, the Royal Horticultural Society, and more specialised groups like the Royal National Rose Society all generate an interest in plants including endangered ones, and help to keep them in cultivation, in some cases through deliberate programmes.

Establishing a collection can be a major commitment that extends into the indefinite future. Even though managers are normally left by most councils to get on with the horticultural development of the parks untrammelled by too many controls this is a step that should only be taken after formal consent has been obtained. Plants from the collection have to be propagated; kept in good health made available for study; cuttings, seeds, or plants have to be shared with enthusiasts or even nurseries wanting to take them up again. They have to be catalogued and recorded. In some cases a reserve collection may also be necessary.

The National Council for the Preservation of Gardens and Plants published their first directory of British National Collections in 1990. It is obtainable from the Council at The Pines, Wisley Garden, Woking GU23 6QB.

Rare breeds

The park can be used to keep breeds of domestic animals that are rare or uncommon or have been supplanted by newer more productive kinds. Herds of highland cattle in Heaton Park in Manchester, and Pollock Park in Glasgow are well known examples. There are many uncommon or rare varieties of sheep goats, pigs, cattle, poultry, horses, and ponies. They can all find a place in the biggest parks or on model farms. In other parts of the world there are game reserves under the management of parks departments. There too endangered species can keep their hold on life.

There are two questions the manager must ask before embarking on the project. Can it be done well enough and on a scale sufficient to attract the public? Secondly do the necessary skills exist or can they be acquired to ensure the contentment and well being of the animals? If so then the collection should be developed to the point at which it is a major attraction. The animals can be bred and farmed to produce an income which can offset the direct costs for example of animal feeds and labour. The range can be extended by exchanges with the stock of other enthusiasts or by purchase because a market exists in these animals just like any livestock.

Although the welfare of the animals is a major consideration they are there for reasons of display. They have to be in attractive surroundings, the pens and paddocks must be well stocked to give lively interest, there should be enough signs to explain to the public what they are seeing, and the enclosures and fences ought to be made of attractive materials which though stockproof should enhance the scene not detract from it as many do. There must be shelter and water. Adequate pasturage should be available elsewhere so that the animals can be transferred when necessary to give a chance to renovate the grass in the pens or simply to prevent it deteriorating in very wet weather.

Horses

Horses have a special and distinct part to play. They are held in particular affection in many countries. The heavy horses are still struggling to keep their place in the modern world. Parks departments can help them. In their turn the horses will help the park by keeping it at the centre of public attention.

The heavy horses Clydesdales, Shires, Suffolk Punch, Percheron in Britain and other favoured breeds elsewhere in the world are as artificial as varieties of lettuce or poodles. They are the product of man. They were developed for pulling ploughs, farm implements, carts, and wagons. For this they require obedient, patient, enduring strength; dinner plate feet to grip the ground; and placid, gentle, sweet, temperate natures. They were bred for labour and during the 19th century they were brought to a peak of handsome perfection.

The Clydesdale Horse which is one of the biggest can be considered as an analogy for the decline of all rare breeds. In 1920 there were still 2,823 registered Clydesdale mares in Britain. It is by the number of these that the success of a breed can best be judged. In that year the stallion Dunure Footprint who had been a major winner at agricultural shows was in such demand that he had to cover a mare every two hours day and night. He was sustained in this high endeavour by the total milk production milk of two cows. The breed was undergoing its last convulsive expansion. By 1930 there were 1,608 registered mares, by 1950 only 273 when the Clydesdale was declared an endangered species by the Rare Breeds Society. By 1972 there were a mere 187. Today there are more, but not many.

Times change. The breed was developed for a purpose. It was replaced and supplanted. Its era over it might be said that it should go too. Yet the heavy horse took generations to bring to perfection. Its survival deserves the same loving attention as all other beautiful things.

The preferred Clydesdale horse for hauling goods on roads or in a park is between six and twelve years old not less than seventeen hands in height, and weighing about seven hundred and fifty kilograms. Geldings are best because they are usually calm and hard to disturb; mares can be used but are flightier; stallions are not recommended for this kind of work at all and they can be hard to handle. Leave them to the specialist. Mares can be sent away to them when breeding is to take place and there is no need to keep them in the department.

The working life of a Clydesdale gelding varies with the individual and with the type of work it is given to do. Clydesdales can haul goods till they are 18 years old but as they get older they get slower so they used to be transferred onto farm work after they were about 12 years. On the short haul work most likely within a park they can be successfully kept on haulage work longer, after that they can be put out to grass or used for children's rides.

A pair of Clydesdales can haul a load of 4 tonnes on the flat; even a single horse can do nearly as well as that, but a pair is showier and makes more of a dash in the world. They are the equine Rolls Royce. Four horses have no parallel for style but they are hard to manage and need a rare skill in the driver. Stick to two is my advice.

Horses can be economical even today and that is what has assisted their mild resurgence. I can remember when the last horse was taken out of service in a park that I used to know. Its tasks included pulling a cart used to gather autumn leaves. Four gardeners were used to load the cart. There was no driver because the horse would move forward at a word of command and could also be ordered to stop which it nearly always did! It was succeeded by a tractor and trailer. This required five staff for the same work because the tractor needed a driver. Labour costs rose correspondingly. The tractor filled the air with fumes. The horse had not been guiltless but its emissions were intermittent and occasional. It had been mostly silent whereas the tractor filled the place with spluttering sound. No city child approached the new equipage with a lump of sugar or a handful of grass. Everyone felt a sense of loss.

Light loads, short hauls, frequent stops. This is the kind of work that suits a horse best and at which it is still likely to be economical even today; gathering leaves, emptying litter baskets, clearing rose prunings or grass cuttings, taking the hay off a wild flower meadow, clearing away spring and summer bedding plants, carting pulverised bark to spread as a mulch in shrub borders; taking out seats after they have been cleaned. Parks have many similar tasks.

The cost of two five year old Clydesdale geldings broken to harness, plus harness and a cart is, at the time of writing, £12,000. They cost about £18,000 a year to run. The price of large motor van is higher, its annual expense is greater, its life is shorter. Carts increase in value as the years go by.

If mares are kept they can be used for breeding but they are off the road for a period before each birth and for up to six months afterwards. It is more usual to have a brood mare whose only role is reproduction. Foals have a high value if they have a good pedigree and are fillies. They are especially appealing to the public.

Local blacksmiths and saddlers catering for the leisure equestrian trade soon relearn the art of dealing with heavy horses. The blacksmith will rediscover the art of retreading the old horse shoe building upon and tempering the iron so that it is given a new economical lease of life. In regular use a shoe lasts less than six weeks. There are still carters anxious to get back to their old work who can pass their skills to a new generation and the amount of voluntary help is a source of constant surprise. Carts and other horse vehicles can be found languishing in sheds and at the back of farm buildings or they can be made specially. Other vehicles like carriages and traps are sold at auction. In Britain the periodic sales at Reading specialise in them.

The technology of the cart is that of fifty years ago, but there are now stronger and lighter materials and new devices like nylon bushes and substitutes for the laboriously cleaned chrome fittings and chains. These make carts easier and lighter to use. There are also improvements to other equipment, horse drawn seed drills and rakes for example, they all help to make the horse more productive and efficient.

There are drawbacks of course. Horses like all other livestock need attention seven days a week and this is expensive to provide even though volunteers ease the burden. They need dry, snug, draft proof stabling and a store for straw, hay and food, though many buildings including garages can be adapted for the purpose and in older parks the former stable blocks are still quite likely to exist. Vets' bills can come as a surprise and heavy horses can die from the disease called grass sickness which is still not fully understood and which cannot be cured. It is possible to insure against this and other hazards and this should certainly be done using the council's general insurers who are likely to offer good deals.

Horses are slower moving than motor vehicles, even a tractor and trailer can get about quicker so they are not really suited for longer journeys except perhaps through city centres where the public like to see them, and where traffic is not likely to move quicker than they can. Routes should be chosen to avoid long steep hills where they will indeed accumulate a queue of exasperated apoplectic motorists toiling along behind them.

There are advantages in bringing back horses and using them in the streets and parks. They bring utility, economy and civic cheerfulness. Nothing is quite so agreeable as a pair of large horses and a cart. Their amiability is in sharp distinction to the menace and aggression of the motor car. Their hoofs make a cheerful rhythmic clatter and the iron shod wheels of the cart grate upon the surface of the road with a continuous burr like the drone of a bagpipe. They elicit smiles from adults and waves from children, they attract the cameras of visitors and tourists. Oil is a finite resource, burning it here produces acid rain which kills trees and poisons lakes somewhere else. The motor car is a powerfully disruptive force exerted against the very fabric of towns. There is a case for considering the use of horses quite apart from economic ones.

In a park horses of all kinds can find a place. Ponies and traps or horses and carriages for children's' rides; stage coaches to take visitors on tours of the city and carry children's parties on joy rides; landaus for wedding parties and to take old people on sight seeing tours; or horses simply to give rides in the park. Opening the stables to the public attracts a steady flow of visitors. These can all be functions of the client.

Most of the haulage work is a matter for the contractor and it would probably be considered uncompetitive to specify the use of horses in tender documents. Even so at least one in-house contractor is using them and outsiders may do so too and will find horses and carts a satisfactory interesting alternative to motor vehicles and tractors and trailers. The work must be planned carefully, there is no chance of hurrying back for a forgotten item with a horse and they should be used for the work they are best at. They should be considered on economic grounds but there is a bonus of valuable, steadily renewed publicity, not to say an aura of self righteousness and a selling point for tourists.

Trees

One of the most important tasks of parks departments is dealing with trees because they are a dominating component of most human settlements. They give scale, proportion, ameliorate the appearance of ugly structures, break the line of severe modern buildings, bring unity to the disparate elements of streets, provide a home for wild life, echo the changing seasons, act as focal points, frame views, divide large inhospitable spaces into smaller friendlier ones, give sense of enclosure and containment, make car parks less desolate and ugly, remind us of nature. They bring shelter, improve human comfort, trap warm air beneath their branches at night, still the force of winds thereby diminishing the heat loss from buildings, reduce air turbulence near tall buildings, absorb noise, trap dust, bind soil particles together so preventing erosion either through wind or water. If they are maintained with respect for their natural form and habit of growth, and given the space they need to grow to the fullness of their beauty, they confer the gift of loveliness, making dull places extraordinary.

If they are so benign why do trees need advocates and why then are they not an automatic component of every development? Park managers are all too familiar with the litany of complaints about them. When young they are the typical target of the urban vandal.

Roots as they develop and expand in girth lift pavements and kerbs, heave walls, disturb foundations. They can cause the subsidence of buildings built on shrinkable clay especially during periods of drought when thirsty roots may suck water out of a soil in which it is not replenished by rainfall. Roots can block drains, a few species for instance of poplar throw up suckers where they are not wanted or expected.

The leaves cause excessive shade in higher latitudes, North or South, though shade may be welcome in lower ones. Aphids inhabit them exuding honeydew which drips onto walls, pavements, and cars parked below making them glutinous and unsightly; later on sooty moulds develop and turn them black. Branches and whole trees occasionally fall sometimes without any evident reason. Trees shed leaves which may adhere to wet pavements making them even more treacherous, not to mention demanding labour to sweep them up.

Fallen leaves block gutters and obstruct drains and downspouts. Bud scales, catkins, and dead flowers fall in spring, fruits in autumn, twigs at any time. Trees sway menacingly in winds creating arboriphobia if not terror in those who live in their shadow. 'Trees are fine outside my neighbours house and remove or prune them at your peril but I do not want one near me' is the silent opinion of householders everywhere. The management of trees in towns calls for iron nerves and high skills of diplomacy and tact.

Only a minority of trees in an area is likely to be owned by the Parks Department but it should try to be involved in discussions and decisions about all of them. It is easiest to do this in respect of trees that are in the ownership of local authorities. They may be in the Highways Department if they are in streets, the Housing Department in housing estates, in the control of School Councils if they are around schools, they may be growing in the premises of the Social Work and other departments. In the case of new developments trees may be included at the choice of the architect.

Liaison with these groups is comparatively easy because they need advice and help and the parks departments are the nearest sources of expertise to hand. Even so getting the work depends on reputation and internal marketing, making sure that advice is asked for whenever it is needed. When it is sought it should be prompt, obliging, courteous and of course reliable. Other departments will come hot foot when things are going wrong for example when there is a public row about the proposed removal of trees for road widening, or when trees are causing a nuisance, or if one falls across a road. But the more important work is to make sure that the trees of an area are healthy and kept in good condition all the time; that new generations are introduced; that the need for replacements is anticipated; and that they are then planted in good time. This needs the initiative of the parks client. It is not likely to be considered by others.

The other form of direct intervention that local authorities can make is through Planning Departments who can make tree preservation orders under the provision of section 60 of the *1971 Town and Country Planning Act,* and initiate the designation of conservation areas in which the trees as well as the buildings and other aspects of the fabric are subject to protection. In Britain they can ensure that trees are preserved or new ones planted when they give permission for new developments, indeed under section 59 of the *1971 Town and Country Planning Act* they are required to do so. Many countries have vested these or similar controls and powers in local administrations. Involving itself in these processes is an important way for the Parks Department to obtain a wider influence on the appearance of the district at large. This is all the work of the client side. Contractors may be asked to prune, plant or remove the trees and deploy the necessary skills but in this they will be employed by the owner even though it may be the parks client that specifies the work, provides the initial estimates of cost and supervises what is done.

Preserving trees

The planning legislation helps to protect trees but it is only as effective as those who apply its rules in each locality. Tree preservation orders are costly to install and are time consuming and difficult to police but they do give some protection to esteemed existing trees. It is not worth applying to every scrubby tree or those that are entering a period of terminal decline. The legislation stipulates that the orders should be applied to trees when their retention 'is in the interests of amenity'. It does not say what is precisely meant by this which gives a good deal of choice and is open to argument.

Orders can be challenged but once they are in place it becomes an offence to cut the tree down, or wilfully destroy it, or top or lop it without permission from the local authority. If authorities suspect that a protected tree is going to be removed or injured they can go to court and obtain an injunction to prevent it. They may need to act quickly and the parks managers should be alert and let the Planning Department know if they suspect that an important tree is under threat. 'Cursed be he that removeth his neighbour's landmark' says

Deuteronomy 27.17. It is the thought that underlies the tree preservation order, indeed the penalties for contravening an order are unfortunately so light that a curse might be the more powerful sanction.

To establish an order each individual tree has to be surveyed and catalogued. The owners and the occupiers must be notified and they can object in which case the order is not effective until it is confirmed. Section 61 of the 1976 Act introduced temporary orders effective immediately and lasting for six months. Not a bad idea. They should be applied as a matter of course when notifications are made. They were introduced because owners not wanting the constraints that an order would place on their freedom of action sometime took out their axes before they were in place. Rear Admiral Hopper giving evidence to the United States Congressional Committee on Defence once said 'It is easier to apologise afterwards than to get permission before'.

Objections can be lodged when orders are proposed. The planning authority confirms the order itself under provisions in the *Local Government Planning and Land Act 1980* but if the order is contested it must hold a public enquiry at which evidence may be called.

The orders do not confer immortality. Trees decay, die back; need pruning to take out dangerous or dead branches; or they may need complete removal. This work can only be done with the consent of the planning authority. Sometimes this power is delegated to the Planning Department — sometimes retained in the jurisdiction of the committee itself. Permission to remove trees entirely is sometimes linked to a requirement to plant others in their place. This should always be done when the conditions are approriate. Advice should be offered to the owner, so that the work is done properly, a well grown tree is chosen and that it is given every chance to survive.

The local authority can enforce an order to replace a tree under section 103 of the *Town and Country Planning Act 1971* and under section 91 it can plant the tree itself and recover the cost of doing so from the landowner. In Conservation areas much the same rules apply except that all the trees are affected, good and bad alike.

The problem with all legislation is enforcement. Local authorities do not have eyes everywhere nor can they afford systematic supervision of other peoples trees. Neighbours sometimes complain but by then the damage is done. Worse still for the enforcement agency the courts take a fairly lenient view of transgressors, sometimes imposing a fine not much more than they would exact for a parking offence. The threat of legal action about trees is more potent than the reality. It is more fruitful to seek the cooperation of owners so that they recognise the value to the community of the trees that they own, understand and accept their responsibilities and know that they can easily obtain sound advice about their treatment and safety from the local authority.

Disputes

There is a lively history of contention about trees. Dangers to people, property or convenience can easily excite the litigious. There is thus a large body of common law about them. This affects trees that local authorities own whether they are in parks or not as well as other people's trees which neighbour local authority property. It is best to avoid an expensive court case by negotiation and through skilled understanding management long before an impasse is reached. A court is not likely to see tree preservation as its overriding aim and is very likely to put human convenience ahead of vegetation.

Trees can be a nuisance in a variety of ways and nuisances can be actionable at law. The branches may grow across the boundary and intrude onto a neighbouring property. The neighbour can cut them back whether the owner likes it or not no matter what butchery is done to the tree in the process. To do the work the boundary must not be crossed and the branches belong to the owner of the tree but that is cold comfort. Better by far that the department gets the work done properly and with respect for the shape and condition of the tree. Prevarication stimulates self help. The same rights apply to roots though they are harder to tackle. Tree preservation orders are no help because they do not transcend the right of a neighbour to abate a nuisance and in any case it is very rare that tree preservation orders are applied to the authority's own trees.

A more serious matter occurs if a tree is responsible for damage to property or injury to people. All trees should be systematically inspected twice a year, once in summer so that the health of the tree is easy to see and again in the winter when dead wood can be spotted. Necessary action should be taken promptly. Records should be kept for future reference. The *Occupiers Liability Act 1957* and the *Health and Safety at Work Act* also affect trees and oblige the person responsible to ensure that they are safe.

There are circumstances when giving bad advice may produce a liability if it eventually results in injury or damage. Watch out!

A designer may be liable if an unsuitable tree is planted which then causes damage. Planting a poplar near a house built on a clay soil might be an example.

District Councils can insist that dangerous trees are dealt with even if they are growing on private property under the *Local Government (Miscellaneous Provisions) Act 1976* Section 23, they can do the work and charge for it if the owner will not cooperate, if the council refuses to use its powers it may become liable itself. Highway authorities have powers to deal with trees that may endanger people using road and can require owners to cut back offending branches when they obstruct a pathway or road.

Roots can cause an actionable nuisance as well. It is not so easy to see early signs of root damage but the inspector should be on the alert for paths or garden walls which show signs of heaving, and should suspect quick growing trees which are near to buildings or in the vicinity of drains as a matter of course. The foundations may be affected by the physical increase in the girth of the roots.

Some clay soils may shrink as the tree takes up water so that foundations shift. On such soils the prudent landscape designer keeps trees away from buildings. Removing well established trees on clay soils can also cause trouble because just as the roots cause sinking by extracting water so their removal lets the water accumulate again. This causes the clay to expand. It can push buildings and walls upwards.

A tree that is an obvious danger can be considered a nuisance and the person affected can go to court to get the matter remedied by an injunction calling on the owner to make the tree safe. If a tree blocks light from a neighbouring house or office or even a greenhouse, though not the garden itself, there is a remedy at law. Sometime the sale of a property includes restrictive covenants and these can affect trees either to protect those that exist or to prevent others from being planted.

The owners of overhead power lines can do great lasting injury to trees near their installations by lopping them to make sure that the branches are kept well clear of their cables. They have the right to do this. Better to keep tree planting clear of these areas. Trees that have been lopped especially by unskilled staff look unsightly for a long time afterwards. The growth of new shoots is so fast after lopping that the process will be needed again all too soon.

The manager should take care that the trees in his care are kept safe and are dealt with promptly when they cause a genuine nuisance. Trees that have poisonous and attractive fruit should be excluded from public planting schemes and trees near buildings should be selected with care avoiding those which are known to cause trouble, generally the ones that grow quickly and have vigorous invasive roots, or are apt to shed branches without warning. Records should be kept of all the the trees in the ownership of the authority, the results of inspections and of the work that was done. If a complaint looks as if it is the precursor to a claim the matter should be passed at once to the council's legal department and handled by them from the outset.

Semi-mature trees

New developments or changes in a familiar landscape beget demands for the use of the so called semi-mature trees. They appear to save the time of waiting for an established landscape to develop. Techniques of moving large trees and machines for the purpose have improved dramatically since this type of tree first became the darling of town planners in the 1960s. Their use has been given a further boost by the garden festivals which in Britain have generally taken place with insufficient time to create a well established landscape in which to set them. The concept goes back to the great landscape gardeners of the eighteenth century and perhaps before. The trees can vary in height from five to fifteen metres and can weigh anything up to twelve tonnes depending a great deal on the size of the root ball which can be as much as three metres across and one deep.

There are two drawbacks. One is the cost which is many times greater than that of a well grown young tree from a nursery. The other is the rate at which the trees establish and start to look at home in their new locations. Some never do, and a proportion die completely. By then the architect or planner who chose to use them will be forgotten. The responsibility and the blame will have settled on the maintenance manager. It is desirable to influence the choice of tree from the outset and to object if a bad one is made.

Young well grown trees will generally look better and grow faster and soon give more weight to the landscape. If good ten year old specimen trees are chosen from a nursery where they have been grown with the skill needed to produce a well balanced head of strong branches and a compact fibrous root system and if they are planted close together in a group their immediate impact on the scene is likely to be just as great as a semi-mature tree which will be twenty or thirty years old and slow to adapt to the new conditions. After a year or two the young trees if they have been planted carefully in well manured fertile soil will be much better.

If semi-mature trees have to be used they should be selected individually. The best source is a nursery in which they will have been transplanted regularly when small. The strongest roots will have been severed every second year so that the root system is kept to a manageable size. If this has not been done the chosen trees should be prepared at least two years in advance by severing the strong roots to encourage fibrous ones to grow.

The tree should be moved in the dormant season, mistrust those who say it can be moved in leaf with the help of clear plastic transplanting sprays which stop or reduce transpiration. It should be lifted with as many of its roots as possible and these should be covered and kept moist during transplanting. The new hole should be big enough to accommodate the whole root system without crushing. The tree should be securely anchored, and the hole filled with top soil which must be rammed into place. As an insurance it is a good idea to plant a group of young trees close by. If the following growing season is dry the tree should be watered by flooding the soil to its full depth and even then a transplanting spray may be needed to reduce the water loss. A lot of trouble? It certainly is and not to be undertaken without good reason.

Planting trees

It goes without saying that trees should be suited to the conditions in which they are to be planted and should not grow bigger than the space that is going to be available but neither should they be so small that they are out of scale.

That makes choosing them complicated enough but add the requirement that trees of several species should be chosen (though planted in groups of a kind) so that a calamity to one type does not mean disaster for the whole scheme; that they should be appropriate in appearance; have features of interest which decorate and adorn the area with flowers, fruit, varied forms interesting leaves, autumn colour; and have roots that will not invade neighbouring drains and foundations, — the process becomes one of high skill. It is too often undervalued.

All plant material should conform to B.S. 3936 part 1. Either the client or the contractor will be responsible for obtaining it depending on the arrangements envisaged in the tender documents. The size can be specified but the quality is more important. It should be obtained from a reputable source, be true to type, free from pests and disease, and with no perennial weeds mingled with the roots. In obtaining quotations the botanical name of the plant should be stated to ensure that all the tenders relate to exactly the same type. Recommended sizes are given in the British standard but nursery catalogues will give a better idea of what is actually available. There is no advantage in specifying something that cannot be obtained.

Before planting it is essential to find out where underground services are. The client should know about them in designing the scheme but contractors should be obliged to check and satisfy themselves. The trouble is that even the owners of cables may not know exactly where they are or at what depth. I remember a group of gardeners planting street trees. To make holes in the iron hard verge of a road is tough work. They were banned from using a crowbar because of the risk of shallow or unrecorded cables or pipes. They used one secretly. It burst through an electric cable. The end of the bar melted.The man pirouetted. The nearby estate was cut off. Instead of reporting it, the squad, fearful of the consequences, finished planting the tree and went away. The Electricity Board came to find it enveloped in a cloud of steam emitted by boiling earth. Telephone and television cables are just as vulnerable. Caution is essential when planting in streets or near developments even when it is supposed that there are no obstructions.

In other respects conventional horticultural advice is still entirely relevant. It deserves repetition because tree planting is one of the most important landscape tasks. It affects the appearance of a place for generations.

It is best to observe the conventional planting season which varies from country to country and even from district to district. It starts a fortnight earlier in the north of Scotland for example compared with the south of England and in some seasons can go on for a month later. Choose the dormant season for deciduous plants, and moist spells at the beginning and the end of it for evergreens. Container grown trees can be planted at any time but they need watering in dry spells if planting is done in the growing season. This adds to the expense. They are dearer to buy. The extra cost is only justified if it is essential to finish off a planting scheme perhaps for an opening or to give an immediate settled appearance to a landscape. It is not justified by impatience.

I once went to an interview for a job that involved supervising contractors who were employed to plant trees on sites scattered up and down the country. The question was asked 'What is the most likely cause of failure'. I answered 'choosing the wrong species for the site'. The right answer was even more mundane. It was 'allowing the roots to dry out before planting'. Thirty years on and desiccated roots are still the most frequent reason for the failure of newly planted trees. Vigilance is good advice for all clients and DSO supervisors. The tree may indeed burst into leaves later on simply because there is sap in the stems but the growth will not be sustained and the plants are quite likely to die or remain stunted.

Holes should be big enough for the root system without cramping; new fertile soil should be imported if existing soil is poor; the base of the hole should be broken up and well rotted compost or manure worked into it; the tree should be at the same depth as in the nursery as shown by the colour change on the stem; planting should be firm; the ground should be lightly forked after planting to admit light and air.

Staking is a vexed question. There is now plenty of evidence to suggest that development of a tree trunk is impeded by a stake. However street trees cannot be left to sway in a wind so they still require support. Where they are likely to be damaged by vandals usually after dark, they may also need a guard though even the best of these do not confer invulnerability. A grease band works wonders if placed at the top of the stake, the hand of iniquity will release it in shocked, slimed revulsion.

Pruning

Pruning is highly skilled work and is difficult to specify. Trees can be easily ruined. The client for most street trees, which are the ones most likely to be pruned, is the Roads Department. They will surely require advice. This should be volunteered because they will not necessarily know they need it. Bad work ruins the look of the whole district not only the individual trees, and may destroy the painstaking husbandry of many years by former parks departments.

Pruning may be needed to make trees safe; reduce the loss of light experienced by neighbouring properties; and allow the passage, unscathed, of double decker buses which are tilted towards street trees by the camber of roads. Older trees of species unsuited to the space available may need pruning to keep them in bounds as a better alternative to removing them entirely. Dead wood should be removed whenever it appears.

Crown thinning is the most common operation. The object is to remove as many branches as necessary to allow more light whilst keeping the tree's natural shape. It also reduces wind resistance and may make a tree safer in gales. The first step is to remove crossing, badly placed and damaged branches then to take out the minimum of live healthy wood to secure the desired effect. The branch being removed must be cut first on the underside to stop tearing as it falls or is lowered, then the stump should be cut flush with its point of origin. Big wounds should be pared smooth with a sharp knife to facilitate healing. Painting with a bituminous paint used to be recommended as an aid to healing and for cosmetic reasons, but recent research has shown this to trap moisture which encourages rot forming organisms.

Lopping, the euphemism for which is crown reduction, should only be done as a last resort, only on broad leaved trees, and only as a precursor to building a new crown. It may alleviate the immediate cause of complaints but subsequent growth is so rapid that they soon return, and the tree is made ugly however well the work may be done. The branches may be shortened to other branches or side growths. Sometimes it may be necessary to cut back to a stump. The work should be directed from the ground so that a semblance of the tree's shape is kept.

Occasionally trees have to be felled. In conservation areas or if the trees are covered by a preservation order, this needs planning permission. Felling is skilled work especially when the space is limited near buildings. In such situations the tree must be taken down in sections and each piece lowered to the ground. The work should only be done by experienced staff. The potential for accidents is high.

Large pieces of timber from tree work should be sold for timber if its quality is good enough. Parks in particular sometimes contain unusual trees and their timber may be valuable. Larger pieces that are not fit for this use should be accumulated and auctioned for fire wood. In most areas demand will be brisk. The best way of disposing of brush and small branches is to shred them using a brushwood chipping machine. This reduces them to a fraction of their bulk and makes carting easy. The product after being stacked for a time can be used as a mulch. The alternative is to burn it but this is undesirable for environmental reasons. Specifications should not only state the desired work they should make it clear how the arisings are to be used.

Trees suffer from a number of diseases and it will almost certainly fall to the client to watch for them. Nothing looks worse than dead trees or is more likely to be the subject of adverse public comment. They should be removed at once.

Most diseases are impractical to control because of the size of the trees and the difficulty of treating them. In some cases there is no cure. Some such as tar spot of sycamore are generally so mild in their effect that they can be safely ignored.

The best remedies are to use a variety of trees even though they are planted in groups of a kind and to ensure that a succession of various age groups is present through a steady programme of new planting even into parks that already appear well stocked. Provision for the work should be made in the annual estimates and in the tender documents. New trees should be inspected to see that they are healthy so that disease is not introduced. Contractors and DSOs should only be allowed to get their plants from reputable nurseries.

Dealing with rots and cavities which are the most frequent disorders can be expensive and before it is undertaken the value of the tree, its projected life, and its importance need assessing carefully and testing against the cost of replacement. If the rot has progressed too far the tree may be dangerous and then should be removed. Shallow rots can be cut out till healthy wood is reached then left. Deeper cavities can be opened in the same way but they should be cut so they let water run out. At one time they would have been filled. Not now. It is best to leave them open so they can be inspected easily. If appearances demand it, the hole can be covered with fine-meshed wire which should be a sufficient disguise.

There are several common diseases on park trees in Britain. The *Plant Health Act 1967* permits orders to be made with a view to preventing the spread of certain diseases, Dutch Elm Disease being an example. Fire Blight and Watermark Disease of Willows are notifiable diseases under the act. Managers should at least know what the the most common diseases are and be able to recognise them.

Anthracnose on London plane is caused by a fungus. The disease causes most trouble in a wet spring. Young leaves and shoots die, the tree looks sparse. Secondary growth later disguises the effect. The shoots develop cankers. Weeping willow suffers from anthracnose too but it is caused by a different fungus. The leaves become distorted and they and the young shoots die. The shoots develop cankers. The tree recovers later in the season but growth can be stunted.

Fire Blight is a bacterial disease which affects the members of the family *rosaceae* which provides a number of important ornamental trees including the whitebeam which is the worst troubled. In the spring the young foliage, shoots, and flowers wilt and then wither turning dark brown or black as if they had been scorched. The tree may be killed. Infected trees should be removed promptly and burnt. Poplar canker is also a bacterial disease. It causes the death of shoots and branches and sometimes kills the whole tree. Avoid susceptible species and types.

Dutch elm disease is all too familiar. There are not many elm trees left in England as a result of it though the disease has not yet reached all parts of Scotland. Removal of infected trees and the destruction of the bark checks the spread of the disease which is caused by a fungus carried by the elm bark beetle. Beech bark disease is caused by a fungus and the beech scale insect. The insect weakens the bark so that the fungus can gain a foothold. It can kill even large and well established trees but it has not become the major scourge that was predicted of it. Honey fungus can also kill trees and shrubs and will march along a hedgerow. Phytophthora root rot can do the same though mainly on water-logged soil.

Gas in the soil can wipe out a row of street trees. Drought kills big trees that cannot adapt quickly enough or adjust to a changing water table. It is becoming a major killer in parts of Britain. Other diseases occur but are sometimes confined to a particular place. Oak wilt is a killer disease of oak trees in North America. Import and other restrictions help to prevent the spread of this and other troubles for example importing christmas trees from Scandinavia into Britain even those given for public display by one city to another is strictly controlled and indeed resisted.

Community forests

The idea of a community forest is not a new one, the Vienna Woods are an example of what is now presented under the name, the Bos Park near Amsterdam is another, more recent. In Britain Epping Forest and the New Forest have many of the characteristics of what is now proposed, so does the residue of Sherwood Forest near Edwinstowe in Nottinghamshire and areas of bush preserved near some Australian cities. Some British cities have extensive woodland and sometimes this is close to Forestry Commission land. If they are not linked together already efforts should be made to make footpaths and plant shelter belts so that they can be read as an entity in future and share in the qualities of what is proposed on a larger scale in the community forests.

The Countryside and Forestry Commissions made a proposal in 1989 to create community forests in England in the grand manner. Twelve are at present proposed and there are two planned in Wales. The first trees have already been planted in the South Staffordshire Forest which is to lie between Walsall and Cannock Chase, Wolverhampton and Lichfield. A forest to be called Thames Chase has been inaugurated. It runs from Brentwood south towards Thurrock and eastwards from Dagenham and Upminster. In the North East of England the first tree was planted in April 1990 in a forest which is to embrace south Tyne and Wear and north east Durham. These are large areas.

The forests will affect recreation in all the urban communities near them. Expect the others to follow and more after that. The idea is one from which every country might learn.

The proposal is to designate forests of up to 15,000 hectares. There is a mixture of reasons for doing this. This will help to heal old scars, and create a better richer environment for wild life and other elements of the flora besides trees. There are landscape and aesthetic considerations. The forests will change and it is hoped improve the appearance of whole tracts of countryside getting rid of eyesores or enveloping them in vegetation, giving cohesion to disparate landscape elements.

They have important recreational potential and will allow access to a wide range of pursuits within the forest. Surveys have shown that more than 80 per cent of the British population visits the countryside for recreation at least once a year. The forests may encourage more.

Villages have amenity and recreational needs. These include access to footpaths, woods and playing fields. Although a rural community seems to be rich in space in practice little of it is accessible or capable of public use.

The forests will eventually permit timber production on a big scale. To do this they will need skilled management. It is true that a wood will sustain itself after a fashion. Some people advocate that it should be left to take its natural course. Some wild woods should certainly exist but they are not likely to permit of economic timber production and doing nothing is not conservation. Most of the woods planted will be cropped with trees and the income they can generate will be one of the motors that may bring them into being. They should be managed to give continuity and planted with a varied range of species to give a diverse sylvan tapestry and to permit recreational use but the main aim must be make them economically viable. Birds and wild mammals and undergrowth will follow.

They are to have a mixture of recreational uses: walking, cycling, horse riding, fishing in the streams and ponds, orienteering, fun runs, picnicking, sitting in the open air, nature study, caravanning, attending festivals, exhibitions, concerts, visiting farms with rare breeds, walking round sculpture and nature trails, and so on. The whole will be harmonised by large scale tree planting. Recognise the formula? It is the urban park writ large.

The forests are not to be in any one ownership. The proposals anticipate the cooperation of people who already own land in the areas. Farmers, local authorities, the forestry commission which are major participants in the scheme, and owners of derelict land. They will be encouraged to participate by grants and of course by cajolery.

There are many grants that can be applied for the purpose and which are also of interest for smaller scale projects in all areas not just those that happen to have been chosen as forests. The Forestry Commission woodland grant schemes; the farm woodland and set-aside schemes run by the Ministry of Agriculture; grants from the Countryside Commission; grants for the restoraion of derelict land; sponsorship from industry and commerce is anticipated. Some help will no doubt be forthcoming from planning agreements and in some areas money may be available from the European Community. It is hoped to stimulate and harness a great voluntary effort.

The idea of the forests represents a great opportunity. If they are a success they will change the face of large tracts of country on the fringe of urban areas and even surround some of them in a sylvan embrace. They will call for considerable skills of land, forest and outdoor recreational and park management, and sensitive aesthetic judgement. A botched job on the scale involved will be an error indeed.

Environmental impact assessment

The European Commission issued a directive on the subject of environmental impact assessments in July 1988. It requires developers seeking planning permission for certain types of development to submit formal statements intended to describe the environmental costs and benefits of what is proposed. It can be expected that more types of development will be included as time goes by. In Britain the statements are prepared by the applicants. In Australia the statements are paid for by the applicant but independent consultants are appointed by the planning authority to make the assessments. In Holland a commission has been appointed to do the work.

The procedure formalises what have long been central considerations of planning committees faced with all proposed developments no matter what their size. The park manager has an interest in both the formal and the informal assessments when these impact on landscape, open space, planting and botanical matters. Planning departments may not always consult. If they do not then make a fuss: first to them but if that yields no result then to members of the council.

Environmental friendliness

Park systems may seem to be environment friendly by definition. Not a bit of it. Some horticultural practices involve the use of lethal chemicals — weedkillers, insecticides, fungicides, growth regulators; parks gardening techniques can swallow peat bogs; green keepers wipe out worms on lawns; conservatories and greenhouses spew out heat generated by burning fossil fuels; mowers, tractors, lorries, and vans, burn various subspecies of oil; all kinds of goods are purchased wrapped in reels of paper and cardboard; park seats are sometimes made from tropical hardwoods ripped out of rain forests so are some kinds of highly durable fencing; bonfires still pollute the air, even leaves are burnt in some places. There is the strongest case for amending some of these practices and telling the public that this has been done so that they can follow the lead.

Some chemicals probably have to be used but they should be a last and not a first resort and should not be applied as a matter of routine. This can be achieved by suitable wording of tender documents. Weed killers should only be used on turf when perfect grass is a necessity. Not many lawns qualify for the treatment. Golf and bowling greens do and so do the finest ornamental lawns where perfection is needed as a foil for flower beds.Such areas will not usually be large. If they are consider redesigning them.

Elsewhere nature should be left to take its course assisted by changes in cultural techniques which include accepting herb rich turf; letting grass get longer occasionally so that it smothers mosses; making sure that the grass grows quicker and better than its opposition on games pitches where a uniform turf with an even texture is desirable; by spiking, top dressing, reseeding with durable modern varieties of grasses; choosing the most advantageous length of cut when mowing.

Weed killers among shrubs can be avoided by close planting so that a weed smothering canopy is quickly established or by the use of ground cover plants and by mulching using bark or compost. Leaves that fall in borders should be left to lie where they are. Soil acting residual weed killers are still the most economical way of keeping weeds down among roses which have an open canopy that lets plenty of light through to allow weed growth beneath but even they can be mulched successfully provided that the material is laid down deeply enough.

Fungicide and insecticides should be seldom needed in parks. They have a place on fine turf to control the variety of afflictions to which it is prone but not on larger grass areas. The need for them on roses, antirrhinums, and some other plants can be minimised by the choice of disease resistant varieties.

The same principles which used to inform the cultivation of farm and vegetable crops should be applied to ornamentals. Rotation of species is possible in flower beds so avoiding a build up of soil borne pests and diseases quite apart from ringing the changes so as not to bore regular visitors out of their minds. No planting scheme should rely too much on a single species. The lesson of Dutch elm disease and the devastation it wrought on the English landscape is evidence enough.

Designers should use a number of different genera. Pests and diseases are attracted to monocultures simply because they find the living so easy. Once installed they can do an exaggerated amount of damage. It is true that roses and daffodils used for mass display have to be planted in large tracts of a single genus but these should be the exception. The mixed border in which shrubs, trees, herbaceous plants, bulbs and annuals are planted together is as good as fungicide at limiting the spread of plant diseases quite apart from its cheerful impact on the landscape.

As for killing worms that should be anathema to everyone. It certainly is to the worms. Only two of the twenty five British species of worms throw casts and even they limit the activity mainly to the Autumn when the moist soil brings them near to the surface. Only on the finest turf are they a genuine problem but on such areas the casts are easily scattered along with the morning dew by switching them away with a long flexible cane nowadays often made of plastic. Killing one species of worm kills them all and robs the soil for the next thirty years or more of a large industrious band of workers continually engaged in improving it.

Good hygiene should be practised where vulnerable plants are grown, for example fallen rose leaves which carry black spot disease from one year to the next should be cleared away so should prunings and with them the clusters of eggs of insect pests. Conservatories should be kept clear of plant debris which harbours pests and may act as centres of fungal infection, the glass should be washed down so that all the winter daylight is admitted and healthy plant growth is promoted. There has been a revival of interest in biological controls and these should certainly be tried. Stocks of most important predators of pests of economic significance are available for purchase, thus it is possible to buy encarsid bugs to kill white fly. In California the Mediterranean fruit fly is a feared pest, troublesome, costly, and efficient at reproduction. It is a serious matter in a state that produces $16 million worth of fruit every year. Biologists have discovered sex. They have found how to sterilise the male flies and they propose to release enough to overwhelm the whole fly population. Enough infertile males and there will not be new generations of flies to cause future trouble. If it works watch out for the same idea to be propounded for other pests of economic importance.

Two hundred years ago carbon dioxide made up 0.28 per cent of the world's atmosphere today it is 0.035 per cent, a quarter more. It absorbs heat better than most of the other gases in the air so it traps the heat that arrives as light, and stops it from radiating back into space. It cloaks the earth like an eiderdown. In the little ice age which lasted from the 13th century to the end of the 18th the river Thames froze solid in winter around London Bridge and glaciers grew in Norway and the Alps. Icebergs drifted closer to the equator. Temperatures then are thought to have been a mere one degree centigrade cooler on average than now. Add the same amount and ice melts at the poles, low lying places get flooded as the seas rise, climate and vegetation changes. Good, says the Aberdonian contemplating a crop of oranges in the garden, bad, says almost everybody else watching a desert spread or familiar plants dying.

The annual carbon dioxide produced by a single British household would fill a British Rail intercity train from one end to the other, it would fill the house itself at least four times over. There would be 20 tonnes of it. Britain is not the worst offender. There are three countries in Western Europe and twelve in the world with even more lamentable records. It not only presages environmental devastation it represents appalling waste.

Parks departments are not blameless either. They are likely to have conservatories, greenhouses, dwellings, mess rooms, tea rooms, restaurants, club houses, and a variety of other buildings each heated with fossil fuel and each contributing its share to the looming cataclysm. Fuel economy makes more than just economic sense. Every building that can be insulated, should be. The temperatures inside should be kept to a tolerable not a luxury level by the minimum necessary heating in cold climates and the minimum cooling in hot ones. In Britain help and advice can be obtained from the Department of Energy and its local agencies.

In conservatories an effort should be made to concentrate on plants that will stand low temperatures in Winter, They include a surprising number of interesting species. Even unlikely ones like cactus not only survive in winter temperatures below 4 degrees centigrade but will not flower if they are kept too warm then. Greenhouses in higher latitudes like other buildings should be insulated and double glazed when possible. The classic gardeners advice of siting them to get the maximum degree of light, sheltering them from prevailing winds which increase heat loss, and keeping the glass clean in winter to admit the maximum light and thus heat, should be followed still.

There are more positive measures. Expect to see more of them. Solar heating panels work even in Scotland. Wind generators though still expensive and visually intrusive are appearing in more and more places. In Durham the departmental greenhouses were at one time heated by the methane produced by a sewerage works, and the former parks manager there managed to get his mowing machines to run on it too. Near Aberdeen a nursery is heated by the waste heat from a whisky distillery. Cheers! These are ingenious remedies for the problem. Those who started them years ago are applauded still. Parks Departments should take the lead not only to stretch budgets and make them go further. They should also proclaim what they have done and take the kudos as well.

Peat is another problem. Good advertising and promotion made it fashionable. It eclipsed all its rivals. The introduction of soiless composts boosted the amount we use. In Britain there are 1.6 million hectares of peat. The problem is that horticultural grade peat is only obtained from a comparatively few areas in which peat bogs are disappearing and with them a unique habitat. One day, in Britain by about 2010, they are expected to be exhausted if the present rate of use is not slowed up. Before that peat will get more and more expensive as stocks get low and shortages occur. Best economise now. Look at composts based on loam again. Mulch with bark or wood-chips. Improve soil with compost not peat. Do not burn leaves and organic refuse stack them and leave them to decompose and then use the product.

The British Horticultural Development Council whose head-quarters is at Petersfield in Hampshire is a national body funded by a levy on more than 3000 producers of horticultural crops. At present they contribute 0.5 per cent of their annual turnover and such is the size of the industry that this produces £3 million. From this sum a number of research projects are funded one of them being into peat and peat substitutes.

The problem with all the feasible substitutes is that they are more expensive — some of them costing two or three times as much. They all have disadvantages of one kind or another especially for use in composts in which conditions are critical. Bark is 1.5 times dearer and it is difficult to obtain a consistent product or a guaranteed supply in the volume likely to be required; polystyrene has problems of electrostatic attraction; perlite and vermiculite are twice the price; municipal solid waste is cheap and abundant but presents problems of eliminating pathogens and can contain heavy metals and glass; coir is two or three times as dear and there are problems of fungal spores; animal wastes are more fertiliser than soil conditioner. Composted straw the use of which might solve another problem; spent mushroom compost which relies heavily on peat itself; pumica, and other materials are all being studied.

Adjust the specifications next time round to make them more environment friendly. Make sure that seats are not bought if they are made from tropical hardwoods even though they may have far off sounding names. Some local authorities ban their use already. Complain when goods arrive in excessive packaging, not only is it waste but you pay for it.

If a tree is removed it should be replaced. If it is then made into paper there is a net reduction in the carbon dioxide in the atmosphere. This book is 40 per cent carbon. As long as it exists the carbon will stay where it is, as safe as if it were in a bank, and doing more good, or less harm, than if it were floating about. A sustainably managed forest yielding its timber for paper on which to express environmental opinions on sustainably managed forests is the ultimate in benign recycling.

Recycle materials — not just paper. Make sure the park restaurant uses a bottle bank. Better still give preference to suppliers who put their product in returnable containers whether bottles or anything else. Old hat? Certainly, but you would be surprised how few departments and DSOs pay heed to these simple easily introduced economies. There is the story of the Aberdonian who went for a hip operation and afterwards asked for the bone to make soup. It is the exaggerated example of recycling and frugal management. Both make good sense.

Quality audits

One of the jobs I have often been asked to do since becoming a consultant is to advise on the quality of park and open space maintenance and how it can be improved and what should be done to develop the service. The fashionable term for the process is quality audit.

Exposing grounds maintenance to competitive tendering is not a new idea nor is it confined to Britain. There is a danger however in the present British arrangements. The skills and the responsibilities which used be involved in managing a park have been abruptly divided between contractor and client. Each is concerned with enforcing tender documents, the client to get his or her money's worth the contractor to ensure payment for every job that is done. In many places the consequence has been that the service has become static, unchanging and unresponsive to shifting public tastes.

Every manager of an open space will be used to receiving generalised complaints. They usually take the line that things are not as good as they used to be, or at least as they ought to be. Complaints like this are so imprecise that it is hard to make sense of them. A quality audit must be specific so that the manager can act on it. Of course it is necessary to get a general impression but this must then be broken down into its detail.

The first point of reference should be the tender document and the management plan, if there is one. Sometimes these are too vague and can be interpreted in a variety of ways. Very often they omit any recognition that there is a service to the public involved. Despite the popularity of the cliche itself they are mostly silent about customer care.

Use of consultants

Not every local authority uses a consultant but on occasions one can be of use in applying a new mind to a problem. They can be used to resolve disputes between client and contractor being independent or both. They can suggest ways in which a parks system might be revitalised either at great cost or in the case of Aberdonians at little.

Standards

At their best contracts are partnerships albeit vigilant ones, but they can become rancorous and ill tempered. Even former friendly colleagues who separately became client and contractor find themselves in permanent mutual exasperation. The main problems arise because of different perceptions of quality and resentment over matters of supervision.

The idea that it might be construed as unfair competition stopped some authorities from insisting in tender documents that B.S.5750 on quality accreditation should be applied to contractors. A system of formal quality monitoring is desirable even where the standard has not been enforced. Both the contractor and the client should be involved in it. It does not in itself produce good work: that can only be the product of well written documents and attentive supervision by both the parties concerned. Firm measures should be taken if standards slip.

Some problems stem from inadequate supervision often on the incorrect supposition that 'in-house' contractors will behave with consistent righteousness whereas in practice they are under the same pressures as private ones and react in precisely the same ways. They have to work to the prices they have given. These may have been pared below the desirable minimum under pressure of competition. They may wish to demonstrate their competence by making handsome profits, they may even be allowed to share in them. The creation of client and contract units and the allocation of staff between them may have left both with insufficient skills — contractors may not recognise problems and deficiencies when they see them. They may deliberately use inferior methods or take short cuts.

Let me illustrate the point by telling you about one system of parks and open spaces that I was asked to look at after there had been a flood of complaints by members of the public. The grumbles were directed to councillors at their surgeries and to the local press who in response started a campaign. It was the client who was the target. The contractor was perceived as doing what he had been told and was almost anonymous anyway. There was a host of problems some of them small in themselves but together they gave the impression of a badly managed service.

First the omission. No one had told the contractor to ensure that litter was removed from the parks before mowing. Early on in the season there was little anyway so the problem went unheeded. However there was a warm spell and the park enjoyed an exceptionally busy weekend. A lot of paper had been left behind. By ill chance the contractor arrived early on Monday and cut the paper scattered grass. The litter was shredded into a myriad fragments. It became a degenerate confetti. The complaints started to flow, the press took them up and supported them by photographs, the public impression of the department plunged.

The mowing machine operators had missed the corners of lawns and verges when cutting the grass. This increased the speed of work which the contractor rewarded unduly. The effect was to make everywhere look unkempt. By the time I saw it the growth was so thick that the mower was unable to tackle it. In the longer term some redesign should be undertaken so that the machines used can do the work more conveniently. This would be to everyone's advantage. In the short term it was simply a matter of enforcing the contract.

Summer bedding plants were doing badly. The problem was that specification had told the contractor to water the plant after planting but not to ensure that the soil was moist to its full depth beforehand. The plants had been put out in a dry spell, had been given insufficient water and had suffered a major set back. In the most important locations a new start was suggested using pelargoniums that had been grown in pots. In less conspicuous places the inferior display could be tolerated but since this was feasible the beds could be eliminated or replaced by something easier to keep.

Some newly planted trees and shrubs were dying and as they were numerous they were very noticeable. 'They can't even grow trees' was a grumble made by a councillor. The contractor had allowed the roots to dry out — it takes time to protect them from desiccation. They had been exposed during their transport from nursery to site and whilst awaiting planting were left to lie on the surface. If they were not dead on arrival the cold drying winds soon finished them off. Apart from the expense of putting things right it is a serious waste of resources and time. It should be given the highest degree of supervision. Once the plants are in the ground it is impossible to tell that anything is wrong until they die in the summer and by then it is not necessarily clear what has been the cause.

Many out of the way corners had been ignored altogether from the start of the season, others were omitted when the operator was pressed for time. This was a failure of supervision by both sides.

The bowling greens had been fertilised (omitting fertiliser or applying less than the amount specified is an old trick) but the material had been applied unevenly with consequent discoloration where too much had gone on and ghastly pallor where there had been too little. The problem arose from the use of an unskilled operator and the absence of an effective training programme.

The greens and other fine turf areas had been watered but not enough had been applied and the turf was suffering from drought. The water that had been applied was put on during the day when most of it had been evaporated by drying winds and the sun. The specification was silent on this point and should be revised next time round. The best time for irrigation is during the later evening or at night. Only if skies are overcast and rain is threatened or falling is it fully effective in the day even though irrigation then elicits wry comments from members of the public.

Examining the effectiveness of a park

The first step is to look at the philosophy of management, what would nowadays be called the objectives, if any clear ones exist. Often they do not. If not they should be evolved and written down so that everybody concerned can read them. They can be elaborated and amended as time goes on. The first aim is to secure the maximum degree of enjoyable use of all parks and open spaces by as many people as possible. They might also be seen as tourist attractions or as means of so improving a run down area that industry is attracted to establish itself there. Firms on the move do quality audits of their own before they settle on a new location in which to set up or expand, environmental factors are becoming ever more significant when these choices are made.

It may be necessary to look at the ways the parks are distributed through an area; whether enough open space is stipulated for new developments; where new ones can be planned. These are matters which properly concern the Town Planner but they are also crucial matters for the Park Manager as well who has an interest in the success of the system, in the hierarchy of spaces ranging from decorative incidental open spaces, small gardens and play areas, through local parks and amenities, right up to the largest urban and country parks.

There is a host of smaller matters that determine the success of an individual park. A great many questions have to be asked. Are people attracted into the parks? If not, why? Are they forbidding in themselves? Too dark and gloomy perhaps? Do people know where they are and what they proffer? Are there programmes of entertainments? Are these imaginative? Do they attract audiences?

Is the fullest use made of grants and other sources of external finance? Is the possibility of sponsorship considered?

Is the park properly marketed and if so where and with what view? Is there an adequate flow of media attention and if not what can be done to stimulate it? Are there regular press releases and press conferences when particularly important matters are to be presented? Is advantage taken of photo opportunities for instance when the first crocus appears?

What are the hours and times of opening and closing if any? Some public gardens are still fenced and gated and present formidable barriers to would be entrants after their official hours of opening are over. The standard hours of closing ignore one of the reasons why at least a proportion of town dwellers use parks and public gardens. Research in America has shown that an increasing number of the patrons are in middle or even late middle age. They are there to court one another. The phenomenon derives from the pioneering American matrimonial system of serial monogamy which generates successive courtships. Public gardens in Britain and elsewhere in the world would be used more if the management kept them open later.

Gardens in the gloaming are full of perfumes that are elusive at other times of day. It used to be the great privilege of being a student at the Royal Horticultural Society at Wisley near Guildford in Surrey that the garden could be explored at dusk or later. The air was laden with scent: Azaleas, Daphnes, Cytisus, Viburnums, Philadelphus, Loniceras, Jasminums, Roses, Primulas, and even in Winter the fragrance of Hamamelis. A garden can be an olfactory paradise when it is most likely to be closed to the public. There is the strongest case for instituting twilight and even better moonlight walks even if permanent opening is not possible.

What is the attitude of the staff to the customers would they prefer to be without them or do they recognise that they are the life blood of the park? Are they friendly do they greet patrons with a smile, will they stop to pass the time of day? When I started work the gardener leaning on his spade dispensing homely wisdom to the passing trade was so familiar that he became a caricature, but he kept people coming back for a friendly word? He survived the widespread introduction of bonus schemes but has largely disappeared with compulsory tendering.

The peripatetic maintenance squad is the best way of maintaining scattered small sites. It is increasingly used to maintain bigger ones as well. Something is lost. Regular staff assumed proprietorship. They knew their regular customers and were often able to address them by name — a recent subject of pride to the Post Office in its advertising campaign.

Is there reference to customer care in the tender documents? The contractor's staff is just as involved as the client. If not there should be and an appropriate clause should be put at the next opportunity difficult as it may be to specify, to manage, and police thereafter. Are children and families made welcome? Are there plenty of things for them to do? Is evidence of vandalism removed promptly? Is graffiti removed the same day that it appears?

Is there a museum or gallery or a library in the park? They sometimes can be found in occupancy of the mansion house around which the original park was built especially in older towns. What is the level of liaison between the managements? Is the opportunity taken of outdoor sculpture exhibitions or indoor interpretive ones? Are readings of children's books encouraged in the playgrounds? Is there an exhibition or a good collection of garden and natural history books in the library?

Are there particular features of interest so that no park is a near duplicate of another? Is there horticultural entertainment? Are there enough trees to give shelter and verdure and homes for wild birds and a sense of enclosure? Are new buildings and features under consideration — conservatories, outdoor ice rinks, an agricultural museum, displays of domestic animals or rare breeds, aviaries? Is the park redolent of loving care?

Is it safe to use? Is it convenient for disabled visitors? I was once challenged to go round a park in a wheel chair to find out for myself how difficult it could be. I did. It was. Afterwards I arranged for other staff to do the same. There was a steady improvement thereafter. Small obstacles were removed. The parks and buildings were made more accessible. Toilets were adapted or built. Ramps were made. More important there was an increased understanding of how difficult parks can be for anyone who is disabled.

Is there a case for a complete or a progressive redesign? Should the introduction of new features be considered? Is there a possibility of joint developments with commercial groups or others? Are the buildings in good order and doing their job well? Do any of them need adaptation or require a change of use? Are any surplus to requirements? Are some ready for demolition?

Are there enough seats? Are they well positioned in sheltered places (facing south in Britain) where people will be attracted to use them? Are they comfortable? Can they be used without extreme postural discomfort and ensuing backache? Are they appropriate in design for the location perhaps rustic log seats for wild or rural places; elaborate reproduction Victorian cast iron for the most formal gardens or close to buildings of the same age group? Are they robust enough to withstand vandalism.

Are there enough litter bins? Are they of appropriate design? Are they emptied often enough? Is there scope for an anti-litter campaign in association with the Tidy Britain Group and others? Is the park clean at the start of every day? Nothing is more apt to induce litter throwing than the existence of ungathered debris. What steps have been taken to deal with the problems that dogs can cause? Can more be done?

Are the entrances placed where they best serve the public. Are there fences? If they exist are they necessary or should they be removed? Do they protect vulnerable areas, or prevent children from running blindly into an adjacent road? Is the fence of such architectural merit as to have an intrinsic value? Is this enough to justify its retention for what it is, rather than for what it does? How well is it maintained? Are there walls around or in the park? Are they clean and in a state of good repair?

Are there prohibitory signs which can be removed? Boards displaying dire warnings or invoking rules are still too often a feature of the entrances to many parks. They destroy the sense of escape and liberty from urban constraints that should be a feature of open spaces. One kind of notice that is usually missing however is one showing the name of the park perhaps supplemented by some information about it and a word of welcome. Are there enough or any directional signs to show motorists and pedestrians how to get to the park? Has there been liaison with the motoring organisations and the Roads Department about this?

Do the details of the layout permit easy efficient economical maintenance? Are there awkward corners that can be amended or irrelevant flower beds that would be better removed or made elsewhere? Is the standard of maintenance needlessly high, or (more often) is it too low? Has there been a value analysis?

Can the individual parks be expanded? There is plenty of evidence that shows bigger parks of more than 20 hectares are in general more attractive than smaller ones? Sometimes a neigh-bouring field or derelict site can be acquired or transferred or a piece of ground that can be developed for some other use ex-changed for a larger piece that cannot. Can one park be linked to another with a footpath or a corridor of open space so that two or more smaller parks start to behave as if they were a single bigger one?

Can the park cater for all age groups? Are there children's play grounds? Do these have places for mothers to sit and watch their children play and talk together while they wait? Is there super-vision, what form does this take? Is the equipment interesting? Was some of it chosen or made specifically for the particular site? Is it properly maintained and regularly inspected? What is the nature of the surface beneath? Is it safe if a child were to fall on it? Is the equipment itself safe to use without also being deadly dull? Has there been a survey to find the level of use?

Playgrounds are easy to judge as to their success or failure by the number of children they attract, how often they feel motivated to return and how long they spend there. Does the park offer scope to climb trees or to play in a secret place among bushes? Have children been asked for their views and advice? Is there scope for play leadership, children's entertainers, mobile playgrounds with portable games equipment, travelling discos?

Does the park contain a restaurant tea room or any other catering facility? Would this increase the use of the park? Would it have enough customers would there be passing trade? Is there scope to offer it to a commercial developer? Would there be competition? Is there a chance of gain in kind, for example might the developer be required to provide a pavilion in return for the site?

Do the paths lead where people want to go? Are they in good order or do they need repair? Are they made of appropriate materials that are sympathetic to the place? Are the path edges treated suitably? In formal settings they should be neat and regularly maintained, elsewhere the standard should be more relaxed. Are there short cuts which would be better acknowledged and paved? Should little used paths be eliminated and grassed over or planted? Would the design look better without them?

Is the permanent planting, of trees and shrubs, sufficient? Is enough replacement planting being done? Are new generations of trees being introduced? Is there enough planting to give a sense of habitability and to provide shelter? If not, where should new plantations be introduced and what should they consist of? Is the colour planting well located, is its quality good enough, is there sufficient to act as a magnet for the public?

Do the games facilities permit supervision to be a single attendant? Are they sufficient, diverse, interesting? Are they in the right place? Are additional ones needed so as to increase income without increasing the cost of getting it? Are different ones needed perhaps to reflect the changing tastes and age range of the park users? How are the facilities managed? Might they be better handed over to the clubs that use them with safeguards for casual public use? Are there coaching schemes? Do they cover enough sports and relate to a wide spread of age groups? Can everyone potentially find an interest?

Is there a big enough wild flower and bird population in the park and if not how can it be encouraged to increase in quantity and range? Are efforts made to draw attention to it and explain it to visitors? Are there guided walks, explanatory signs pamphlets, books, slide shows, and videos for use in talking to groups clubs and schools?

What is the level of public participation? Have local people been consulted about what they want? Have community and other groups or even individuals been asked to join in planting schemes? Is there a council inspection? Are members of the staff asked what they think?

Is there a systematic scheme of staff training not only in the techniques of what they do but in customer care and quality control and public presentation?

Progressive improvements

In the days before competitive tendering the best parks managers looked forward to the Winter months. Routine maintenance slackened off then and there was time to do a variety of labour intensive jobs that could not find a place in the capital programme either because there was not enough money there or because they would be scorned if they were put forward.

Big and small jobs were done. Trees were planted, woods made, shrub borders refurbished, paths realigned or new ones built, adaptations were made to make the park easier to maintain in summer, playgrounds were extended or constructed.

As an example let me cite my own experience. In a succession of winters I made the largest heather garden in the country in Hazlehead Park in Aberdeen and went on to make major azalea and rose gardens there, as well as undertaking a variety of smaller improvements and adaptations. All the other parks and open spaces were developed and adapted and enriched in similar ways. The process was common throughout the country. Managers even looked forward to the advent of Winter. The result is a rich national heritage. The public respond to novelty and change and regular customers were glad to note and observe progress

Where it was not done the parks gradually died. Generations of trees are still missing in some of them. Borders are old and tired. The park system became out of date and irrelevant.

Tithonus was an ancient Greek who was badly treated by fate rather like a poll tax defaulter. His problem was his girl friend. She had attracted the attention of the god Jupiter and she asked him to give Tithonus immortality. Jupiter having an eye to the main chance did so. The problem was that she had failed to ask for eternal youth so Tithonus was condemned to millennia of senescence. He grew so old and shrivelled that he was mistaken for a grasshopper and was eventually eaten by a crow. It is a parable of what can happen to a park. It may be ever so well maintained but unless there is a constant renewal of its fabric its senescence is inevitable and after that follows disesteem and falling attendances till it is left to a few romping dogs. For the crow in the story, read developer.

The process is affected by compulsory tendering because unless adequate provision is made in the documents none of these progressive often unheralded improvements and changes will be made. The specifications that I have been asked to read and comment on, have contained few references to development work and the majority none at all. Moreover many contractors have altered the seasonal pattern of employment for parks maintenance staff so that they work longer hours in the summer and shorter ones in the winter. Personnel are no longer automatically available to do the work and there is little or no pressure to look for worthwhile Winter tasks in order to keep a workforce productively engaged.

This is not a lament. It is the recognition of a long term problem that ought to be addressed if the parks concerned are not to enter into a long slow decline.

Development should be anticipated and written into the tender documents and remembered when annual estimates are prepared. A full programme should be developed. It is not enough that the emergence of the ideas should be left to chance. They affect the future of the service and what it will be like tomorrow. Pindar who died in 438 BC said in the *Olympiads* (1.51) The days that are still to come are the wisest witnesses. Shakespeare in *King Lear* (V.i. 107) says 'How many things by season season'd are..... To their right praise and true perfection'.

10 Britain in bloom

The Britain in Bloom campaign is worthy of study by park managers in every country in the world. Its principles are capable of use everywhere. In those countries where equivalent competitions do not exist it is in everyones interest to introduce them or put pressure on the appropriate national organisations to do so.

The campaign is an annual competition designed to produce improvements in the environment through the 'imaginative use of trees, shrubs, flowers and landscaping'. It is an important vehicle for changing the appearance of towns and villages. It is now organised by the Tidy Britain Group which is an independent, though Government funded body whose concern is to encourage tidiness by means of education and proselytising.

It is possible to turn up a refined horticultural nose at the kind of gardening evoked by the name Britain in Bloom. It smacks of the Victorian floral confection. To that extent the competition is badly named. It is really concerned with things that should often engage the thoughts of park managers — liveability, the quality and interest of the surroundings we collectively create for ourselves, community effort.

Growing flowers and caring for the way places look is only a fraction of what most modern departments do. Those who see it as having an abiding importance are sometimes represented as being spiritual Victorians; hangovers from an era when the embryo leisure and recreation service really did put most of its resources into gardening, even into bedding schemes. Fashion has swung too far the other way. For half a century we have been tugged along by recreational triumphancy. Parks departments have for the most part been subsumed into bigger units that have it as their main concern.

There is a tendency in wildlife groups to denigrate horticultural flowers and indeed wild ones are just as showy in their fleeting seasons. In the event planting flowers and trees is still the activity that most citizens notice and comment on, favourably if it is done well, critically if it is done badly. It is important to everybody but especially to the majority of people who do not take part in sport, or attend concerts, the theatre, borrow library books or recognise the subtle beauty of natures myriad shades of green. Planting flowers should not be done apologetically, it should be done with panache and flair and in the grand manner.

The competition was based on a French idea developed on the instructions of President de Gaulle who wanted to see La Belle France materialise. He appreciated that one of the quickest ways of realising this was by comparatively simple and easily made horticultural improvements. In achieving these the efforts of everyone could be harnessed. He succeeded in establishing a campaign with such effect that the idea was imported to Britain in 1963. There are now several European countries in which similar schemes operate and representative communities, mostly winners in the respective national competitions, compete in the Entente Florale competition.

Part of the reason for bringing the campaign to Britain was to get tourists to come here and to persuade them to return and bring their friends. It was also concerned from the outset with the quality of life. After all if a place is not fit for a tourist to visit fleetingly then it is certainly not fit to live in. It is a matter of civic cheerfulness.

It is said that the competition is not primarily about winning! Hooey! This Olympian view is possible for the organisers who indeed have deeper motives of environmental improvement but the entrants are almost certainly imbued with a powerful competitive urge. Not all can win but the competition is subdivided into a filigree of regions and classes. Add a plethora of trophies for special aspects of the competition and winning something becomes distinctly feasible if not in the national then at least in the regional campaigns. So it should be. A pat on the head is universally efficacious. It is a powerful motivation and incentive. It produces the desired result of making towns and villages more interesting to visit and better to live in.

There are advantages for a department in entering the campaign besides winning. The visit by the judges gives a fillip to the local effort. It provides a focus to the year's programme, supplies an incentive; encourages the staff to put an extra gloss on their work; allows the client to get an extra effort from the contractor; gives the chance to demand a response from the whole community; it engenders civic pride, and generates as little else can, a strong sense of community endeavour.

The Britain in Bloom competition has undergone a number of changes over the years and there is no doubt that these will continue in future. They have been made in the light of experience but they are also a response to a steadily increasing number of entrants. More than 1,000 communities now enter the competition.

There are now four different categories based upon size of population. They are subdivided so as to ensure that like is judged against like at least in the regional competitions. One submission from each category can then be put forward by each region to the national campaign. There is an important qualification. Only regions with more than 75 entries overall can put an entrant into all four categories; those with between 50 and 74 entries can only put entries into three; between 26 and 49 can put two forward; and below this only one. The region can choose for itself which category it elects to enter if it cannot get into them all.

The categories are composed as follows:

Villages
Small villages with populations not exceeding 600 people;
Large villages with populations of between 600 and 2,000 people but these communities must be truly rural not small market towns or urban in nature, and not be attached to a larger area.

Urban areas
Urban Communities are defined for the purpose of the competition as having a maximum population of 5,000 people though without a stated minimum. These areas might include large villages on the fringes of towns, small market towns, and distinct communities within a city or a town.

Towns
Small towns with 2,000 to 10,000 people;
Towns with between 10,000 and 25,000 people;
Large towns with between 25,000 and 70,000 people.

Cities
Cities with between 70,000 and 150,000 people;
Large cities with more than 150,000 people.

The organisers have bowled another googly at competitors. Early on in the campaign it became evident that a few communities were winning frequently. It was assumed that others would be put off from entering if this state of affairs continued. This may or may not have been true but the advisory committee that suggests how the campaign should be run thought that it was, so the rules were changed to make sure that the trophies were spread around. If a city wins it is excluded from the national competition for the following two years and if other communities win in their sections they cannot go forward in the following year.

There are three stages of judging. The first is a knock out competition. The second seeks to find regional winners each region submitting entries into the national competition. There are seventeen regions. The third and last stage is judging for a series of national trophies.

There are formidable organisational problems. The campaign is a major piece of horticultural management. It is by far Britain's biggest garden competition. Hundreds of judges are involved in the early stages of the competition. There is a large amount of paperwork as entry forms are invited, gathered in and collated. The judges have to be selected and given instructions, routes have to be carefully worked out, local organisers notified transport arranged, hotels booked, and the press and media informed. Afterwards the judges marks have to be assembled and their comments recorded and published. The winners have to be told the losers encouraged. The process has to be repeated at each stage of the competition. Even when the judging is over regional and national award ceremonies have to be arranged and the maximum publicity obtained.

The standard advice for examination candidates is to read the question. It is the same for entrants into the Britain in Bloom campaign. It is essential to know what the judges are looking for and to make sure that each element is given attention in preparing for a visit. Fairness requires easily understood criteria which different sets of judges can interpret in the same way. They are asked to look at the following:

Effort, enthusiasm, commitment and overall floral impact;
Where appropriate, commitment from the private sector;
Individual and corporate efforts by hotels, banks, shops, factories, garages, schools etc;
Participation by residents and the community;
Efforts made towards improvements since the last competition where this applies;
Photographic evidence of earlier plantings or other achievements prior to judging.

The best way of understanding the way in which this expresses itself in practice is by reading the comments of the national judges which are printed and circulated each year to the finalists and to the press. They are also given to delegates at the annual Britain in Bloom seminar and every effort is made to publicise them.

By the nature of things the judges are urbane and polite in what they say. Their comments thus have to be interpreted. Perhaps I might take a moment to explain by examples from a previous year's report. In this they said that 'Despite the difficult summer weather, standards were generally high'. (The use of the word generally means that in some places at least standards were low.)

'Attention to maintenance, the planting of flowers, and land-scaping developments continued' (the word continued indicates mild disappointment. After all attention could have improved, increased or even intensified). 'It is appreciated that financial cuts and a difficult economic climate had created problems'. (By this they meant that they had seen that things were slipping badly, they did not like it and had heard the same excuse wherever they went). 'Cooperation between the business sector and the Britain in Bloom organisers, is essential to the overall effect' (That is to say that there was no cooperation at all in some places and not enough anywhere). 'It was apparent that in some places hanging baskets troughs and window boxes had been allowed to deteriorate, this was regrettable since it was evident from the regional judges reports that these features had previously made a greater impact'. (This is the nearest these amiable people get to downright condemnation. It means that things were very slack indeed and that the earlier judges probably needed their back teeth sharpening). The detailed comments about individual places are couched in even gentler terms. Even so they are essential reading for all competitors.

The judges look to see what improvements are made each year and at the degree of community effort rather than at inherited loveliness. This made it possible for Middlesbrough in the North East of England to win the national trophy for cities on two occasions even though they faced the opposition of beautiful cities with, on the face of it, a much better chance of success.

Judges place great emphasis on the degree to which every section of the community participates. They hope to find that commerce, industry, local authorities and private gardeners are contributing with equal effect. Every year the national judges comment on the failure of commercial interests in some place or other to play their full part. It is the most frequently cited reason for failure to win.

Great efforts are made to try to ensure that the judging is seen to be fair. This is much harder than it seems because every place has different features and attributes and is affected in different ways by the weather, on this last point judging has to take place within a short span of time so that each community is as nearly as possible at the same stage.

It is necessary to compare communities together that are not too dissimilar in character. That is why the structure of the competition is so complex. It seeks to group communities of broadly similar size, and it tries to ensure that the number of entries in the national competition is related, to the size of the entry region by region.

The problem of making fair comparisons has sometimes given rise to exasperated questions demanding to know for example how an industrial city with a gloomy Victorian inheritance of mean streets and grimy buildings can compete with a glamorous holiday resort or spa town which was built to give delight in the first place and has never had to dirty its hands with making steel or building ships or producing chemicals or digging coal. It is not easy to make the necessary allowances but the judges have to try.

The comments made by the judges are also important because they set horticultural trends. Naturally those who compete pay great attention to what they say. If for example they applaud the use of hanging baskets then over a period of years more will appear. They are the most important single influence on horticultural fashions in the country. The consequences are visible everywhere.

The number of flower and plant containers has multiplied, buildings are now peppered with window boxes where there were none before, hanging baskets are no longer merely suspended from the projecting parts of building but are strung from the arms of specially introduced poles lining the streets, (this process reached its apotheosis in Plymouth in 1990 which produced the largest concentration of streetside hanging baskets in the civilised world). Bus shelters are festooned with flowers tumbling from the top and sides of gro-bags, more importantly attention is paid to plantations of trees and shrubs in city centres and to structure planting which makes a more substantial enduring contribution to a place.

Success in the competition needs a lot of organisation locally. The recommended way is to start a committee, it is the British tradition. 'Not another committee' sighs the municipal functionary. The judges will certainly want to see one. They will even offer a recipe. Mix together local authority departments concerned with parks, leisure, tourism, cleansing, client and contractor sides, add the chamber of commerce, youth organisation and voluntary groups like the Rotary club, the WRI and townswomens guilds. Simmer annually. In fact the members should represent all those that ought to be contributing to the campaign. They can give advice, that is easy, but they should also be prepared to approach other people in the group they represent to try to get their support. In some places they also get involved in raising money for the campaign.

The leadership is usually provided by the Parks Department under whatever name it is known. In some respects it has the most to gain because success in the competition will bring it great prestige. It can administer the work of the committee, give horticultural advice, and of course manage the areas it controls itself in a way that will set an example to others and impress the judges when they come.

It can organise and sustain community involvement for example in planning and arranging sponsored planting schemes, and in organising and paying for local garden competitions.

In smaller communities leadership may be taken by individuals using their own enterprise and enthusiasm. Their endeavours should be supported to the full. A department can help in a variety of ways: by providing secretarial support; helping with advice; giving a place to meet; judging a garden competition; giving the trophies and sponsoring the prizes for it; and improving the standard of maintenance of all the fragments of ground that a local authority owns even in the smallest community - verges, the local park, the space round a war memorial, the playground or even the village green. These areas are often conspicuous and nearly always capable of being improved in appearance by better or more appropriate maintenance or by planting for decoration and to reduce the future cost of upkeep. The expansion of the competition in recent years has been mainly from smaller communities. They are arguably more important than cities for the same reason that white sheep are more important than black ones, there are more of them.

Involving private gardeners and the owners of commerical premises is not as easy as it seems and may take patient work over a period of years. It has to be done because the judges place equal emphasis on them.

First commerce. It is very desirable to have one or more representatives of local traders and businesses on the committee. They have to be willing to impress on their colleagues that there are advantages in the publicity and the flow of visitors that stem from success in the competition. It is a help if participation is made easy. For example the department may be able to provide window boxes or hanging baskets or flower tubs if the trader will sponsor them. It is then just a matter of selling the service. In hard times when the economy is static or in recession even this may be difficult but not everybody suffers equally or at the same time, so when it is hard to get new shops into the scheme it may still be possible to get banks and professional offices or garages to take part. 'Keep trying' is the motto.

Encouragement can be given by means of an annual competition to find the best shop, factory, hotel, garage, office block, school, church, or other building. It may be subdivided into districts and different categories. The prizes need not be large. Many towns give a plaque for display by the winners with a prize intended to be put towards further displays for example plant vouchers. These are often presented at a civic or other reception so that competitors, judges, and committee can get together and compare notes. The maximum publicity should of course be obtained for the winners.

Businesses are an important element in the competition not just because the marking system gives them so much weight, but in general. They occupy prominent positions, fill city centres, and stand conspicuously beside main roads.

Private gardeners have a crucial part to play and the easiest way of encouraging them is by means of a local gardens competition. The one that I ran for many years depended on two important assumptions namely that everybody would want to enter but that only a few would take the trouble to submit an entry form. Every front garden was therefore looked at by the departmental foremen and the district superintendents as they went round the town. They submitted a list of the best ones in their areas. Independent judges from outside the department were then invited to assess the gardens and to identify the winners. To make sure that the effect was spread uniformly the city was divided into several districts and to give the maximum spread of prizes, the winners and the runners up were all given awards and everyone shortlisted was invited to a civic reception each year. The maximum local publicity was obtained through the press and local radio and television, during the process of judging, when the winners were announced and when the prizes were presented.

Garden advice is also important but the easiest way of reaching a large number of people is through the press and the local gardening correspondent. If there is no garden column my recommendation is to volunteer at once to supply one every week. They are usually about 800 words in length.

Giving garden advice can also be the province of an official employed to answer individual enquiries; arrange for soil to be tested; name plants; identify pests and diseases; recommend cures; arrange exhibitions, displays, demonstrations and open days; produce information sheets; and generally help private gardeners to contribute to the appearance of their own premises and collectively to that of the whole community. Many local authorities provide an advisory service of this kind but the range of what they offer is very variable.

If this seems a lot of trouble to go to then consider that private gardeners maintain as much as a quarter of the surface areas of some towns and are likely to control an even bigger proportion of a village. They have a major effect on the appearance of a place. I went so far in my own city as to arrange for the owners of neglected gardens to be contacted individually to see if they needed advice or if necessary to direct them to where they could get help. In a well maintained community even a single neglected garden can give a disproportionately bad impression. Local horticultural societies and flower shows should be encouraged and supported.

When the judges arrive what do they look for? First of all they hope to get a friendly enthusiastic welcome from the people most concerned with the local effort. Often this will be the park manager but at some point he will want to introduce the chairman of the committee, the representative of commercial interests and other enthusiasts. The judges should see the whole community taking part. They hope to be taken on a properly planned route and be given a plan and documentation about it. Later in the day after visiting several other places the information will be a valuable *aide memoire*.

The route should be planned in detail so that no time is wasted and that the judges can leave to their next destination punctually. They have an exhausting schedule and a delay in one place may cause problems further on. Refreshments should only be provided if these are asked for by the organiser. Suppress a sense of hospitality. Judges bulging already, have only a little time and this should be used in seeing things that are distinctive and individual. One cup of coffee looks very like another.

Naturally the route should include the best places. It should offer a view of all the elements to which marks are attached. That means showing a variety of parks, open spaces, verges, shops, garages, offices, other commercial buildings, churches, community buildings, and good quality private gardens. In travelling along a route that picks out the best of these the judges will also be inadvertently shown some of the others. Self interest suggests that the effort to improve the amenity of a town or village should encompass all of it. In any case the campaign is not a narrow exercise in winning a trophy. It is part of an important environmental improvement project.

Reginald Arkell in his book *Old Herbaceous* has his gardener hero giving advice to his friend the station master as to how to win the best kept station competition. He ascertained when the judging took place and suggested that every spare bit of ground in and around the station should be filled with Michaelmas Daisies since their brief season of glory would coincide with the visit of the judges. It was of course cynical advice and ignored altogether the question of whether the place was attractive at all the other seasons of the year. None the less the station master took the advice and won the competition.

The Britain in Bloom judging occurs over a more protracted period but the first judges tend to arrive with the first roses in June; the regional judges come in late July when the flower are still interesting; and the national judging starts at the end of August when the second flush of blossom is at its best on many varieties. Roses are the Britain in Bloom equivalent of Michaelmas Daisies. There are many plants to supplement them including all the traditional summer bedding plants, annuals, many herbaceous perennials, the summer flowering varieties of heather, flowering shrubs and foliage plants of all kinds. The judges are naturally most influenced by what they can actually see, try as they might to consider what things are like at other times.

Like residents the judges have an interest in what a place looks like all the year long, and will be glad to see photographs or press cuttings which show it at other seasons. Presentations should be lively and interesting. Judges can be bored just like everybody else. They will never be bored by press photographers or reporters nor by interviews for radio and television. They welcome the chance to give a point of view. Press interest indicates community interest.

The judges spend a lot of time cooped in motor cars so they are often glad to get out and walk. The opportunity should be used to show an area of concentrated interest like a town centre or the middle of a village or an important park. Otherwise it will waste time.

The judges look for interesting or novel planting schemes, for innovation and invention, they look at the way flowers, trees and shrubs have been introduced and cared for, they hope to find high quality appropriate landscaping, well used and well maintained, interesting public parks and open spaces interlaced with other developments, they want to feel the affection that is lavished on private gardens, the pride with which public buildings are managed and maintained, and the public spirit and cooperation that has motivated the owners of commercial premises and offices and factories in improving the appearance of their property

They are not just looking at horticultural cosmetics. It is the air of civic pride, quality, loving care that impresses the judges.

They also examine the negatives of a place. They look for the absence of litter — remember that the organisers are the Tidy Britain Group — they want to see freedom from graffiti and vandalism. In any case the best way of controlling this is to remove it as soon as it appears. Leaving it encourages more. Britain in Bloom participation revives in a community that most efficacious of all anti-vandal measures, neighbourly disapproval, which acted as a potent check upon exuberance of all kinds until a generation ago. They also want to see that no land has been left derelict. There is no excuse for it in any case. The techniques of temporary landscaping are well known and have even been improved by the various national garden festivals.

Parks' staff should take the initiative in the Britain in Bloom campaign. They have it in their grasp to lead the whole community in a general effort, it gives them the chance to make valuable contacts within the community, to publicise their own existence and the things that they stand for, it allows them to display their skills. If the community wins they get an added bonus and a boost to their public standing and to the esteem in which they are held. It is close to the heart of their function.

Planning

Planners affect the work of Parks Departments. The problems of compulsory tendering in Britain and cash shortages everywhere have diverted attention from the form and pattern of open space in towns. It is of more enduring significance.

Structure and local plans set the framework in which local issues are decided. The structure plans explain the broad outline of policies. Local plans must conform to them but they are more specific and add detail and local references. The parks service is affected by both. The plans identify the need for recreational facilities; explain the standards that are proposed; identify deficiencies; and point out where new parks and open spaces can be introduced. Larger communities may be divided into several localities each with its own plan.

Plans set out a minimum area of open space for each thousand people. It is often based on the National Playing Fields Association proposals. The problem is discussed elsewhere but the normally accepted standard is not enough to allow the development of large urban parks as well as the network of green spaces and playgrounds for which it is intended. Parks staff can put forward counterviews of their own and should do so. It is no good grumbling later. If they cannot persuade the planners they should submit a reasoned case to the planning committee so that councillors can discuss more generous standards. Plans are subject to extensive public consultations through often ill attended meetings. After the local procedures have run their course the plans must be approved by the Secretary of State for the Environment, or for Scotland or Wales as appropriate.

The plans should be taken seriously because they are used to regulate future development decisions. If a matter goes to an appeal the appropriate Government Ministers place reliance on local plans.

'I will lift up mine eyes to the hills...' said the psalmist *Psalm* 121. No parks client should be so engaged with the details of his work as to ignore the significance of structure and local plans and the broad view they take of a community and its needs.

Tree preservation orders are the lesser stuff of which planners are made but they affect the concerns of park managers and often require their cooperation. Conservation areas are a grander vision but with much the same effect on nobler vegetation. Some structures in parks are subject to planning control for example listed buildings. New developments also require planning permission which seeks to ensure that the building and its projected use are acceptable and conform to the local plan. Planning permission is required for such matters as floodlights around an all weather football or hockey pitch or tennis courts and the permission may contain conditions which for instance can limit the hours during which the lights can be used or requiring them to be shielded to protect neighbouring properties from annoyance. Smaller changes which depart only in a minor way from the zoning as open space are not subject to control. They are the so called *de minimis* changes.

Building controls are intended to ensure the structural soundness and safety of buildings, and conformity with the regulations that prevail at the time. Even buildings that are to be pulled down and have the necessary planning approval also require a building warrant.

Planning gain

In order to ease the passage of their proposals developers sometimes offer a *quid pro quo*. They are naturally interested in seeing that their scheme is approved with the minimum delay and if this can be achieved by giving a community asset in return for agreement then — there it is. A planning gain has been accomplished. The council may think that giving permission is worth the gain, the developer is saved the trouble and expense not to mention the doubt and delay of going to an appeal if the council disapproved. Everybody is happy — probably.

Agreements are possible under section 106 of the *Town and Country Planning Act 1990* or Section 33 of the *Local Government (Miscellaneous Provisions) Act 1982*. Detailed advice was given in the *Department of the Environment circular 22/83*. Similar ones were issued also in 1983 for Scotland and Wales. The agreements can be used to include parks, open spaces, a length of riverside, playgrounds, recreational buildings, or pitches as part of a bigger development which of course has to fund it. Some of these things can be demanded as part of planning permission in the normal way but planning agreements produce extras on which the authority cannot insist and might never even get except by way of an agreement. They are a way of paying back to the community some of the value it confers or adds when it allows developments to take place.

The gain should be directly related to the development; be necessary to secure a balance of uses if a large comprehensive development is proposed; be appropriate, and reasonably related to the development in scale and kind. That leaves plenty of scope. The park's service is the likely heir to whatever is provided and should keep an eye on the possibilities and have clear idea of what might be obtained and what the community needs most.

As an example of the scale of some proposals, in 1990 a major development was proposed at Newcastle upon Tyne that would affect eight hundred hectares of the City's green belt. Half would be developed for industry and housing. The rest would become the Newcastle Great Park.

Councils are also major landowners and some of the sites they own, for example on the edge of a park or playing field are valuable. They make developers' mouths water. In exceptional circumstances those concerned might suggest that ground could be leased for an appropriate use in return for something the community might value more than the integrity of the space. There is an example of changing facilities being provided in playing fields in return for a site on which to build a restaurant, in itself a useful asset. Beware. It is a heady prospect. Local authorities under financial pressure may take the idea further than is either wanted or expected.

Derelict land

In the decade to 1989 12,000 hectares of derelict land were reclaimed in Britain. Some of it was restored for agriculture some became urban park, some nature reserve, some forest, some was used for recreation. Occasionally the land was serving a more useful function as it was, providing a home for wild flowers, becoming colonised by trees and scrub offering the perfect adventure playground for children. Much of it however was derelict in the fullest sense degenerate, unsightly, abandoned. There is still a lot of such land and more is being produced. It is also an international problem.

A number of grants are available for restoring land that has been so damaged by industrial or other activity that it is incapable of beneficial use without reinstatement. This definition has survived since the *Ministry of Housing and Local Government Circular 68* which was issued in 1965. It includes sites that have been subject to mining extraction, spoil heaps, abandoned workings and industrial sites. Rubbish tips and extractive work now normally have conditions that require reinstatement by whoever is responsible. The *Derelict Land Act 1982* is intended to bring derelict land into use and improve its appearance.

There are no longer serious technical barriers to restoration. Considerable experience has been accumulated. A great deal is known about the mechanical processes including ground modelling, drainage, problems of methane generated by tipped organic material, the formation of soils and the most suitable plant species to pioneer difficult sites.

In the past derelict land has been an important source of parks. The playing fields on Hackney Marshes in London are based on rubble from the blitz. Berlin used the rubble of its buildings which they call *truemmer,* to make green hills. The Mound which is a green space in the heart of Edinburgh is made from excavations from the foundations of the eighteenth century New Town. Napoleon III used former gypsum workings to make Buttes Chaumont Park in Paris. Every year I get post cards showing the famous Butchart Gardens near Vancouver which were made from a quarry. Most places can tell similar tales. Derelict land was important in the past. It will be in the future, some of the most interesting sites with the greatest potential for parks and gardens are todays mineral workings and tips.

Tourism

The tourist industry is one of the most important in Britain and the same is true in many countries. There are several sources of statistical information. The *United Nations Year Book* and the *OECD Tourist Statistics* which are also published annually both analyse aspects of the trade. In 1986 13.772 million tourists and visitors came to Britain; 1.429 million visited Australia and were sprayed with disinfectant there; 0.733 million visited New Zealand; 100,000 visited Zimbabwe though that figure sounds what the Scot from the North East would call an *Och-tae-hell* estimate; the USA received a precise 23.358501 million tourists; and even Tonga got 0.035 million. Internal tourism is even harder to measure but is numerically more important.

Tourism is a material factor in the local economy of many countries and individual cities. Places that once seemed unlikely tourist destinations like Bradford in Yorkshire now recognise their potential and promote themselves for the purpose.

To know what tourists want it is only necessary to draw on personal interests. Diversity, change, fine scenery, a sense of history, comfort, novelty. Parks and gardens are likely to figure high in any list of attractions. More people visit the National Trust gardens than their other properties. The Royal Botanic Gardens at Kew attracted 1,206,881 visitors in 1989; 914,748 people went to the equivalent in Edinburgh. Between 1988 and 1989 the British Tourist Authority estimate there was a 12 per cent increase in visitors to gardens. The *British Tourist Authority Visitor Survey* in 1988 found that 31 per cent of all overseas visitors said they were attracted here by the landscape and scenery.

Local tourist brochures nearly always show a scene in a park. It will probably depict flowers in the Victorian tradition, conservatories, outdoor entertainments, amenity planting, outdoor games. These are the tourist promotor's perception of what makes a locality interesting to visitors. A park system well managed for the purpose can be in the front line of efforts to attract tourists, to persuade them to stay longer, to get them to return and advise their friends to follow. The same degree of customer care that ought to be offered to the resident should be extended to them as well.

Grants can sometimes be obtained for particular projects and the tourist boards are also able to give advice and encouragement. They should certainly be consulted and their views obtained when schemes that might get their support are proposed.

Preserving open spaces

There is steady pressure for development and redevelopment in many areas and open spaces often occupy prime attractive sites. The public will often rush to protect the space if it is known to be at risk. The *1990 Town and Country Planning Act* defines open space as land laid out as a public garden or used for the purpose of public recreation, or land which is a disused burial ground. Local Authorities are not allowed to dispose of this kind of space or to appropriate it for another purpose unless they first advertise their intention to do so in a local paper for two successive weeks and then take into account any objections. There are circumstances when the greater public good may demand the release of open space if it permits the advantageous development of a much bigger area and especially if it is replaced within the scheme. Otherwise there is an interest in seeing that open space is busy throughout the year and is kept and extended — not diminished.

The *Acquisition of Land Act 1981* stepped up the pressure to preserve space. It requires that land wanted for redevelopment which has to be bought by a compulsory purchase order and which has an open space on it can only be purchased if the Secretary of State is satisfied that suitable alternative open space is provided. This must be just as advantageous to the public and no less in area. That should be the minimum objective in respect of any open space that is lost. Planning authorities can give themselves planning permission. New legislation is being considered which will oblige them to show that they have behaved well when they gave consent to themselves.

The merit of the minimum standards of open space and play space that are put forward from time to time, is that they can be used to demonstrate that there is a shortage, usually in older urban centres. The best protection however is public fuss. This is most likely to arise if the management of the space has ensured that it is busy, enjoyable, interesting, liked or admired.

Public involvement

The park system takes up just under 40 per cent of local authority leisure spending. The proportion has fallen in the last two decades because of the increase in the number of indoor facilities. It also employs capital resources which far exceed the value of all the other leisure facilities combined. The great size of the investment alone suggests that the public should be consulted to find what they want from it.

Parks should also be appraised to assess how successful they are. Comparisons are sometimes made with other authorities. These are often on the basis of spending on parks per thousand of the population. The figures ignore the quality of what is done, and how well it serves the community. To find out more about public reaction it is desirable to make a systematic survey not just of the existing customers but of those who might be expected to visit the parks but do not.

Parks are usually free and a whole day's visit need not involve spending even a penny, well, perhaps a penny. It is not possible therefore to apply the commercial test of success, whether the income is more than the expenditure. Other measures have to be used in making a cost/benefit analysis. How much use is made? Whether this is considered of high quality by the customers? What factors would enhance their enjoyment? What value is added to neighbouring property? What effect is there on the levels of vandalism or bad behaviour? What are these compared with those in similar areas? What are the direct costs and income? The service should be the best for the price.

There is also the problem of uneven amounts of use during a week, or through the year. Parks are very apt to attract joggers and dog walkers in the mornings, older people and mothers and toddlers during the day, youths playing football in the evenings, organised sports on Saturdays, and crowds looking for relaxation on Sundays. The high peak is usually on Sunday afternoons. The different uses fit together quite well but few parks work to their full capacity most of the time. Address the problem by studying the potential market and catering for what it wants so that the park is busy more often and for longer.

11 Demographic changes

Changes in population take place all the time. The relative proportion of the different age groups changes accordingly. The statistical study of the phenomenon is called demography. They are important influences on the use made of parks, and recreational facilities of all kinds.

Shakespeare discusses one aspect in *As You Like It* (II VII 139). 'And one man in his time plays many parts..... His acts being seven ages. At first the infant,..... Mewling and puking in the nurses arms.' There has been a surge in the number of births in Britain since 1985. The first fruits of this renewed endeavour among twenty five to forty four year olds have already had an effect in parks. Family groups pushing prams are appearing in larger numbers. Parents or grandparents with push chairs are visibly more numerous. They need pleasant, safe, interesting places to walk or sit and talk with others. The first harbingers of the higher birthrate are now the newest clients of playgrounds after years of quietly declining use.

The effect of the boom is now reaching the kindergartens and nursery schools. During the decade the British school population is expected to grow by more than 800,000. This suggests that facilities which may have been under threat of redundancy for years should in fact be retained. In any case open space once lost is generally irrecoverable, buried beneath development. The presumption should be in favour of retaining it no matter what the trend of the moment might be.

'And then the whining schoolboy, with his satchel, ... and shining morning face, creeping like a snail..... unwillingly to school.' Shades of the playground in his mind and heroes of the football field. He needs space in which to run and play and climb and splash. In Britain a falling birthrate during the 1970s produced a decline in the school populations in the 1980s. It made playgrounds less busy; reduced the attendances at football coaching classes in parks; gave the bird population a rest from bird-nesting boys.

In a year or two the number of school children will rise again and the facilities that have been underused for a decade will be in demand once more. They should be spiffed up now in anticipation so that they can compete effectively for the trade.

Energetic programmes should be developed to involve the young in the activities of the department. Planting trees with the help of schools, sponsored bulb planting, helping with the park animals, football coaching, the revival and extension of children's summer entertainment programmes, and as time goes by, the return of the pop concert in the park. Expect more pressure about playgrounds and the quality and interest of what they contain. Families that have been deferred arrive later in life. Parents are thus more influential and experienced. They will be more aware of deficiencies, complain with greater force, present suggestions more often. There is more point than ever in consultation, marketing, explanation of policies and services.

'And then the lover,..... Like a sighing furnace with a woeful ballad..... Made to his mistress' eyebrow.' I know a man who says he did not know that parks were open in the day until he reached the age of thirty three, and borders after dark are in themselves pre antenatal. The reduced birthrate in the late 1960s and in the years which followed has now expressed itself in a large fall in the number of sixteen to twenty four year olds. This in turn has reduced the demand for such pursuits as squash and team games which are largely the province of that age group.

Courtship in parks has not declined proportionately. In this respect Shakespeare took too short a view. The human capacity to emit the love sick sigh is not reduced by age. Changes in social patterns particularly those that affect divorce mean that courtship can occur two or three times in a lifetime, and there are celebrated cases in which it is perennial. The park is still the top resource for the purpose.

Managers should hone their romantic senses. They should plan secluded arbours, sweet flowers, pleasant walks, grassy glades, take a hint from eighteenth century furniture designers, and introduce the courtship bench on which two people though sitting side by side are also facing one another. None are made yet, the enterprising manager should place an order now and start a trend, they should also ensure that no path is so narrow that two people cannot walk side by side, and that no park is closed in moonlight.

'Then a soldier,..... Full of strange oaths, and bearded like the pard,..... Jealous in honour, sudden and quick in quarrel,..... seeking that bubble reputation..... Even in the cannon's mouth.' Beating a ball about a course, seeking to cling to passing youth by jogging. There is a story of the man told he should run ten miles a day to keep from getting fat who after weary months found himself 3,000 miles from home. There has been an increase in Britain in the number of people between twenty five and forty four years old. This group has a wide range of opportunities in choosing how to use their leisure time.

The desire for eternal life and the retention of a retreating youth have become a fetish. This is generating an interest in health and fitness. Jogging of course but also aerobics can take place in parks. In some countries exercises habitually take place in the parks and open areas. There is a case for refurbishing the once popular exercise tracks and there is no need at all to abandon health and fitness to the indoor club. The increased demand for golf, and thus courses and driving ranges, and ski slopes artificial or otherwise, are expressions of the increase in this group and of the money at its disposal.

'And then the justice,..... in fair round belly with good capon lin'd..... With eyes severe and beard of formal cut,..... Full of wise saws and modern instances.' The great consulted, presidential, sitting in the club and organising others, the volunteer, the gardener liking flowers and neat mown grass or urging that a place for wild life should be found within the town.

There are more people of this age group in the Western World than there have ever been. Its number will continue to grow. It is affected by early retirement which often occurs two thirds through the average life span. There are more potential volunteers. They can do all manner of tasks that would be ignored if they had to be paid for.

Parks should continue to provide the fullest range of facilities and attractions, golf, bowls, gardens, flowers, allotments, restaurants, conservatories, concerts, tea dances in the afternoon, outings some of them by pony and carriage, accommodation for clubs. The park is their natural leisure constituency.

The group has expanded not only because the baby booms of earlier years are feeding it with new recruits but also because people are living longer. They are remaining active till later in life. In the oldest groups there are many more women than men left alone and often lonely, late in life. They generate an increased demand for the gentle leisure pursuits of the park, walking, studying natural history, sitting in the open air, socialising, drinking tea, listening to music. The park is already well adapted to provide for them and to some extent they are one of its specialities.

'The sixth age shifts into the lean and slippered pantaloon,..... With spectacles on nose and pouch on side,..... His youthful hose well sav'd, a world too wide..... for his shrunk shank; and his big manly voice,..... Turning again towards childish treble, pipes..... And whistles in his sound.' A place to sit in the sun's grateful warmth to meet with others who are also old, and reminisce, and watch the passing show. Conservatories, a room to play a game of cards, the means to make a cup of tea, encouragement to sprightliness, concessions and free use.

'Last scene of all,...... That ends this strange eventful history,...... Is second childishness, and mere oblivion,...... Sans teeth, sans eyes, sans taste, sans everything.' Access for those who can no longer walk unaided, wheelchairs to assist the volunteer, liaison with the groups who help the aged, and then, sans park, excepting corners for memorial seats and trees.

Managers should keep an eye on social and demographic trends and anticipate the changes they bring. The statistics are generally easy to obtain in spite of the reduction in the range and amount of official statistic gathering in recent years following a policy of getting only those that have direct relevance for the Government, and not even all of them. The figures for births from which all the rest flow are the most accurate of all.

When the information starts to emerge from the most recent census it should be studied with care for the implications it has on the parks service and the requirements it will face in future. Regional and even local variations to the national pattern have a marked effect.

Parks have been out of the fashionable gaze for a generation. Watch out! They are due for a revival. The interest in the environment, the desire to keep green places in towns, the gains from recreation in the open air, reaction against the carbon dioxide spewing motor car, the need to spend leisure near to home, population changes, all point to a resurgence of parks. Managers should be promoting them, publicly asserting their importance, enunciating their own philosophy. If they fail someone will steal their clothes. Napoleon said to his marshall who were prevaricating at the time 'If you are going to take Vienna, take Vienna'. No caveats, no reservations, no procrastination, no delay. There is something to sell, sell it.

John Ruskin in The Lamp of Memory says:

'The idea of self denial for the sake of posterity of practising present economy for the sake of debtors yet unborn, of planting forests that our descendants may live under their shade, of raising cities for future generations to inhabit, never, I suppose, efficiently takes place among the publicly recognised motives of exertion. Yet these are not less our duties; nor is our part fitly sustained upon the earth unless the range of our intended usefulness include, not only the companions but the successors of our pilgrimage.'

It is the privilege of what we do. It goes beyond demography, even beyond professional self interest.

Bibliography

Abercrombie P 1944 *The Greater London Plan* HMSO London

Advice manuals 1990 Countryside Commission Publications, Albert Road, Manchester

Allen M 1962 *Design for Play* Hawn, London

Badmin, Combes, Raynor *Leisure Operational Management* (2 vols) Longman, Harlow, Essex

Bengtsson A 1970 *Environmental Planning for Children's Play* Crosby Lockwood, London

British Standards British Standards Institution, Linford Wood, Milton Keynes MK14 6LE

Butler G 1982 *Introduction to Community Recreation* 5 edn. McGraw Hill, New York

Carlson, MacLean, Deppe, Petersen 1985 *Sport and Recreation an Economic Analysis* Wadsworth, Belmont, California

Chadwick E 1842 *The Health of Nations* Edited extracts of his papers, London

Chadwick G F 1961 *The Works of Sir Joseph Paxton* The Architectural Press, London

Chadwick G F 1966 *The Park and the Town* The Architectural Press, London

Chancellor E 1907 *The History of the Squares of London Topographical and Historical* London

Chancellor E 1925 *The Pleasure Haunts of London During Four Centuries* New York

Civic Trust 1970 *Reclamation of Derelict Land* London

Civic Trust 1977 *Urban Wasteland* London

Conservation Handbook Series British Trust for Conservation Volunteers, 36 St Mary's St, Wallingford, Oxon OX10 OEU

Cranz G 1982 *The Politics of Park Design. A history of urban parks in America* The MIT Press, Cambridge, Mass.

Crowe S 1956 *Tomorrows Landscape* The Architectural Press, London

Eckbo G 1949 *Landscape for Living* Dodge, New York

Ellis M J 1973 *Why People Play* Prentice Hall, New Jersey

Freud S 1973 *The Complete Works* Hogarth Press, London

Geddes P 1915 *Cities in Evolution* New edn 1949 Williams and Norgate, London

Gilbert, Macrory 1989 *Pesticide Related Law* British Crop Protection Council

Godbey G 1985 *Leisure in Your Life* 2nd edn Venture Publishing, State College. PA 16803

Goodale T, Godbey G 1988 *The Evolution of Leisure* Venture Publishing, State College. PA 16803

Gratton C, Taylor P 1985 *Sport and Recreation in Economic Analysis* E and F N Spon, London

Gratton C, Taylor P *Economics of Leisure Services Management* Longman, Harlow, Essex

Greater London Council 1968 *Surveys of the Use of Open Space* Greater London Council, Planning Department

Hawkes J 1951 *A Land* Cresset Press, London

House of Lords Select Committee 1973 *Report on Sport and Leisure* HMSO London

Howard E 1902 *Garden Cities of Tomorrow* Reprint 1951 Faber and Faber, London

ILAM 1988 *Maintenance of Grounds and Open Spaces A guide to tender and contract documents* Longman, Harlow, Essex

Jacobs J 1962 *The Death and Life of Great American Cities* Jonathon Cape

Jeckyll G 1889 *Wood and Garden* Longman, London

Jeckyll G 1908 *Colour for the Flower Garden* Country Life, London

Joseph 1989 *Sociology for Business* Polity Press, Cambridge

Kerr W 1962 *The Decline of Pleasure* Simon and Schuster, New York

Land Capability Consultants for the DOE 1989 *Cost Effective Management of Reclaimed Derelict Sites* HMSO London

Lindsay, Hoving 1965 *New York City's Parks, Yesterday and Today* New York

Lovejoy D and Partners *Spons Landscape Handbook* 3rd edn. E N Spon, London

Olmstead F L 1852 *Walks and Talks of an American Farmer in England* Putnam, New York

Olmstead Jr F L, Kimball T 1973 *Forty Years of Landscape Architecture* The MIT Press, Cambridge, Mass.

Repton H 1803 *Observations of the Theory and Practice of Landscape Gardening*

Robinson W 1883 *The English Flower Garden* John Murray, London

Royal Town Planning Institute 1976 *The Urban Crisis Leisure in the Urban Environment* Royal Town Planning Institute, London

Scott M 1985 *The Law of Public Leisure Services* Sweet and Maxwell, London

Sillitoe K K 1969 *Planning for Leisure* HMSO London

Stock E 1898 *The Municipal Parks Gardens and Open Spaces of London: Their History and Associations* London

Tansley A G 1961 *The British Islands and Their Vegetation* (2 vols) Cambridge University Press

Townley, Grayson 1984 *Sponsorship of Sport, Arts and Leisure* Sweet and Maxwell, London

Tunnard C 1938 *Gardens in the Modern Landscape* The Architectural Press, London

Wallwork K A 1974 *Derelict Land* David and Charles, Newton Abbott

Walsh R G 1987 *Recreation Economic Decisions, Comparing Benefits and Costs* Venture Publishing, State College. PA16803

Wells T, Bell S, Frost A 1990 *Creating Grasslands with Native Plant Species*. Nature Conservancy Council, Northminster Hse, Manchester

Wright F L 1932 *The Disappearing City* New York

Wurman, Saul, Levy, Katz 1972 *The Nature of Recreating. A Handbook in Honour of Frederick Law Olmstead: Using examples from his own work* The MIT Press, Cambridge, Mass.

Index

Abercrombie, Sir Patrick, 119
Aboreturn, Derby, 6
Aboreturn, Nottingham, 6
absenteeism, 63
Acquisition of Land Act 1981, 229
address lists, 89
Adventure playgrounds, 149
Advertising, 86–8
Advertising Standards Authority, 87
After dinner speaking, 96
Ambush marketing, 83
amount of space, 131
anthracnose, 195
aquares, 3
Arts Council, 18, 44–5
Audit Commission, 40

beech bark disease, 196
Bills of quantities, 59
Birkenhead Park, 6
Birmingham Botanic Gardens, 6
bonus schemes, 64
booklets, 175
Bos Park Amsterdam, 196
Botanic Gardens, 9
Bourneville, 8, 19
Britain in Bloom campaign, 214
British Code of Advertising Practice, 87
British Horticultural Development Council, 202
BS 5750 1987, 57
building controls, 225
busking festival, 33
butterflies, 166
by-laws, 39

Capital employed, 74
carbon dioxide, 201
carpet bed, 84
cashless pay, 109
casual staff, 63
casual supervision, 131
casual users, 113, 117, 118
Catering, 118–9
Catering and recreation management, 113–27
central nurseries, 62

Central Park Commissioners, 163
Central Park New York, 9, 10, 25, 124
Changes to specifications, 53–4
Children's farms, 150
Children's playgrounds, 128–159, 210
Choosing a contractor, 119–20
Circulation space, 140
civic pride, 103
client, 115
Client officers, 73
climbing frames, 135
climbing nets, 136
club houses, 123
Clydesdale Horse, 181
collectors, 124
Community forests, 196–8
community involvement, 220
Community management, 122
competitive tendering, 203
Complaints, 121,123–4
Compulsory competitive tendering (CCT), 47
compulsory purchase order, 229
computer assisted design, 27
conditions of contract, 56
conservation areas, 187
conservatories, 201
Consultation, 78, 138–9
consumer surveys, 121
contention about trees, 188
contour slides, 137
Contract failure, 120–1
contractors, 64, 67, 73, 118
Corbusier, 14
Cost control, 73–4
Countryside Act 1968, 35
Countryside Acts, 42
Countryside Commission, 18, 167
Countryside Commission for Scotland, 21
courtship in parks, 232
Cremore Gardens, 3
cricket wickets, 107
cross border trading, 60
cross boundary tendering, 65
crown thinning, 193
Crystal Palace, 6
customer surveys, 23

dangerous trees, 189
day work, 59
Demographic changes, 231–4
demographic shifts, 79
Department of the Environment, 2
Derelict land, 226
Design, 23–7
design brief, 23
Direct Mail, 89
Direct Service Organisations, 48
Disabled children, 157–8
disabled people, 175
disabled visitors, 209
distribution of play spaces, 130
dog toilets, 107
dog wardens, 107
Dogs, 105–7
Downing, Andrew Jackson, 8
DSO management, 61–2
Durham, 202
Dutch elm disease, 196
Duthie Park, Aberdeen, 5

Education Act 1944, 37
Education Act 1988, 37
enclosure of common land, 4
Entertainments, 124–7, 156–7
Environmental friendliness, 199–203
Environmental impact assessment,
    198–9
Environmental Protection Act 1990,
    35
equipment, disposition of, 134
Equipment, selection of, 135
Equipped playgrounds, 130
Exhibitions, 81–2

Fair Play for Children Campaign, 158
fences, 29, 102, 146–7, 210
Fidelity insurance, 111
fire blight, 195
first aid equipment, 107
floral litter, 29
flower and plant containers, 219
flowers, 102
fly posting, 89
folly marketing, 84
Food and Environmental Protection
    Act 1985, 110
Forestry Commission, 42, 175
formal bedding, 28
formal play equipment, 129
Forms of tender, 116–8
framework planting, 161

franchising, 117–8
freelance coaches, 115
fuel economy, 201
Functions of parks, 12–33

games facilities, 211
garden advice, 221
Garden Cities Association, 7
Garden Cities of Tomorrow 1902, 7
Garden Festivals, 26, 38, 190
gardening writers, 93
General Household Survey, 13
German standards, 142
golf, 108
Golf courses, 122–3
golf professionals, 122
graffiti, 29, 88, 103–4
grass sickness, 183
Grays Inn, 3
Greater London Development Plan, 20
Greater London Plan, 19
Green Belts, 7
Griffin, Walter Burley, 8
Ground maintenance, 54–6
grounds maintenance specifications, 55
group picnics, 32

Hampstead Garden Suburb, 8
hanging baskets, 219
Harmful chemicals, 110–1
Health and Safety at Work Act, 35,
    139, 188
Health and Safety at Work Act 1974,
    141
Heaton Park Manchester, 180
Hierachies of open space, 18–22
hierachy of use, 21
Herbert, George, 15
Hidcote, 24
hockey, 107
Holidays, 63
honey fungus, 196
horse vehicles, 183
Horses, 180–4
Horticulture as recreation, 17–8
horticultural chemicals, application of,
    66
horticultural varieties, 24
horticulture, 17,29
Howard, Ebenezer, 7, 19

independent advisor, 120
Industrial Revolution, 4
Inflatable equipment, 151–2

inspection of playgrounds, 145
Institute of Leisure and Amenity
    Management, 43–4
Institute of Marketing, 32
Insurance, 111–2, 146
international events, 125
Interpretation, 173–4
Interpretation centres, 177–8
Isaiah, 1

Jeckyll, Gertrude, 6

Kelvingrove, Glasgow, 6
Kick–a–bout games, 150–1

landscape designers, 24
landscaping rose, 29
Law of Public Leisure Services, 34
lawns, 68
Leisure Management Direct Services
    Organisation, 114–5
leisure explosion, 14
leisure time, 14
Letchworth, 8, 19
Litter, 104–5
litter bins, 209
local and structure plans, 132
local gardens competition, 221
Local Government (Miscellaneous
    Provisions) 1976, 38
Local Government (Miscellaneous
    Provisions) Act, 38
Local Government Act 1948, 36
Local Government Act 1972, 35, 37
Local Government Act 1974, 39
Local Government Act 1988, 38, 48
Local Government Commissioners,
    39–40
Local Government Planning and Land
    Act 1980, 38
Local structure, 45–6
Location, 130–2
loose fill materials, 144
lopping, 189, 194
Loudon, John Claudius, 6

maintenance, economy of, 27
maintenance, grounds, 49,54
Management buy–outs, 75–6
management fee, 117
management plan, 204
Manchester, 21
Marine insurance, 111–2
marketing, 77

Material responsibility, 45
Mathematical checks, 59
Measurement plans, 173
Melbourne Botanic Gardens, 9
Member involvement, 60–1
Mill, John Stuart, 35
minimum hours, 119
ministerial responsibility, 45
mobile patrolman, 177
Moses, Robert, 9
motor vehicles, 25
multistemmed trees, 30

National Council for the Preservation
    of Gardens and Plants, 179
National Curriculum, 14
National flower shows, 82
National Garden Festivals, 124
National Parks and Access to the
    Countryside Act 1949, 42
National plant collections, 178–9
National Playing Field Association
    standard, 131
National Playing Fields Association
    1, 146, 158
National Trust, 174
native plants, 161
nature conservation, 160
Nature trails, 174–6
New Towns, 19, 26
Nostalgia marketing, 83–4
notice boards, 101
notices, 101, 107
Nottingham, 1
Nunawadding, City of, 15

Occupiers Liability Act 1957, 142
Office of Population Census and
    Statistics, 17
Olmstead, Frederick Law, 9, 19, 28
Ombudsman, 39
open day, 82
Open Spaces Act 1906, 35, 36
overhead projectors, 95
Overheads, 74–5

paddling pools, 156
Parc Guell, 27
park attendants, 177
Park Commissioner for the City of
    New York, 10
Park rangers, 176–7
parks and open spaces client, 50
parkways, 9, 10

path surfaces, 175
paths, 25, 29, 134, 211
Paxton, Sir Joseph, 6
peat, 202
Peoples Park, Halifax, 6
performance bond, 120
Performance reviews, 71–3
pergolas, 29
permanent planting, 211
personal accident policy, 111
Pheonix Park, 3
philosphy of management, 207
physical education, 14
Physical Training and Recreation Act, 8
Physical Training and Recreation Act 1937, 36
phytophthora, 196
Piccadilly Gardens, 21
pioneer species, 162
Planning gain, 225–6
planning permission , 225
Plant Health Act, 195
planting, 25
planting flowers, 215
Planting trees, 191–3
play fashions, 148
Play leadership, 157
Play sculpture, 152–3
playground accidents, 139
playground design competition, 139
playing surfaces, 107
pleasure gardens, 4
Poisonous plants, 98
Pollock Park Glasgow, 180
Ponds, 30, 171–2
poplar canker, 195
Port Elizabeth, 45
Port Sunlight, 8, 19
Portable playgrounds, 148–9
poisonous fruits, 98
Posters, 88–9
Pre-School Playgroups Association, 158
preservation orders, 225
Preserving open spaces, 228–9
Preserving trees, 186–8
press conference, 93
press release, 91, 92
Pricing, 31
private gardeners, 221
private gardens, role of, 132
Progressive improvements, 212–3
prohibitory signs, 210

Promotions, 79–81
Pruning, 193–6
public consultation, 23
Public Health Act 1847, 5
Public Health Act 1848, 36
Public Health Act 1875, 36
Public Health Amendment Act 1890 36
Public involvement, 229–30
Public liability insurance, 111, 125
public meetings, 78
public participation, 212
public planting programme, 103
Publicity, 89
pulverised bark, 145

Quality audits, 203–4
quality control, 57, 69–71, 121
quality forum, 70

Ranelagh Gardens, 3
Rare breeds, 180
Rare Breeds Society, 181
Regents Park, London, 6
Repton, Humphry, 6
resilient surfaces, 144
retirement, 15
Retiro Park Madrid, 45
Risk managment, 98–112
Robinson, William, 6, 160
Rooking equipment, 138
romantic senses, 232
root damage, 189
rotation of species, 200
Royal Botanic Gardens Kew, 228
Royal National Rose Society, 23

Safety, 139–41
safety policy, 142
Safety surfaces, 143–5
safety zones, 140
San Antonio, 26
sand, 144, 153–4
sand pits, 153
sand tables, 153
Scottish National Heritage, 176
season tickets, 109
Seats, 147, 209
Security, 109
see–saws, 138
Select Committee on Public Walks, 5
Selecting contractors, 65–7
self guided trails, 174
Semi–mature trees, 190–1

service level agreements, 75
set–aside, 167
shelters, 135
short cuts, 28
shrubs, 29
signs, 175
skin irritations, 8
slide show, 95
Slides, 136–7
sliding surface, 137
Small open places, 22–3
sponsored paying, 32
specifications, 56–9
sponsored planting, 32
Sponsorship, 2, 31–3
sport and leisure management, 117
Sport risks, 107–9
Sports Council, 17, 18, 43, 158
sports development officers, 114
St George's Park, 45
St James Park, 20
Standard specifications, 142–3
standards, 54
standards, upkeep of, 55
structure and local plans, 224
sub letting, 115
supervision, 69, 121
swing heights, 136
swing seats, 136, 140
Swings, 136

Talks, 94–7
tape link–ups, 95
television, 16
Tidy Britain Group, 104, 214
topiary gardens, 24
topography, 133
Torbay Parks department, 82
Tourism, 227–8
Tourist Boards, 44
Town and Country Planning Act 1990, 228
Town Improvements Act 1847, 5
Toxocara canis, 106
tree guards, 102
tree preservation orders, 186
Trees, 184–6
Tapes of playground, 129

undesirables, 109–10
unfair competition, 118
ultra vires, 34
Undesirables, 109
Unemployment, 14

University Park Nottingham, 166
unsocial hours, 114
upkeep, cost of, 27
urban amenities commission, 18–22

value analysis, 71
Value for money studies, 40–2
Vandalism, 99–103
vandalism, copy cat, 100
Vaux, Calvert, 9
Vauxhall Gardens, 3
vehicle insurance, 111
Victoria Park, Aberdeen, 6
volunteers, 15

Water, 155–6
Wealth of Nations, 32
weed killers, 30
weed killers, selective, 166
Welwyn Garden City, 19
wetproof surfaces, 144
Whirling equipment, 138
wild flower meadows, 168–9
wild flowers, 165
wild flower mixtures, 30
wild life groups, 214
wishing well, 32
Woods and shelter beds, 162–5
Woodthorpe Grange Park Nottingham, 45
working conditions, 63

Zoo Licensing Act 1981, 38